D0948456

The Psychology
of Learning Science

The Psychology of Learning Science

Edited by
Shawn M. Glynn
Russell H. Yeany
Bruce K. Britton
University of Georgia

LAWRENCE ERLBAUM ASSOCIATES, PUBLISHERS
1991   Hillsdale, New Jersey   Hove and London

Lawrence Erlbaum Associates, Inc., Publishers
365 Broadway
Hillsdale, New Jersey 07642

Library of Congress Cataloging-in-Publication Data

The Psychology of learning science / edited by Shawn M. Glynn, Russell
H. Yeany, Bruce K. Britton.
      p.   cm.
   Includes bibliographical references and indexes.
   ISBN 0-8058-0668-7
   1. Science—Study and teaching (Elementary) 2. Science—Study and
teaching (Secondary) 3. Learning, psychology of. I. Glynn, Shawn
M. II. Yeany, Russell H. III. Britton, Bruce K.
   LB1585.P78 1991
   507.1'2—dc20   90-22511
                                                                        CIP

Printed in the United States of America
10 9 8 7 6 5 4 3 2 1

Contents

Preface   vii

List of Contributors   ix

Part I: Frameworks for Learning Science

1. A Constructive View of Learning Science   3
   *Shawn M. Glynn, Russell H. Yeany, and
   Bruce K. Britton*

2. Learning-theory-based Science Teaching   21
   Audrey B. Champagne and Diane M. Bunce

3. A Conceptual Change Model of Learning Science   43
   Edward L. Smith

4. Students' Conceptual Frameworks: Consequences for
   Learning Science   65
   Reinders Duit

Part II: Conceptual Development and Learning Science

5. Developmental Patterns in Students' Understanding of
   Physics Concepts   89
   Joseph Stepans

6. Developing Students' Understanding of Chemical
   Concepts   117
   Joseph S. Krajcik

7. Conceptual Development in Astronomy   149
   Stella Vosniadou

8. Children's Biology: Studies on Conceptual
   Development in the Life Sciences   179
   *Joel J. Mintzes, John E. Trowbridge, Mary W.
   Arnaudin, and James H. Wandersee*

Part III. Methods and Media for Learning Science

9. Science Activities, Process Skills, and Thinking   205
   Michael J. Padilla

10. Explaining Science Concepts: A Teaching-
    with-Analogies Model   219
    Shawn M. Glynn

11. Learning Science in Software Microworlds   241
    Patricia E. Simmons

Author Index   259

Subject Index   265

Preface

This book bridges the gap between state-of-the-art research and classroom practice in science education. The contributors are from several different disciplines, including not only science educators, but cognitive scientists and psychologists as well.

This book is about teaching and learning science concepts in elementary and high school. The concepts of interest are in the areas of physical science and biology. This book has three parts: Part I is Frameworks of Learning Science; Part II is Conceptual Development and Learning Science, and Part III is Methods and Media for Learning Science. The chapters in each part provide overviews of current research on learning science concepts and illustrate, in concrete ways, how the findings of this research can be applied in elementary and high school science classes.

The contributors have drawn clear connections among theory, research, and instructional application. Their ultimate goal is to have science teachers put their ideas to use in their classes. Toward this end, the contributors have included in their chapters explicit models, illustrations, and examples drawn from actual science classes. We thank Hollis Heimbouch and Linda Eisenberg of Lawrence Erlbaum Associates for their support and excellent advice.

Shawn M. Glynn
Russell H. Yeany
Bruce K. Britton

List of Contributors

Mary W. Arnaudin, Department of Biological Sciences, University of North Carolina at Wilmington, Wilmington, NC 28403.

Bruce K. Britton, Department of Psychology, University of Georgia, Athens, GA 30602.

Diane M. Bunce, Department of Chemistry, The Catholic University of America, Washington, DC.

Audrey B. Champagne, School of Education, SUNY at Albany, Albany, NY 12222.

Reinders Duit, IPN—Institut für die Pädagogik der Naturwissenschaften an der Universität Kiel, Olshausenstr. 62, D-2300 Kiel 1, Federal Republic of Germany.

Shawn M. Glynn, Departments of Educational Psychology and Science Education, 325 Aderhold Hall, University of Georgia, Athens, GA 30602.

Joseph S. Krajcik, Department of Educational Studies, 610 East University, University of Michigan, Ann Arbor, MI 48109-1259.

Joel J. Mintzes, Department of Biological Sciences, University of North Carolina at Wilmington, Wilmington, NC 28403.

Michael J. Padilla, Department of Science Education, 212 Aderhold Hall, University of Georgia, Athens, GA 30602.

Patricia E. Simmons, Department of Science Education, 212 Aderhold Hall, University of Georgia, Athens, GA 30602.

Edward L. Smith, Department of Teacher Education, Michigan State University, East Lansing, MI 48824.

Joseph I. Stepans, Science and Mathematics Teaching Center, University of Wyoming, Box 3371 University Station, Laramie, WY 82071.

John E. Trowbridge, Department of Biological Sciences, University of North Carolina at Wilmington, Wilmington, NC 28403.

Stella Vosniadou, Center for the Study of Reading, University of Illinois, Champaign, IL 61820; Aristotelian University of Thessaloniki, 73 Queen Sophias Avenue, Athens, Greece.

James H. Wandersee, Department of Curriculum and Instruction, Louisiana State University, Baton Rouge, LA.

Russell H. Yeany, Department of Science Education, University of Georgia, Athens, GA 30602.

FRAMEWORKS FOR
LEARNING SCIENCE

1 A Constructive View of Learning Science

use

Shawn M. Glynn, Russell H. Yeany, and Bruce K. Britton
University of Georgia

If the students of today are to prosper in the 21st century, they must understand the basic facts, principles, and procedures of science. In other words, the students must be scientifically literate.

The world is becoming increasingly technical; science teachers are responsible for preparing students for this technology. Science teachers should emphasize the quality of their students' learning rather than just the quantity: Conceptual understanding is more important than rote memorization. Science teachers should emphasize the process of science rather than just the content, because students who understand the process are better prepared to acquire science content on their own. Science knowledge changes quickly and the updating of one's knowledge is a lifelong activity.

Conceptually based, process-oriented instruction calls for a lot of hard work on the part of both teachers and students. Teachers and students must actively organize, elaborate, and interpret knowledge, not just repeat it and memorize it. *+ + use CONSTRUCTIVISM*

PSYCHOLOGY OF LEARNING SCIENCE

The psychology of learning science holds the response to the challenge of increasing students' understanding of science. Throwing more science facts and principles at the students is not the answer. Increasing the number of students' laboratory activities is not the answer either; a trendy emphasis on "hands on" will not, by itself, increase students' understanding of science. What is additionally needed is a "minds on" emphasis in the learning of

→ reflection is needed

3

science. For example, high school students should be required to understand what is meant by important concepts in biology (e.g., photosynthesis and mitosis-meiosis), chemistry (e.g., chemical equilibrium and the periodic table), physics (e.g., gravitational potential energy and electromagnetic induction) and earth science (e.g., plate tectonics and precipitation). To test students' understanding, they should be asked to explain these ideas. When the students' explanations are not clear, they should be required to clarify them. The students must be able to explain concepts using their own words rather than repeating the words of a textbook author.

Teachers should require students to reason scientifically. One way they can do this is by modeling scientific reasoning for their students. In effect, teachers and students should become collaborators in the process of scientific reasoning. Together, teachers and students should construct interesting questions about science phenomena; simply telling students the answers has little lasting value. Teachers and students should guess, or hypothesize, about the underlying causes of science phenomena. Teachers and students should collect data and design scientific tests of their hypotheses. And finally, teachers and students should construct theories and models to explain the phenomena in question. Throughout all stages of this collaboration, teachers and students should be constantly "thinking out loud" (Glynn, Muth, & Britton, 1990). By means of the "thinking out loud" technique, teachers can help students to reflect on their own scientific reasoning processes (that is, to think metacognitively) and to refine these processes.

TRADITIONAL TEXTBOOKS AND METHODS

Why are teachers not routinely modeling scientific reasoning for their students? To some degree, the fault may lie with traditional textbooks and methods of instruction.

A school science curriculum can be placed on a continuum from "textbook-centered" to "teacher-centered." In a textbook-centered curriculum, the textbook is the engine that drives the curriculum. A textbook-centered curriculum aspires to be "teacher-proof," or able to support teachers who may lack important knowledge, training, and experience.

In a teacher-centered curriculum, a textbook may still play an important role, but the teacher has much more control over the methods of instruction. The teacher-centered curriculum assumes that the teacher knows a great deal about science, about methods of instruction, and about the way that children learn and develop.

Currently, the curriculum of the United States tends to be textbook-centered. According to Bill Aldridge (1989, p. 4), executive director of the National Science Teachers Association, "Consider the typical situation in the

United States. Children study science in elementary school mainly by reading about it." U. S. publishers refer to their product as a "program" rather than a textbook, because the "teacher's edition" prescribes precisely how concepts should be taught, and the textbook is accompanied by a host of resource materials, such as videotapes, software, overhead transparencies and masters, laboratory manuals, study guides, test item banks, posters, and motivational activities (e.g., physics fairs, competitions, and conventions).

Unfortunately, the present textbooks and associated methods of instruction are not particularly effective. According to the American Association for the Advancement of Science report, *Science for All Americans:*

> The present science textbooks and methods of instruction, far from helping, often actually impede progress toward scientific literacy. They emphasize the learning of answers more than the exploration of questions, memory at the expense of critical thought, bits and pieces of information instead of understandings in context, recitation over argument, reading in lieu of doing. They fail to encourage students to work together, to share ideas and information freely with each other, or to use modern instruments to extend their intellectual capabilities. (1989, p. 14)

The present science textbooks and methods of instruction do not yet take into account recent discoveries in the psychology of how students learn science. Discoveries about the constructive nature of students' learning processes, about students' mental models, and students' misconceptions have important implications for teachers who wish to model scientific reasoning in an effective fashion for their students. Eventually, these discoveries will have a significant impact on textbooks, methods of instruction, curriculum courses for future science teachers, and in-service workshops for current science teachers. But there is a need for something to be done now to communicate these discoveries to teachers, textbook authors, and college professors who train science teachers. *The Psychology of Learning Science* was written to address this urgent need.

CONSTRUCTIVE ASPECTS OF LEARNING SCIENCE

Learning, the process of acquiring new knowledge, is active and complex. This process is the result of an active interaction of key cognitive processes, such as perception, imagery, organization, and elaboration. These processes facilitate the construction of conceptual relations.

Science teachers sometimes view students as human video cameras, passively and automatically recording all of the information in a lesson or a textbook. Instead, teachers should view students as active consumers, who are selective and subjective in their perception. The students' prior knowledge, expectations, and preconceptions determine what information will be selected out for attention. What they attend to determines what they learn. As a result, no two students learn exactly the same thing when they listen to a lesson, observe a demonstration, read a textbook, or do a laboratory activity. Ideally, students will challenge the information they are presented, struggle with it, and try to make sense of it by integrating it with what they already know.

How can teachers help students to learn science concepts meaningfully? The answer is to help students learn concepts *relationally*. That is, students should learn concepts as organized networks of related information, not as random lists of unrelated facts. Unfortunately, standardized tests of science achievement frequently fail to distinguish between students with relational learning and students with rote learning. If the students are asked to use the concepts in creative problem solving, then the advantage of relational learning over rote learning becomes apparent.

In order to learn a concept meaningfully, students must carry out cognitive processes that construct relations among the elements of information in the concept. Students should then construct relations between the concept and other concepts. Without the construction of relations, students have no foundation and framework on which to build meaningful conceptual networks. The meaningfulness of these networks depends on both the elements of information that comprise the networks and the relations that weld the elements together.

ORGANIZATIONAL AND ELABORATIVE PROCESSES

The most important questions that psychologists and science educators must answer are: (1) What processes should science students perform and what relations should they construct in order to comprehend science concepts? and (2) In what ways can these processes and relations be supported by instruction?

It is known that organizational and elaborative processes play a particularly important role in science learning. Studies done of experts and novices in fields such as physics (e.g., Chi, Feltovich, & Glaser, 1981) and medicine (Feltovich, 1981) have shown that experts not only have more knowledge than novices, but also better organized and elaborated knowledge.

Organizational processes are essential for building conceptual networks. Science teachers can support students' organizational processes by techniques such as *concept mapping*. A concept map is an effective way of depicting both the elements of information in a conceptual network and the hierarchical relations among the elements. Relations of other kinds, such as causal and temporal, are also specified in the map. The teacher can construct a concept

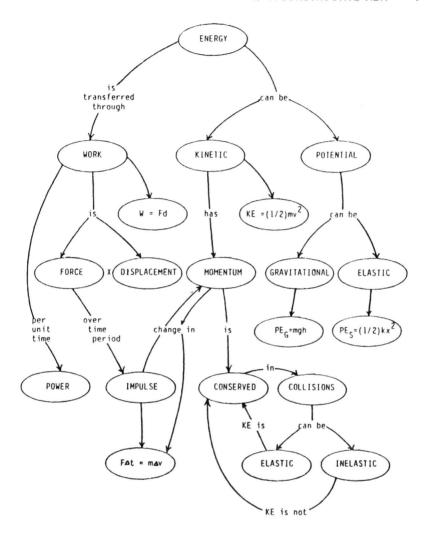

FIG. 1.1. A teacher's concept map. From "Building an Organized Knowledge Base: Concept Mapping and Achievement in Secondary School Physics," by William J. Pankratius, 1990. From *Journal of Research in Science Teaching, 27*, p. 328. Copyright 1990 by the National Association for Research in Science Teaching. Reprinted by permission.

map and use it to plan a lesson. For example, Fig. 1.1 shows a high school physics teacher's map of the unit "Conservation of Energy and Momentum," which includes the concepts of work, power, energy, and momentum.

Students should construct their own concepts maps. The teacher can use the students' maps to diagnose and remediate misconceptions (see Fig. 1.2).

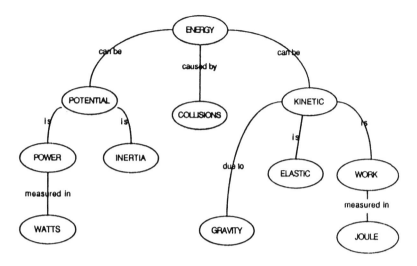

FIG. 1.2. A student's preinstruction concept map. From "Building an Organized Knowledge Base: Concept Mapping and Achievement in Secondary School Physics," by William J. Pankratius, 1990. From *Journal of Research in Science Teaching, 27*, p. 329. Copyright 1990 by the National Association for Research in Science Teaching. Reprinted by permission.

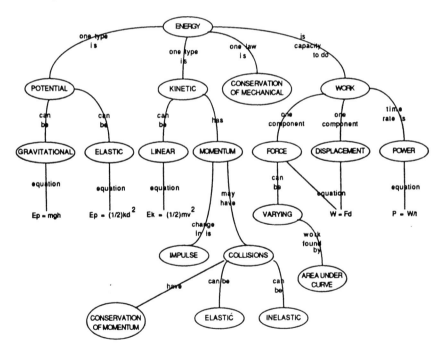

FIG. 1.3. A student's postinstruction concept map. From "Building an Organized Knowledge Base: Concept Mapping and Achievement in Secondary School Physics," by William J. Pankratius, 1990. From *Journal of Research in Science Teaching, 27*, p. 331. Copyright 1990 by the National Association for Research in Science Teaching. Reprinted by permission.

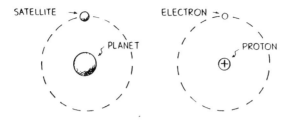

FIG. 1.4. An analog drawn between a gravitational field and an electrical field. From *Conceptual physics* (p. 496) by Paul G. Hewitt, 1987. Menlo Park, CA: Addison-Wesley. Copyright 1987 by Addison-Wesley Publishing Company, Inc. Reprinted by permission.

As the student learns more and more about the concepts in question, their concept maps will evolve, becoming more sophisticated, and eventually approximating those of the teacher (see Fig. 1.3). By comparing the concept maps that students produce over the course of instruction, the teacher can trace developments in students' conceptual networks. Concept mapping should be an active, constructive activity: It is unproductive for the teacher simply to present a concept map to students and instruct them to memorize it.

By means of elaborative processes, students connect new elements of information with elements they already know. Helping students to draw an analogy, such as that illustrated in Fig. 1.4, is an effective way of promoting elaborative relations (Glynn, 1989; Glynn, Britton, Semrud-Clikeman, & Muth, 1989). At the same time, teachers should ensure that students understand that analogies are double-edged swords. That is, an analogy can be used to explain correctly and even predict some aspects of a new concept; but at some point every analogy breaks down. At that point, misconceptions can begin. Students must understand this.

THE HUMAN INFORMATION-PROCESSING SYSTEM

Students are selective in their cognitive processing of information because their minds, which can be conceptualized as information-processing systems, are quite limited in the ability to learn large amounts of unfamiliar information quickly. When performing cognitive processes and constructing conceptual relations, students must work within the limitations imposed by their information-processing systems.

The human information-processing system includes our conscious mind, or *working memory* (Baddeley, 1990), where mental work is done, and our *long-term memory*, where the products of learning are stored. Working memory is analogous to a cognitive workbench. Mental operations are performed on this workbench, but it is a relatively small workbench on which only a few operations can be performed concurrently. If working memory is asked to process too much information too fast, learning breaks down: for this reason, working memory is often referred to as the "bottleneck" of the human information-processing system. Ideally, the information in working memory is rehearsed, integrated in various ways with the information in long-term memory, and stored in long-term memory for future use.

Long-term memory is analogous to a set of file cabinets or a computer hard disk. Long-term memory is virtually unlimited in its storage capacity and its information storage and retrieval functions are enhanced by the processes of organizing and elaborating information.

The *executive control* coordinates the learning and reasoning that is taking place in the information-processing system (Britton & Glynn, 1987). The executive control monitors the interaction between the working memory and the long-term memory. Under the supervision of the executive control, intellectual products are crafted on the cognitive workbench of working memory, conceptual information and tools are retrieved from long-term memory, and the products of reasoning are stored in long-term memory for future applications.

A COGNITIVE MODEL OF SCIENTIFIC REASONING

It is possible to use the human information-processing system components to develop a model of what takes place in a science student's mind when he or she reasons about science phenomena. As can be seen in Fig. 1.5, the science student typically responds to a problem-solving environment created either by the student, the teacher, the textbook, the lab manual, or a combination of these sources. The environment contains questions, observations, and conclusions, some of which may be provided for the student.

Under the supervision of the executive control, the student carries out cognitive processes and constructs relations in working memory that have an impact on the questions, observations, and conclusions in the problem-solving environment.

When reasoning in working memory about a science phenomenon, the student draws upon relevant facts, principles, and skills stored in long-term memory. These skills should include the basic and integrated science process skills routinely performed by scientists working in many disciplines. The basic skills include observation, classification, and communication, metric measurement, prediction, and inference; the integrated skills include identifying variables, constructing a table of data, constructing a graph, describing relationships between variables, acquiring and processing data, analyzing investigations, constructing hypotheses, defining variables operationally,

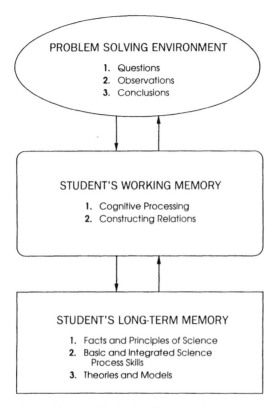

FIG. 1.5.   A cognitive model of scientific reasoning.

designing investigations, and experimenting (Funk, Okey, Fiel, Jans, & Sprague, 1979; Yap & Yeany, 1988).

The products of the scientific reasoning carried out in working memory are returned to long-term memory for future applications. The final products of a student's scientific reasoning are theories and models.

THEORIES AND MODELS: SCIENTIFIC AND PERSONAL

In science, "the term theory is used to describe an organized body of principles and assumptions that account for a set of phenomena along with the rules for its application" (Neimark, 1987, p. 212). According to Neimark, a good theory serves two very important functions: (1) Summarizing a great deal of knowledge economically by incorporating it in a limited set of general principles, and (2) leading to specific, testable predictions. A *model*, on the other hand, is a simplified, physical representation of a thing or process. The representation can take many forms, such as a diagram, a flow chart, a computer program, or a physical replica. Hoffman (1980, p. 407) describes the relationship between theory and model:

> According to the semantics of the word, a model instantiates some of the structure of the theoretical entities in a real substantive thing. The theory *describes* the structure in a symbolic representation. A model, thus, can be distinguished from the theory and hypotheses it instantiates and from the metaphor used to express the theory in terms of, or by reference to, the model. In the model, the universe of discourse of the theory is instantiated by a physical thing with visualizable parts and relations that somehow correspond with the theoretical entities and their relations.

A scientific theory may have associated with it one or more models. For example, when explaining the theory of atomic structure, the Rutherford, Bohr, and Schrodinger models can all be useful; although the Schrodinger model is considered to be the most accurate, because it is most consistent with observations. Likewise, a theory of light could include a particle model and a wave model. Or, a theory of human behavior could include a behavioral (stimulus–response) model and a cognitive model.

We distinguish between *scientific* theories and models and *personal* theories and models because this distinction is important for science education. Scientific theories and models are the current views of phenomena commonly accepted by experts in the science community. Personal theories and models, on the other hand, are the intuitive, preinstructional beliefs of individual students about science phenomena. When students are persistently and systematically questioned, their personal theories are usually found to be qualitative rather than quantitative. Personal theories and models, unlike their scientific counterparts, are often fragmentary and internally inconsistent (e.g., see Stepans, Beiswenger, & Dyche, 1986).

Personal theories are essentially stories that students have constructed, adopted, or adapted to explain complicated, but familiar phenomena, such as weather, biological processes, and gravity. Personal models are the ways that students simplify and physically represent the major characters, objects, and events in their stories.

Personal theories and models are often based on the students' experiences in activities that predate formal schooling, including play, television cartoon shows, and fairy tales. A three-year-old child may explain weather phenomena, for example, with a fanciful story about angels playing in heaven. In this story, there are models to explain thunder, rain, lightning, and wind. The rolling sound of thunder, according to the child, is the sound of the balls rolling down the alley when the angels are bowling. When the balls pass through the clouds, the clouds are "broken" and the water in the clouds spills out. Lightning "strikes" when the angels knock down the bowling pins. And wind is caused by the angels flapping their wings. Usually, a young child does not construct a personal theory and models entirely from scratch, of course; the child may adopt and adapt the imaginative tales of a parent, a grandparent, an older sibling, a friend, or TV characters.

SCIENCE MISCONCEPTIONS

Scientific theories and models and students' personal theories and models often conflict sharply with one another. The students' personal theories and models may incorporate many misconceptions about the way the world works. Unfortunately for the science teacher, the students' personal theories and models often work quite well in the students' everyday life. It is only in the science classroom, under controlled conditions, that the science teacher is able to demonstrate to the students the shortcomings of their beliefs. Frequently, the students are reluctant to give up their misconceptions, preferring instead to believe that some theories work fine in the "real world," while other theories work better in science class. The students tend to compartmentalize and insulate their personal theories and models in order to protect them from the discrepant events they observe in science class. Understandably, the students find it disconcerting to accommodate and change their long-held beliefs. It is easier to memorize the facts they learn in science class, repeat these facts on tests, but continue to apply their personal theories and models outside of school.

What are some examples of students' misconceptions? Anderson and Smith (1987) found that many fifth graders believe, before instruction, that plants get their food directly from soil, water, fertilizer, or sunshine. After 8 weeks of traditional, textbook-based instruction, 90% of these fifth graders still had their misconceptions; they still had not learned that plants get food only by making it themselves. Many of the fifth graders observed by Anderson and Smith also believed that light travels faster at night and that electricity gets used up in a light bulb.

Stepans, et al. (1986) found that 75% of the ninth graders they tested believed that a crumpled piece of aluminum foil weighs more than an uncrumpled one. The authors commented that this disheartening finding is reminiscent of the old joke: Which weighs more, a pound of feathers or a pound of steel? Stepans and his colleagues also asked students of various ages to explain concepts related to how objects sink and float in water. The students performed poorly at all academic levels. In many instances, the only real difference among young and older students was that the older students used more sophisticated terminology. Elementary school students used terms such as "heavy" and "weight," high school students used "density" and "surface tension," and college students used "displacement" and "mass." Unfortunately, the high school and college students had little understanding of the terms they used; the students were able to use the scientific jargon but did not actually understand the phenomena. Many older students, in fact, tried to hide their ignorance by using scientific jargon. The preoccupation of students with jargon is to be expected; high school science texts often introduce more new vocabulary words per page than even foreign-language texts (Carey, 1986).

Standardized tests of science achievement may fail to detect the discrepancies from accepted knowledge in students' personal beliefs, particularly if the tests are assessing factual recall. It is not unusual for students to begin a schoolyear with misconceptions, take science classes and receive good grades, and end the schoolyear with the same misconceptions. To make matters worse, the students' misconceptions sometimes interact with the information being taught in such a way that new misconceptions are created.

The identification of common misconceptions is a popular activity among science teachers who wish to bring students' personal beliefs into line with accepted science knowledge. The identification and cataloging of misconceptions has definite practical value, but it is not enough. The more important task is to determine why students develop beliefs that conflict with accepted science knowledge. The specific questions to be answered are: What are the cognitive mechanisms responsible for the development of personal theories and models, and why are these theories and models, once developed, so resistant to change?

TEACHING FOR CONCEPTUAL CHANGE

To counteract misconceptions and facilitate conceptual change, teachers should encourage students to question what their physical senses tell them because their senses often give a biased view of the way the world really works.

Teachers should stress to students that *the process of perception is relative*: No two individuals perceive (i.e., see, hear, and taste) exactly the same thing when they observe a sensory phenomena. Optical illusions, such as those found in introductory psychology textbooks, could be shown to students to help convince them that perception is a relative process.

In science class, demonstrations can be carried out to refute the misconceptions that exist in the personal theories and models of students. However, these demonstrations will be discounted by the students as unrealistic unless the teacher can connect the demonstrations to the students' real-world experiences. Posner and his colleagues (Posner, Strike, Hewson, & Gertzog

1982; Strike & Posner, 1985) believe that the following conditions should exist in order to bring about conceptual change in students:

1. The students must be dissatisfied with their existing conceptions.
2. The students must have a minimal understanding of the new conception.
3. The new conception must appear initially plausible.
4. The new conception should have explanatory and predictive power.

How can a science teacher create Posner's conditions in the classroom? The work of John Clement is a step in the right direction. Clement and his colleagues (e.g., Clement, Brown, & Zietsman, in press) have had considerable success coping with students' misconceptions by using demonstrations that build upon the students' real-world experiences. Clement noted that many students refuse to believe that static objects can exert forces. For example, many students refuse to believe that a table exerts an upward force on a book sitting on the table. However, all students agree that a spring exerts a constant force on one's hand when one holds it compressed. Clement has developed a "bridging strategy" to help convince students that the book on the table is analogous to the compressed spring. He presents the students with a intermediate, bridging example, such as a book resting on a flexible board (see Fig. 1.6). The students, drawing an analogy from the spring to the board to the book, are then more willing to believe that the table exerts an upward force on the book. More importantly, the students are more receptive to the general idea that even apparently rigid objects are springy to some degree.

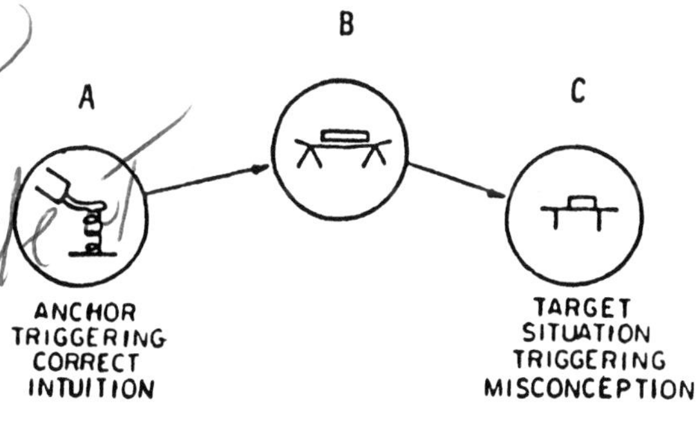

FIG. 1.6.   A "bridging strategy" for conceptual change. From "The Use of Analogies and Anchoring Intuitions to Remediate Misconceptions in Mechanics," by John Clement, 1987. Paper presented at the meeting of the American Educational Research Association. Reprinted by permission.

LEARNING SCIENCE: CONSTRUCTION AND
RECONSTRUCTION

We view the learning of science as a process of construction and reconstruction of personal theories and models. Empirical studies of how students develop their conceptions about phenomena in physics (McCloskey, 1983; Smith, Carey, & Wiser, 1986; Viennot, 1979; J. White & Glynn, 1990; Wiser & Carey, 1983), biology (Carey, 1985), and astronomy (Vosniadou & Brewer, 1987), all support the view that learning is a process of constructing and reconstructing personal theories and models. Barbara White and John Frederiksen (1986) have, in fact, developed instructional software in the area of electricity, which is based on this view. Their software guides the learner through a progression from simple to advanced models of electrical circuits.

Science teachers should view instruction as a process of helping students acquire progressively more sophisticated theories and models of science phenomena (e.g., electricity, gravity, and photosynthesis). Teachers should take students' beliefs into account when developing curriculum plans. Science teachers should expect students to come to their classes with personal theories and models which, in many cases, depart markedly from scientific theories and models. In these cases, the teacher's task is to help the students reconstruct their beliefs to bring them into line with accepted scientific knowledge. Science teachers should point out to students that theories and models, both scientific and personal, are always flawed to some degree and subject to revision. Since theories and models are always flawed, they necessarily contain misconceptions—this is the "dark side" of any theory or model.

It is natural for students to progress through a sequence of theories and models because the stage of intellectual development that the students happen to be in (i.e., preoperational or concrete operational) imposes limitations on the sophistication of the theories and models that can be understood. For example, elementary-school children usually are taught to think of electricity and magnetism as two different forces. It may not be until high school that the children are taught that these two forces are actually manifestations of one electromagnetic force: Electric currents produce magnetic fields, but changing magnetic fields also produce electric currents. To teach the more sophisticated view to young children is considered impractical by many science teachers. Consequently, the children are taught a simpler, more easily comprehended theory and science teachers put themselves in the awkward, but perhaps unavoidable position of deliberately teaching misconceptions. Usually, these deliberately taught misconceptions are straightened out later when the children are at a higher stage of intellectual development. If these misconceptions are not straightened out, then the children will carry them into adolescence, and perhaps adulthood, adding to the problem of scientific illiteracy.

The way children acquire scientific knowledge appears to parallel the , way human cultures have acquired scientific knowledge, that is, through a process of conceptual construction and reconstruction of theories and models. Sometimes children's intuitive models even resemble those of early cultures; for example, children sometimes believe the earth is flat, cold is a thing, temperature and heat are the same, a continuous external force is necessary to keep an object moving, and moving objects stop when the force they have absorbed (impetus) dissipates. Even when children do not develop the same models as human cultures have, the process of model construction and reconstruction appears to be similar. To this extent, ontogeny recapitulates phylogeny.

SUMMARY AND CONCLUSIONS

Because the world is becoming increasingly technical, all students must have a basic understanding of science. Elementary and high school science teachers are responsible for preparing students for the high-tech world of the 21st century.

In science classes, teachers should emphasize the process of science rather than just the content, because students who understand the process are better prepared to acquire science content on their own. Conceptually based, process-oriented instructional methods should be used. Teachers and students must actively organize, elaborate, and interpret knowledge, not just repeat it and memorize it. Students must be able to explain concepts using their own words rather than repeating the words of a textbook author.

Teachers should help students to reason scientifically. One way they can do this is by modeling scientific reasoning for their students. In effect, teachers and students should become collaborators in the process of scientific reasoning.

To learn a science concept meaningfully, students should carry out cognitive processes that create relations among the elements of information in the concept. Students should then create relations between the concept and other concepts.

We developed a model of what takes place in a science student's mind when he or she reasons about a science phenomenon. The student typically responds to a problem-solving environment that contains questions, observations, and conclusions. The student carries out cognitive processes and creates relations in working memory, which have an impact on the questions, observations, and conclusions. When reasoning, the student draws upon relevant facts, principles, and skills stored in long-term memory. The final products of a student's scientific reasoning are theories and models. We distinguished between scientific theories and models and personal theories and models. These often conflict sharply with one another. Students tend to compartmentalize and insulate their personal theories and models in order to protect them from the discrepant events that they observe in science class.

To counteract misconceptions and facilitate conceptual change, teachers should encourage students to question what their physical senses tell them. In science class, demonstrations can be carried out to refute misconceptions; however, these demonstrations will be discounted by the students as unrealistic unless the teacher can connect the demonstrations to the students' personal theories, models, and real-world experiences.

Finally, we described the learning of science as a process of construction and reconstruction of personal theories and models. Science teachers should help students acquire progressively more sophisticated theories and models. Teachers should take students' theories and models into account when developing curriculum plans.

REFERENCES

Aldridge, B. G. (1989). Essential changes in secondary science: Scope, sequence, and coordination. *NSTA Report*, January/February, 1, 4.

American Association for the Advancement of Science. (1989). *Science for All Americans*. Washington, DC: Author.

Anderson C. W., & Smith, E. L. (1987). Teaching science. In V. Richardson-Keehler (Ed.), *Educator's handbook*. (pp. 84–111). New York: Longmans.

Baddeley, A. (1990). *Human memory*. Boston: Allyn & Bacon.

Britton, B. K., & Glynn, S. M. (Eds.). (1987). *Executive control processes in reading*. Hillsdale, NJ: Lawrence Erlbaum Associates.

Carey, S. (1985). *Conceptual change in childhood*. Cambridge, MA: MIT Press.

Carey, S. (1986). Cognitive science and science education. *American Psychologist, 41*, 1123–1130.

Chi, M. T. H., Feltovich, P. J., & Glaser, R. (1981). Categorization and representation of physics problems by experts and novices. *Cognitive Science, 5*, 121–152.

Clement., J., Brown, D. E., & Zietsman, A. (in press). Not all preconceptions are misconceptions: Finding "anchoring conceptions" for grounding instruction on students' intuitions. *International Journal of Science Education.*

Feltovich, P. J. (1981). *Knowledge based components of expertise in medical diagnosis* (Tech. Rep. No. PDS-2). Pittsburgh: University of Pittsburgh Learning Research and Development Center.

Funk, H. J., Okey, J. R., Fiel, R. L., Jans, H. H., & Sprague, C. S. (1979). *Learning science process skills*. Dubuque, IA: Kendall/Hunt.

Glynn, S. M. (1989). The Teaching-with-Analogies (TWA) model: Explaining concepts in expository text. In K. D. Muth (Ed.), *Children's comprehension of text: Research into practice*. (pp. 185–204). Newark, DE: International Reading Association.

Glynn, S. M., Britton, B. K., Semrud-Clikeman, M., & Muth, K. D. (1989). Analogical reasoning and problem solving in science textbooks. In J. A. Glover, R. R. Ronning, & C. R. Reynolds (Eds.), *A handbook of creativity: Assessment, theory, and research* (pp. 383–398). New York: Plenum Press.

Glynn, S. M., Muth, K. D., & Britton, B. K. (1990). Thinking out loud about concepts in science text: How instructional objectives work. In H. Mandl, E. De Corte, S. N. Bennett, & H. F. Friedrich (Eds.), *Learning and instruction: European research in an international context* (Vol. 2, pp. 215–223). Oxford, England: Pergamon Press.

Hoffman, R. R. (1980). Metaphor in science. In R. P. Honeck, & R. R. Hoffman (Eds.), *Cognition and figurative language.* Hillsdale, NJ: Lawrence Erlbaum Associates.

McCloskey, M. (1983). Intuitive physics. *Scientific American, 248,* 122–130.

Neimark, E. D. (1987). *Adventures in thinking.* San Diego: Harcourt.

Posner, G.J., Strike, K. A., Hewson, P. W., & Gertzog, W. A. (1982). Accommodation of a scientific conception: Toward a theory of conceptual change. *Science Education, 66,* 211–227.

Smith, C., Carey, S., & Wiser, M. (1986). On differentiation: A case study of the development of the concepts of size, weight, and density. *Cognition, 21,* 177–237.

Stepans, J. I., Beiswenger, R. E., & Dyche, S. (1986). Misconceptions die hard. *Science Teacher,* September, 65–69.

Strike, K. A., & Posner, G. J. (1985). A conceptual change view of learning and understanding. In L. H. T. West, & A. L. Pines (Eds.), *Cognitive structure and conceptual change.* Orlando, FL: Academic Press.

Viennot, L. (1979). Spontaneous reasoning in elementary dynamics. *European Journal of Science Education, 1,* 205–221.

Vosniadou, S., & Brewer, W. F. (1987). Theories of knowledge restructuring in development. *Review of Educational Research, 57,* 51–67.

White, B. Y., & Frederiksen, J. R. (1986). *Progressions of qualitative models as a foundation for intelligent learning environments.* (Report No. 6277). Cambridge, MA: Bolt, Beranek, & Newman.

White, J., & Glynn, S. M. (1990, April). *Children's mental models of gravity and their predictions of the vertical motion of objects.* Paper presented at the National Association for Research in Science Teaching, Atlanta.

Wiser, M., & Carey. S. (1983). When heat and temperature were one. In D. Gentner & A. Stevens (Eds.), *Mental models.* Hillsdale, NJ: Lawrence Erlbaum Associates.

Yap, K. C., & Yeany, R. H. (1988). Validation of hierarchical relationships among Piagetian Cognitive Modes and integrated science process skills for different cognitive reasoning levels. *Journal of Research in Science Teaching, 25,* 247–281.

2 Learning-theory-based Science Teaching

Audrey B. Champagne
State University of New York at Albany

Diane M. Bunce
The Catholic University of America

INTRODUCTION

Over the past 15 years, significant developments in psychological theories of learning have occurred. A strategy for science teaching based on these theories of learning and consistent with the nature of scientific inquiry is presented in this chapter. The strategy is cyclical and reflects the iterative nature of both learning and scientific inquiry. The strategy enables students to develop: (1) scientific understanding of the natural world; (2) the understanding that scientific knowledge is the product of a process engaged in by a community of scientists; and, (3) skills in the processes of learning science. When this strategy is employed, students act as a community of novice scholars. The teacher is at once coach and referee—coach in the sense of setting tasks for the student which will improve the students' performance as individual scholars, and referee in the sense of helping the collective develop and apply community standards for evidence and argument.

THE TEACHING STRATEGY

The teaching strategy may be viewed as complementary learning and instructional cycles (see Figs. 2.1 and 2.2). The learning cycle has three phases.[1] Each

---

[1]The proposed learning cycle has structural elements in common with the learning cycle used in the Science Curriculum Improvement Study program. The learning cycle proposed here is less preoccupied (concerned) with obtaining closure on a canonical explanation for physical events as is the Karplus learning cycle. This learning cycle is also adaptable to a broader range of instructional tasks and learning activities.

21

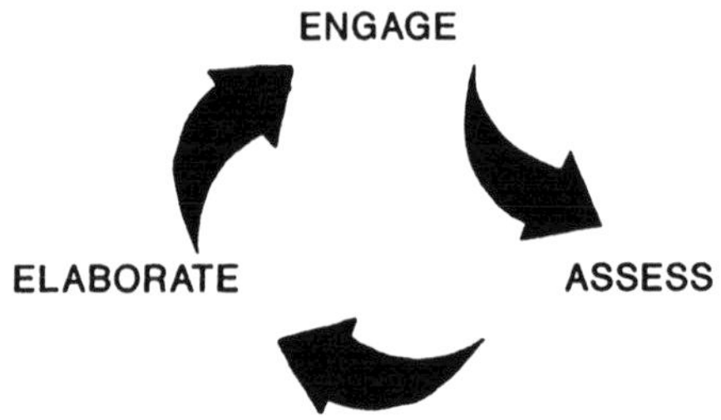

use

ENGAGE

ELABORATE   ASSESS

FIG. 2.1.   The learning cycle.

phase is named according to a stage in the learning process. The phases are engagement, elaboration, and assessment. The learner engages in an academic task, elaborates the task, and assesses his or her progress toward satisfactory completion of the task. Engagement, elaboration, and assessment are advanced via interactions with other learners under the guidance of the teacher.

The complementary instructional cycle also has three phases, which correspond to the phases of the learning cycle. The teacher sets the academic task, monitors interactions among the students and evaluates students' learning. An academic task is a goal-directed activity designed to produce lasting, cognitive change in the student. Solving problems, doing projects, explaining natural events and phenomena, and making decisions are examples of academic tasks appropriate to the teaching strategy. Memorizing definitions of scientific terms, practicing problems, or completing worksheets are instructional tasks that are a part of school science instruction, but not appropriate for this teaching strategy.

The integration of the phases in each cycle occurs when the strategy is

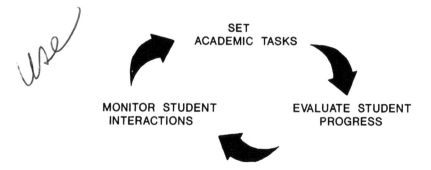

use

SET
ACADEMIC TASKS

MONITOR STUDENT   EVALUATE STUDENT
INTERACTIONS   PROGRESS

FIG. 2.2   The instructional cycle.

activated by the teacher's presentation of an academic task to a class. The active engagement of all students in the academic task is accomplished by making each student responsible for developing an approach to the instructional task and a justification for that approach. The individual plans are presented to the group where students discuss merits of the plans. The group's goal is to identify and execute a small number of promising approaches to accomplishing the task. During the group discussion, students present and defend their approaches to the academic task. This discussion results in better definition of the task as well as the identification and gathering of information that is necessary for its successful completion. As a result of the group's discussions, the group's conception of the task and possible strategies for its completion are elaborated.

The teacher monitors the group's progress and intervenes when necessary. The teacher's intervention is tailored to advance the group's progress toward accomplishing the academic task.

Observations of student discussions provide the teacher with valuable information about all aspects of student achievement including: their science conceptions, the meaning they attribute to science terms, assumptions that students use in developing arguments, and the logical quality of their arguments. This information modifies the teacher's instructional planning. When the teacher's plans are well matched with the students' previous learning, the prediction is that students' further achievement will be enhanced.

Student assessment of their progress toward accomplishing the academic task and the teacher's evaluations of both the group's and individual student's progress are ongoing activities. The result of the student assessment and teacher evaluations shape the subsequent steps in the process.

The Teaching Strategy, the Goals of School Science, and Scientific Inquiry

The proposed teaching strategy is particularly appropriate for school science because it: (1) is in accord with the goals of school science; (2) approximates the processes of scientific inquiry; and (3) is compatible with psychological theories of how people learn. The teaching strategy's purposes are consistent with the goals of school science. These purposes are to enable the student to gain scientific understanding of the natural world, an understanding of how scientific knowledge develops, as well as developing skills in the process of learning science.

Among the goals of school science are for the student to come to understand how scientific knowledge is generated and the scientific community's rules of evidence and argumentation. The proposed teaching strategy provides the opportunity for students to understand the process of scientific knowledge generation by participating in a similar process at a level commensurate with their level of development.

The proposed teaching strategy also provides students with the opportunity to experience how the meaning of concepts and principles evolves in the scientific community. Scientific knowledge develops as concepts and principles are advanced and refined by the scientific community. The process is the result of new information and reinterpretation of existing ideas in the light of the new information. Students participating in a group approach to an academic task develop community knowledge in a manner consistent with the processes of scientific inquiry. The group's understanding of principles and concepts evolves as new information becomes available, and the relation of that information to the concept or principle is discussed by the group.

In addition to conceptual understanding, the application of scientific knowledge is a valued goal of science education. Our discussion in the body of the text focuses on the use of the model to generate scientific knowledge. An example in Appendix A extends the model to the application of scientific and mathematical information to make personal decisions. All three phases of the learning cycle share attributes with the processes by which scientific knowledge is produced. The individual student proposing an approach to an academic task is analogous to the scientists planning an approach to the investigation of a problem. There are two significant differences. First, the student's task is in most cases externally imposed. In contrast, the scientist's problem is generally self-defined. A second important difference is the knowledge base of the mature scientist who already has available considerable information relevant to the problem as well as an understanding of the scientific community's intellectual standards. The consequence of these conditions is that the individual scientist proceeds much further than the student toward elaboration of the task before engaging in private discussion with his peers and brings a much more sophisticated product to the larger community. The analysis and debates of students engaged in the proposed teaching strategy approximates the rigidly prescribed ways in which the personal knowledge of the scientist becomes scientific knowledge. Individual scientists present the results of their work to the scientific community via articles in journals and presentations at meetings. The quality of the work is evaluated by the community, and only work that meets the community's standards becomes scientific knowledge. Evidence presented by the scientist is evaluated according to scientific community standards. The argument that connects empirical evidence to the conclusions is evaluated according to the scientific community's standards of rational argumentation. Not only is this teaching strategy consistent with the goals of school science, but it is also in accord with the tenets of psychological theories of learning.

Psychological Theories of Learning and Implications for Teaching

Psychology provides (1) theoretical explanations for educators' observations that listening to lectures, reading texts, and doing cookbook labs are an ineffective means for developing understanding of scientific principles, and (2) a rationale for instruction that employs verbal interaction among peers to develop conceptual understanding of science and the application of scientific knowledge in personal and social contexts. The explanations and rationale are based on five psychological principles:

scientific knowledge is complex;

experts' knowledge is tacit;

learners construct understanding;

personal theories about the natural world influence the extent and quality of science learning, and

social interaction produces cognitive change.

Scientific Knowledge Is Complex and Experts' Knowledge Is Tacit

These two ideas are the products of work by cognitive scientists. Workers in this field seek better understanding of human intelligence by studying the artificial intelligence of computers. They design computing systems that perform complex tasks, such as the diagnosis of infectious diseases, mineral exploration, or the performance of mathematical operations. The computer systems' information bases and decision strategies are based on the information and reasoning strategies used by experts to solve the problems. The model of human cognition represented in the computer program is empirically verified by the extent to which the computer's solution of the task resembles that of the human expert.

The products of this research illustrate the overwhelming complexity of the knowledge and mental processes that experts call upon in the solution of cognitive tasks. In addition, the researchers have discovered that experts are not explicitly aware of the knowledge or thinking strategies that they are using—thus the conclusion that experts use information and reasoning strategies of which they are not aware.

Cognitive psychologists have studied the information and reasoning strategies necessary to perform academic tasks, including physics problem solving, arithmetic operations, and geometry proofs. This work illustrates the complexity of the knowledge base and reasoning skills required for this academic task. An example from psychologists' studies of arithmetic computation that illustrates the complexity of the knowledge base required for elementary arithmetic is presented in Table 2.1. Under the usual conditions of completing an academic task, the person doing the task is not conscious of the full range of knowledge and procedural skills that are necessary to

TABLE 2.1
Knowledge is Complex: An Example from Elementary Arithmetic

Elementary arithmetic operations—addition, subtraction, multiplication, and division—are performed on numbers. Numbers contain information that is used in performing the operations. Central to understanding arithmetic is knowing the information coded in number symbols.

Some of the information coded in the symbol is expressed in these propositions:

A number symbol is composed of digits.
A digit is a part of a number symbol.
There are 10 digits.
0 is a digit.
1 is a digit.
2 is a digit.
3 is a digit.
4 is a digit.
5 is a digit.
6 is a digit.
7 is a digit.
8 is a digit.
9 is a digit.
Each digit has a position in the symbol.
Each digit has a value name.
The digit's value name depends on its location.
Each digit has a value.
The rightmost digit's name is "ones."
The rightmost digit has a value of the digit's value times one.
The digit to the left of the rightmost digit has a value of the digit's value times 10.
Etc.

This is only a partial list of the propositions that can be written. A complete list of propositions will contain more than 100 propositions. Obviously, it is not possible to tell an elementary student all the propositional information coded in a number symbol. The problem is more than there being too much information to convey. Much of the information that adults use is tacit.

$$\begin{array}{r} 113 \\ -\ 49 \\ \hline \end{array}$$

For example, when adults do subtraction with regrouping, they are not explicitly aware of the information coded in the number symbols on which the computational procedure is based. They do the regrouping in a purely procedural way, crossing out the digit in the 10's place, writing the digit that is 1 less above it, and putting a numeral 1 in front of the 1's digit. They cannot explain why in subtracting 1 from the digit in the 10's place they add 10 to the digit in the 1's place.

complete the task. These only become evident when the person is asked to "think aloud" as he or she completes the task or is asked to explain his or her actions. These products of cognitive research help explain why lectures are not an effective means of instruction. Stated simply, there is too much to tell the students, and the teacher is not aware of all that needs to be told. Consequently, much of the knowledge students need to know is not *explicitly* communicated by the teachers. Successful students are the ones who can fill in the gaps for themselves. The attribute that we call academic aptitude may, in fact, be the ability to make the inferences necessary to fill in the gap between what is necessary for academic success and what the teacher teaches.

Learners Construct Understanding

Personal Theories About the Natural World Influence the Extent and Quality of Science Learning

Research conducted in the constructivist framework demonstrates that students interpret classroom experiences in terms of what they already know. Students actively seek to relate new information, ideas, and experiences to the existing knowledge that seems most appropriate. It is often the case, however, that the new information gets associated with existing knowledge that is different from what the teacher intended. In the constructivist framework, learning is more a process of refining existing knowledge than the simple accretion of new knowledge. The addition of new information is an important part of learning. But the information is always added to existing knowledge that may either facilitate or impede the addition of new information. The effects of students' prior knowledge on their science learning has been the object of considerable study over the past 15 years. This research shows that students begin their formal study of science with theories about the natural world already in place. These influence students' interpretation of science instruction and persist in the minds of students even after they have completed science courses. These theories are called by different names: misconceptions, naïve theories, noncanonical theories. They are theories that develop as the result of children's experiences and are unexamined in any formal sense. That is to say, the validity of the empirical basis and assumptions or logic of the theories have not been examined. Research on spontaneous theories of the natural world relies heavily on the statements people make as they are interviewed about their observations and interpretations of natural phenomena. For example, spontaneous theories about the motion of objects are investigated by describing to the students a demonstration of objects in motion. Students are asked to predict the results of the demonstration and explain their prediction. After observing the demonstration, the students are asked to describe their observations and explain any discrepancy between their prediction and observations. These interviews yield important information about the spontaneous theories students bring to the physics classroom.

Students' spontaneous theories are not easily changed by exposure to traditional instructional methods. This fact is particularly striking in the context of mechanics. The typical student brings a theory of motion to physics class that has elements that are more like the Aristotelian perspective than the Newtonian one that is taught in physics. The Aristotelian perspective persists with many "successful" physics students, that is, with students receiving high grades in introductory physics courses (Champagne, Klopfer, & Anderson, 1980; Gunstone & White, 1981). This research provides empirical support for what physics teachers have long observed, namely, that traditional instruction does not facilitate an appropriate reconciliation of preinstructional knowledge with the content of instruction (Ausubel, 1963).

Other work (Champagne & Klopfer, 1982; Champagne, Klopfer, & Anderson, 1980; Champagne, Klopfer, Solomon, & Cahn, 1980) demonstrates that prior knowledge affects students' comprehension of science instruction. Students' conceptions influence (1) their understanding of science texts and lectures, (2) their observations of physics experiments and, (3) their interpretations of observations.

The products of this work are descriptions of how students interpret physics lectures and textbooks in the context of their everyday understanding of scientific terms rather than in the way the teacher or text is using the terms. Consequently, students often do not recognize significant differences between what is in the text or lecture and what they already believe.

Prior conceptions also influence what students remember about the text they read. For example, when asked why they believe that heavy objects fall faster than lighter ones, many said that they had read it in a book. The students related that the books they read said that Galileo had proven that heavy objects fall faster than lighter ones. The students recall, quite accurately, that Galileo asserted that a gold coin will fall faster than a feather. They forget, however, the crucial part of Galileo's argument that in a vacuum, where there is no air resistance, both would fall at the same rate. The students recall the part of Galileo's argument that is consistent with their idea that the heavier object falls faster and forget the part of the argument that in fact explains why coin and feather will fall at the same rate when air resistance is absent or controlled. This part of Galileo's argument, that all objects fall at the same rate in a vacuum, is forgotten because it does not fit students' conceptions.

Students' observations and interpretations of experiments are similarly influenced by their unexamined beliefs about the natural world. A group of students observed an aluminum and plastic block fall after predicting a comparison of the times they would take to fall. When the demonstration was completed (the objects fall at the same rate), the students were told that they could experiment on their own with the equipment to test their predictions and observations.

One student grabbed the two blocks and weighed them on a balance. His prediction was that the aluminum block would fall faster than the plastic block, and his observation contradicted his belief that heavier objects fall faster. He resolved the contradiction by reasoning that, despite the difference in the materials from which the two blocks were made, they must be the same weight, because they fell at the same rate. He tested this hypothesis by weighing the two blocks.

Two other students who also predicted that the heavier object would fall faster experimented by dropping the blocks from a greater distance above the floor than they had been dropped in the demonstration. One student climbed onto a table and dropped the blocks, while the other put her head on the floor to watch them fall. These students reasoned that the blocks had, in fact, fallen at different rates, but that the difference in descent times was too small to be observed over the short distance (approximately 1 meter) used in the original demonstration. They tested this hypothesis by designing an experiment that used a more sensitive procedure, that is, dropping the blocks from a greater height, to illuminate any difference in the blocks' rates of fall. A plausible explanation for the students' behavior is that they were testing for the effects of air resistance or the idea that objects falling in a fluid reach a maximum velocity. However, there was no evidence from what they said that either of these ideas were being tested.

Most formal science instruction imparts scientific theories without any regard for the students' spontaneous theories. When the tenets of the scientific theories conflict with spontaneous theories or describe a world that does not fit with the students' personal experience, they are rejected outright or accepted as theories that apply only in the context of formal science and are useful only to the extent that they are interesting or are necessary to achieve a good grade in the course.

Students, even the academically able, well motivated, and high achieving, harbor a sense of dissatisfaction with their science understanding. Often during an interview, a student who has just completed a science course expresses frustration with the inability to explain a point by blurting out something to the effect: "I don't understand it, not any of it. You know what you do, learn what they tell you, and give it back to them on the test."

There is ample empirical evidence that traditional methods of teaching science, those relying on lecture and laboratory done in cookbook fashion, are not effective. Contemporary psychological theory helps explain these observations. The teaching strategy being proposed here takes into consideration the importance of the knowledge the student brings to instruction and provides opportunities for the student to make that knowledge explicit, and expose it to assessment by the student's peers and teachers. Social psychology provides empirical evidence that these kinds of social interaction improve science learning.

Social Interaction Produces Cognitive Change

The influence of social contexts on children's cognitive development is an area of research in social psychology. The contemporary view of the relationship is that cognitive growth results from social interaction.[2] "Cognitive abilities are (1) socially transmitted, (2) socially constrained, (3) socially nurtured, and (4) socially encouraged." (Day, French, & Hall, 1985, p. 51) These ideas are the contributions of the Russian psychologist, Vygotsky, to the understanding of conceptual development in children.

Vygotsky distinguishes between two types of concepts: spontaneous and scientific (Vygotsky, 1986). Spontaneous concepts are the conceptual products of the child's reflections on everyday experiences. Scientific concepts are the product of formal schooling. Spontaneous concepts, like spontaneous theories, are slow to change. Vygotsky's theory recognizes the importance of child–adult dialogues in concept growth. In these dialogues, the child's spontaneous concepts come into contact with the adult's scientific ones and, as a result, the spontaneous concepts are modified. In Vygotsky's view, scientific concepts develop as the result of dialogues between student and teacher.

Reports of the effects of interactions in formal educational settings describe various conceptual changes, including, elaboration of concepts, becoming aware of one's own learning processes, raising cognitive level, and improving problem-solving capabilities. The work of Smith et al. (1981) demonstrates that when students with different ideas are asked to reach agreement, achievement and retention are promoted. The positive effects of working cooperatively on achievement, retention, and critical reasoning skills have been reported (Johnson & Johnson, 1975; Johnson, Johnson, Holubec, & Roy, 1984; Slavin, 1983).

Social interactions are stimulated by various tasks. These include solving problems—for example, determining how many rectangles there are in a plane geometrical figure (Perret-Clermont, 1981); defining a taxonomic system (Caravita & Giuliani, undated); or reaching consensus on an explanation for a physical phenomena (Champagne et al., 1985b). Social interactions are conducted in different ways. In some instances, students are

---

[2]This perspective is different from that of Jean Piaget, whose theory attributes the development of reasoning structures to interactions with the physical world. There have been studies conducted in the Piagetian framework demonstrating that changes in performance of conservation tasks when children who are not conservers interact with children close in age who are conservers. The change in conservation behavior is interpreted in the Piagetian framework to mean that reasoning structures have undergone a developmental change.

assigned specific roles (Johnson & Johnson, 1975), and in others, the classroom is structured around an activity as in the Teams-Games-Tournament strategy (Slavin, et al., 1985). The social—psychological research reported here supports the contention that a teaching strategy that promotes teacher–student and student–student interaction should be effective in promoting cognitive growth, but gives little insight into what the mechanisms are that promote growth.

Students learn about higher-order thinking skills through observations of the teacher who models in interactions with students and observations and interpretations of physical events, the skills that he or she expects the students to develop. Moderation of group interactions by the teacher also contributes to students' understanding of science concepts, principles, and the development of higher order thinking skills. The psychological mechanisms by which these affect learning are related to principles from cognitive, behavioral, and social psychology. An example is students' use of scientific terminology.

The posited effects of the teaching strategy on the development of the higher-order thinking skills—learning-to-learn, problem solving, scientific inquiry—are based on a principle from behavioral psychology. The principle is straightforward, creates an environment in which the student can exhibit the desired skills and where the skills can be refined by feedback from the teacher and peers. According to the principles of behavioral psychology, student behaviors that approximate desirable behavior are rewarded. As the behavior becomes more frequent, the reward schedule is modified—the desired behavior is awarded only occasionally.

Peer interaction is more effective than teacher lectures in conveying scientific knowledge because peers' explanations are simpler than adults' and as a consequence are better understood by the learner. To say it another way, the distance between two students' understanding is far less than the distance between a student's understanding and a teacher's, hence communication of ideas is facilitated. Often a peer is quicker to identify a point of confusion than a teacher. The interactive nature of the teaching strategy is based on an interpretation of a tenet of cognitive psychology, proposed by David Ausubel and elaborated by Novak (1977). It is that assimilation of new ideas is contingent on how closely the new idea fits with what the student already knows.

IMPLICATIONS OF LEARNING THEORY FOR THE TEACHING STRATEGY

If one accepts the premise that learning is an active process, an essential feature of any academic strategy is to engage the learner. Engagement is achieved by assigning the student an academic task. The teacher's responsibility is to select a task that will contribute to the student's learning, be interesting to the student, and appropriate to the student's mental and physical capabilities. Examples of tasks include:

applying an example of a scientific principle; solving some kind of problem—it might be a textbook problem or a real world problem—qualitative or quantitative;

giving a scientific explanation of a physical event—changes in the length of day light or the rate at which objects fall;

making a political or social decision;

planning a project or experiment.

The most effective means of ensuring active participation is to require each student to prepare a written proposal for approaching the task. Younger students whose writing skills are not well developed may have to draw a picture, make an audiotape, or dictate their plans. The process of writing a preliminary approach to the academic task focuses the student's attention on the task, and gives the teacher the opportunity to reflect on his or her understanding of the task, recall information that is pertinent to the task, and to organize the best preliminary strategy for completing the task. In some cases, the strategy may be as simple as formulating questions to achieve better definition of the tasks.

This written statement is important to the student's participation in the group discussions that follow. Presumably, the student has developed some commitment to the product of his or her thinking and will be motivated to share ideas with other students and to defend the wisdom of his or her thinking against the work of the other students in the group. Refinement of the plan comes from the feedback provided by the teacher and one's peers. Questions and comments let the student know how well people understand the presentation and gives him or her a sense of the strengths and weaknesses of one's ideas. Since the group's task is to work toward developing consensus, the student must listen carefully to the presentations of others in the group. As a result, one will be exposed to new information and ways of thinking about the academic task. This new information will improve the student's understanding of the task and enable him or her to modify his or her ideas to accommodate the new information and alternative ways of thinking about it. The student's conception of the task and information necessary for its completion will be extended as a result of the group interaction.

The elaborate phase begins with individual presentations to the group. After the initial presentations by each member of the group, students need the opportunity to reconsider their ideas in view of the presentations they have heard. As the discussions proceed, the group moves toward consensus. Consensus may mean agreement on a project plan, a strategy for the completion of the task, or an explanation for an observation. Consensus can also mean agreeing to disagree. In any one of the situations described, there may be two or more plans, strategies, or explanations that have equivalent face validity. In this situation, the ideal solution is to test the alternative ideas. However, this is a situation in which the teacher may decide to intervene and steer the group to one or another of the proposals.

While participating in the group activities, the student has the opportunity to refine and practice many important skills, including science learning and assessment skills, at the same time as learning about science and its applications to his or her personal and social life. The student will have practiced composing a well-structured argument and its presentation, both in written and spoken form. He or she will also have practiced defending an idea to one's colleagues and experienced modifying one's ideas in the face of new information. There will be ample opportunity to practice listening skills, which are important to the process of analyzing the quality of one's peers' ideas, and identifying points of similarity and difference in the ideas presented by the members of the group. Furthermore, the student will be developing the skills necessary to assess the quality of one's own ideas as well as those of other students. Integral to the application of assessment skills are criteria on which to base quality judgments. The opportunity to teach students about these criteria arises quite naturally in the group interactions. Inevitably, as students present their ideas, controversies arise within the group over the quality of information and the reasonableness of assumptions and arguments. When controversy arises, the group is presented with the challenge of developing standards for evidence and logical argumentation. The teacher, in the role as coach and referee, has a major responsibility in helping the group to recognize the need for standards and in helping the group set the standards. Once the standards have been set, the teacher takes responsibility for seeing that they are upheld, while at the same time, helping the members of the group learn to take responsibility for monitoring themselves. As group standards become explicit, individual students learn about these criteria and their application.

These criteria approximate those used by the scientific community. This is a case where the development of science learning skills and understanding the nature of science intersect and illustrates the correspondence between the instructional processes of the teaching strategy and the goals of school science. The strategy proposed provides students the opportunity to learn to assess their own progress toward completing the academic tasks as well as assessing their own understanding of science content and development of science-related skills.

CONCLUSION

The proposed teaching strategy is well matched to many of the goals of science education. Furthermore, it is congruent with the tenets of contemporary psychological theory. Implementation of the strategy presents a challenge to the teacher. The most significant challenge is knowing how to manage the intellectual flow of the group's inquiry. The teacher is constantly faced with decisions about content and process. Should a teacher redirect a good discussion, even if he or she knows that it is leading the students down the garden path? When should the emphasis be on learning how to engage fruitfully in discussion? How much does the teacher press the group to reach closure on one task and move on to another? These are questions the teacher faces on a day-to-day basis.

Selection of the academic tasks is a challenging problem for both the curriculum designer and the teacher. The teacher must judiciously balance the instructional agenda against the group's activity-generated agenda. The curriculum designer sets a generic instructional agenda which may be more or less well matched to the teacher's students. In the case where the students' knowledge and thinking skills are not adequate to the academic task set by the curriculum, the teacher must set new tasks to allow the students to gain the necessary skills. Often the teacher gains insights into these deficiencies as a result of observing students in group discussions. Teachers and curriculum designers are not the only source of instructional tasks or activities. As students work on a task, they generate new questions and expand the narrowly defined task presented by the teacher. A significant conceptual challenge for the teacher is to determine which of the possible academic tasks is the most appropriate for the students.

Orchestrating the teaching strategy is a supreme test of the teacher's pedagogical skill. The challenge to the teacher is great, but so are the rewards. No other method of teaching science has such a strong psychological basis, is so congruent with the nature of science, and affords the teacher such an intimate view of his or her student's progress.

ACKNOWLEDGMENT

An earlier version of this paper was commissioned by the Biological Science Study Committee as a part of a project supported by the International Business Machines Corporation. This version is being published with the full knowledge and consent of BSCS.

REFERENCES

Anderson, J. R. (1976). *Language, memory, and thought.* Hillsdale, NJ: Lawrence Erlbaum Associates.

Anderson, R. C., Reynolds, R. E., Schallert, D. L., & Goetz, E. T. (1977). Frameworks for comprehending discourse. *American Educational Research Journal, 14,* 367–381.

Ausubel, D. (1963). *The psychology of meaningful verbal learning.* NY: Grune and Straton.

Bongaarts, J., & Potter G. (1983). *Fertility, biology, and behavior: An analysis of the proximate determinants.* New York: Academic Press.

Caravita, S., & Giuliani, G. (undated). *Discussion in school classes: Collective modeling of schemata.* Mimeographed paper.

Champagne, A. B., & Klopfer, L. E. (1981). Structuring process skills and the solution of verbal problems involving science concepts. *Science Education, 65,* 493–511.

Champagne, A. B., & Klopfer, L. E. (1982). A causal model of students' achievement in a college physics course. *Journal of Research in Science Teaching, 19,* 299–309.

Champagne, A. B., Klopfer, L. E., & Anderson, J. H. (1980). Factors influencing the learning of classical mechanics. *American Journal of Physics, 48,* 1074–1079.

Champagne, A. B., Klopfer, L. E., DeSena, A., & Squires, D. (1978). *Content structure in science instructional materials and knowledge structure in students' memory.* University of Pittsburgh, Learning Research and Development Center Publication Series.

Champagne, A. B., Klopfer, L. E., & Gunstone, R. F. (1981 April). *A model of adolescents' understanding of physical phenomena and its application to instruction.* Paper presented at the meeting of the American Educational Research Association, Los Angeles.

Champagne, A. B., Klopfer, L. E., & Gunstone, R. F. (1982). Cognitive research and the design of science instruction. *Educational Psychologist, 17* (1), 31–53.

Champagne, A. B., Klopfer, L. E., and Gunstone, R. F. (1985a). Effecting changes in cognitive structures among physics students. In A. L. Pines & F. H. T. West (Eds.), *Cognitive structure and conceptual change.* New York: Academic Press.

Champagne, A. B., Klopfer, L. E., & Gunstone, R. F. (1985b). Instructional consequences of students' knowledge about physical phenomena. In A. L. Pines & F. H. T. West (Eds.), *Cognitive structure and conceptual change.* New York: Academic Press.

Champagne, A. B., Klopfer, L. E., Solomon, C. A., & Cahn, A. D. (1980). *Interactions of students' knowledge with their comprehension and design of science experiments.* University of Pittsburgh, Learning Research and Development Center Publication Series. (1980/9) (ERIC Document Reproduction Service No. ED 188 950).

Day, J. D., French, L. A., & Hall, L. K. (1985). Social influences on cognitive development. In D. L. Forrest-Pressley, G. E. MacKinnon, & T. G. Waller (Eds.), *Metacognition, cognition, and human performance: Vol. 1. Theoretical perspectives.* New York: Academic Press.

Gunstone, R., & White, R. (1981). Understanding of gravity. *Science Education, 65* (3), 291–299.

Johnson, D. W. (1980 April). *Student–student interaction: The neglected variable in education.* Paper presented at a symposium entitled Psychology and Education—State of the Union, at American Educational Research Association's annual meeting, Boston.

Johnson, D. W., & Johnson, R. (1975). *Learning together and alone: Cooperation, competition, and individualization.* Englewood Cliffs, NJ: Prentice Hall.

Johnson D. W., Johnson, R., Holubec, E., & Roy, P. (1984). *Circles of learning.* Alexandria, VA: Association for Supervision and Curriculum Development.

Novak, D. (1977). *A theory of education.* Ithaca, NY: Cornell University Press.

Perret-Clermont, A. N. (1981). *Approaches psychosociologiques de l'apprentissage en situation collective.* Dossiers de Psychologie. Neuchatel, France: Université de Neuchatel.

Slavin, R. E. (1983). *Cooperative learning.* New York: Longman.

Slavin, R. E., Sharan, S., Kagan, S., Hertz-Lazarowitz, R., Webb, C., & Schmuck, R. (Eds.). (1985). *Learning to cooperate. Cooperating to learn.* New York: Plenum Press.

Smith, K., Johnson, D. W., & Johnson, R. (1981). Can conflict be constructive? Controversy versus concurrence seeking in learning groups. *Journal of Educational Psychology, 73,* 651–663.

Vygotsky, L. (1986). *Thought and language.* Cambridge, MA: The MIT Press.

APPENDIX A
THE TEACHING MODEL APPLIED TO BIOLOGY

The teaching model can be applied to engender scientific understanding of the natural world and the application of that knowledge to making personal, social, and civic decisions. The examples from physics in the body of the text have as their purpose to develop conceptual understanding. They stop short of developing the skills to apply that knowledge. The example developed here is from human biology and relates to a problem of national concern: teen-age pregnancy. The goal of the experiences is to help teen-agers understand the physiology of conception and the implications this knowledge has for their behavior with regard to sexual activity. This goal is not different from that of conventional instruction, which has been remarkably unsuccessful in changing behaviors that lead to teen-age pregnancy. While we recognize that attitudes, values, and societal conditions are factors that influence sexual behaviors, knowledge and its implications are also essential to making choices. Conventional instruction does not integrate values, societal conditions, or decision making with the development of conceptual understanding. Because the teaching model has the potential to engender conceptual understanding and to foster integration with life experiences, we believe it can be more influential in determining behaviors than conventional instruction. One reason for the lack of impact of conventional instruction on individuals' behavior is that students have not internalized the content. Instead, such knowledge is held in memory until the science test is completed and then is forgotten. If such knowledge is not integrated with the students' life-related beliefs, no real learning or modification of behavior can be expected to result. If the same material is taught using the Teaching Model, students will be provided with opportunities to examine their previously held knowledge, to integrate new knowledge, and practice the use of that knowledge in making personal decisions.

A SUMMARY OF THE UNIT

The unit described here begins with students assessing the probability that engaging in a single act of sexual intercourse will result in pregnancy. This discussion requires students to define probability and the factors that they believe affect conception. They both write and discuss these ideas with their peers, which provides the teacher with important information about their current understanding of these topics. The teacher uses this information for planning. For instance, it is unlikely that the students' conception of probability or the factors that influence conception will be adequate for making decisions. The teachers can identify gaps in the students' understanding and misconceptions and plan for ways to provide the necessary information and to challenge misconceptions for the purpose of changing them. This may involve the mathematics teacher's joining with the biology teacher in developing and implementing this unit.

What follows is a script for the unit. It is illustrative of the mechanics but contains little content information. Following the script is some information relevant to the physiology of human conception.

The application for the Teaching Model described here includes setting the Academic Task, assessing the probability of conception; providing opportunity for individual response (Engagement); class discussion (Monitoring Student Interactions); external information gathering (Elaboration); small-group discussion (Elaboration); class discussion (Monitoring Student Interaction/elaboration); Evaluation and Assessment. The two parts of the model, Elaboration and Monitoring Student Interaction, go hand in hand and are repeated during the operation of the model.

Instructional Cycle (Teacher)	Learning Cycle (Student)
Set Academic Task Question posed to class: What are your chances of becoming pregnant or causing your partner to become pregnant if you engage in a single act of intercourse?	
	Engage Students estimate "chances" of becoming or causing partner to become pregnant. Explain how they arrived at their estimate.

Monitor Student Interaction
Teacher leads CLASS DISCUSSION of responses by recording estimates for class analysis

Elaborate
CLASS DISCUSSION

Teacher arranges students into SMALL GROUPS to discuss the relative advantages and disadvantages of different ways of expressing probability. Aim of the small-group discussion is a better understanding of the meaning of probability statements.

SMALL-GROUP DISCUSSION—students may have sought outside information to help defend/explain their position.

Teacher organizes a CLASS DISCUSSION to elicit different opinions of probability from small groups. The teacher asks for meaning of students' statements such as: "What does 0% probability mean? What does 1 chance in 10 actually mean?" Teacher then helps class organize and categorize the probability information discussed.

Evaluate
As a result of class discussion, the teacher has better understanding of student knowledge. In evaluating student learning, the teacher must judge how closely students, both individually and as a group, have come to the canonical definition of probability. The teacher must also decide if students can identify the unresolved issues that have arisen during the discussions.

Assess

If student understanding is insufficient, the teacher has the option to initiate a second round of discussion and information gathering. To help the teacher evaluate the student's understanding, the teacher can require an essay response of each student. As a result of this evaluation, individual tutoring by teacher or peers may be a reasonable option.

Students clarify individual definition of probability and enter into group consensus of a probability definition.

After a definition of probability has been agreed on, emphasis shifts back to the biological question of the original academic task.

Monitor Students' Interactions

Elaborate

Teacher organizes a CLASS DISCUSSION. Students are asked if they want to change or keep their original estimate of the chances of becoming or causing a partner to become pregnant. Next, the discussion deals with identifying the biological factors involved in students' estimates.

Students go to outside sources to check and support the factors identified in class.

Teacher organizes class into SMALL-GROUP DISCUSSIONS.

Individual students must present and defend their positions by identifying what is or is not a factor and by elaborating the parameters and corresponding probabilities of each parameter.

Teacher organizes CLASS DISCUSSION to survey groups' positions and to encourage development of a parameter hierarchy. Questions for discussion might include: Which parameters are important? Which could be ignored? What are the probabilities of each factor? How can several parameters and probabilities be combined?

Evaluate

Once again, the teacher is able to examine through class discussion and monitoring of small-group discussion, what the students' original knowledge of the situation was and how close they have come to the canonical view of the problem. In this model, students help to create and integrate "new" knowledge with existing knowledge, and the teacher in role as coach has an opportunity to observe the outward signs of this process.

Assess

Students are able to judge how much they know about the topic by how comfortable they feel in defending their positions to peers. They should also be able to identify what they still would like to find out about the subject.

SOME SAMPLE PARAMETERS GLEANED FROM OUTSIDE SOURCES
Courtesy of the Guttmacher Institute (Bongaarts & Potter, 1983)

1. There are four requirements for successful conception:
   a. The woman's cycle is ovulatory (95% of cycles are)
   b. Insemination occurs during fertile time (about 2 days near middle of cycle)
   c. Insemination leads to fertilization (This happens in about 95% of the cases if the first two conditions are met)
   d. Fertilization results in a recognizable conception (This happens in 50% of the cases if the first three conditions are met)

2. One intercourse in 6 days around time of ovulation results in 17% of women becoming pregnant.
   Two intercourses = 34% pregnant
   Three intercourses = 41% pregnant

3. Based upon the four requirements for conception, the following chart relates the number of intercourses within a 26-day menstrual cycle and the resulting chance of becoming pregnant as a result:

1 intercourse/26 days	3.5% pregnant
2	6.8
3	10.0
4 (once a week)	13.0
5	15.9
6	18.7
7	21.3
8 (twice a week)	23.8
9	26.2
10	28.4
11	30.5
12 (three a week)	32.4
13	34.2
14	35.9
15	37.4
20 (five a week)	42.9

4. Fertile periods for females are brief intervals around time of ovulation.

5. Sperm does not become fertile until 6 hours after insemination and remains fertile for 24 to 48 hours.

6. The ovum remains viable for 12 to 24 hours after release.

7. Risk of conception is zero until beginning of fertile period. It rises to 47.5% and after the 2-day period of ovulation declines to zero. This means the risk of becoming pregnant is zero before the 8th day of the menstrual cycle and after the 23rd day.

8. Male sterility is cause of couple sterility in one-third to one-half of all cases.

9. The factors that have the greatest effect on population fertility are:
   a. rising age at marriage;
   b. decreased length of time of effective breast feeding and its resulting influence on the shortened length of time before conception can occur again.

3 A Conceptual Change Model of Learning Science

Edward L. Smith
Michigan State University

Most people would probably agree that learning science with understanding is desirable for all students. However, not all teachers accept this as a feasible goal for their teaching, nor do all students adopt this as a goal for their learning. Many teachers believe that only those students with high aptitude and motivation will understand the science they teach, while the others will at least be exposed to the subject matter. Many students approach the tasks of instruction with the goal of simply getting them done, meeting the requirements for an acceptable grade, and memorizing information or procedures necessary to pass the tests.

However, revolutionary developments in cognitive psychology and social constructivist theories of knowledge, together with associated research on the learning and teaching of science, have led to new understanding of why the goal of learning science with understanding has been so elusive for so many students. These developments have also demonstrated that such learning is an attainable goal for at least a large majority of students. The purpose of this chapter is to describe a view of learning science with understanding that has developed from and guided much of this research.

AN EXAMPLE OF LEARNING SCIENCE WITH UNDERSTANDING

To illustrate this view of learning, I shall describe a pattern of discourse that occurs in the elementary science methods course that I teach. It follows a pattern very similar to Minstrell's (1982) work with high school physics students on the problem of an "at rest object."

I begin by presenting the students with the following problem:

Situation:	A book on a table
Question:	Does the table push on the book?
Common responses:	No, the table can't push.
	Yes, if it didn't push, the book would fall.
	No, the table is just in the way so the book doesn't fall.
	No, the book pushes on the table because gravity pulls on it (the book).

A conflict arises here in which many students hold positions that they defend energetically with arguments. The class usually divides into two camps, one arguing the impossibility of inanimate things such as tables pushing, while the other argues the essentially Newtonian view that the push of the table is necessary to balance the pull of gravity and prevent the book from falling. The students' justifications are often punctuated with words such as "impossible," "must," and "can't," which, along with their enthusiasm, reflect a degree of conviction to their views.

At this point, a different problem is introduced:

Situation:	A book placed on a student's hand
Question:	Does the hand push on the book?

Some of those who argued that the table did *not* push on the book assert:

Yes, her hand is pushing on the book, after all, hands can push.

Others argue: No, her hand is just *holding* the book.

As additional books are piled on, more students shift their response, agreeing that the hand is indeed pushing on the book. Returning to the book-on-the-table problem, some, but by no means all, of the students have shifted to the view that the table does push, arguing that it is really no different than the book on the hand situation.

At this point, the concept of "force" is introduced as a push or pull on an object by another object and having a direction and a size. Examples such as a hand holding a briefcase and a finger pushing a button are discussed. Next, the use of arrow diagrams to represent forces is introduced and practiced with the same examples. A diagram such as that in Fig. 3.1a is developed for the

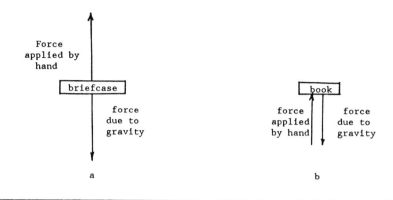

FIG. 3.1.   Arrow diagrams representing forces on objects. (a) Diagram
cooperatively prepared by teacher and students for the briefcase problem.
(b) Diagram prepared cooperatively for the book on the hand problem.
(c) Diagram by students who believe that the table cannot exert a force.
(d) Diagram reflecting the Newtonian description.

briefcase example through class discussion. There is usually consensus that
the force of the hand on the briefcase is equal to and in the opposite direction
to the force of gravity.

With this background, the discussion returns to the book-on-the-hand
problem, resulting in a diagram similar to that in Fig. 3.1b. Finally, the book
on the table is reconsidered. Students draw and discuss the alternatives in
Figs. 3.1c and 3.1d.

Common responses: It seems funny but the table must be exerting an
upward force, otherwise the book would be moving
down.

I guess it must be exerting a force on the book, but how
does it know how hard to push?

At this point, most of the students argue that the table must be exerting a force on the book, even though the idea is still somewhat counterintuitive for some of them.

The idea is made more plausible through discussion and diagramming of forces exerted by varying numbers of books in a pile on the table.

> Common response: The table pushes back with however much force the books push on it.

This leads to the articulation of the idea that the table exerts a force in reaction to whatever force is applied to it, equal in size and opposite in direction to that applied force. This is a statement in everyday language of Newton's third law.

Following this demonstration lesson, we discuss the experience and the students' responses to it. Students often describe the experience as unique. They contrast the experience to their typical experience in science classes. Many report the sense that they really understand, rather than having memorized something for the test. Further, they report seldom, if ever, having had this kind of opportunity to argue and debate their ideas until they felt confident that they did understand.

I think the students are right. I would argue that the students have developed an understanding of the forces involved in the book-on-the-table problem. Although further work is necessary to generalize these ideas, and further conceptual difficulties remain to be overcome, an important beginning has been made in their understanding of Newtonian forces. But what does it mean to claim that they understand and how does such understanding come about?

WHAT DOES IT MEAN TO UNDERSTAND?

I propose two criteria for understanding in science: *connectedness* and *usefulness in social contexts*. The first criterion deals with the structure of a person's knowledge. An idea is understood to the extent that the learner has appropriately represented it and connected it with other ideas, particularly with the learner's own prior knowledge and beliefs. Learning with understanding can thus be contrasted to learning of isolated bits of information. Many students and even some teachers view the learning of science as primarily the learning of many definitions and facts that are to be memorized and reproduced or recognized for testing purposes. Such learning fails to meet the connectedness criterion for understanding.

The second criterion deals with the function of a person's knowledge. An idea is understood to the extent that the learner can use that idea in successfully performing significant tasks appropriate to the social context in which they occur. This criterion incorporates three aspects: (1) The learner should be able to carry actually out various kinds of tasks. (2) The tasks should be generally recognized as worthwhile. (3) The learner should be able to perform the tasks in the social context where they are valued and in a manner judged appropriate by the participants in that context. Another way of expressing this criterion is that the learner should be able to participate successfully in a community of people who share, use, and value scientific knowledge.

The following sections of this chapter will elaborate on these criteria and their implications for learning and teaching science.

UNDERSTANDING AS CONNECTEDNESS

Structure and the Criterion of Connectedness

Consideration of the criterion of connectedness of knowledge is intimately tied up with the idea of the structure of knowledge. Bruner (1960) argued the importance of structure in a book in which he attempted to synthesize the results of a conference that had considerable impact on the science curriculum reforms of the late 1950s and the 1960s. Schwab (1964) and others attempted to characterize the structure of knowledge in the disciplines and its relevance for education. Prevailing psychological theories at that time, however, had very limited capacity to elucidate the structure of knowledge or what it meant to understand subject matter.

The identification of understanding with connectedness was evident in Ausubel's (1968) notion of "meaningfulness." In this view, a concept is meaningful to the extent that it is nonarbitrarily related to other concepts in the individual's cognitive structure. Ausubel contrasted meaningful learning to rote learning in which concepts are learned in isolation.

Contemporary cognitive psychology has explained comprehension and learning in term of incorporation of new information into knowledge structures referred to as schemata or frames. Science educators have adapted these theoretical developments in efforts to describe the conceptual structure of subject matter knowledge and the cognitive structure of individuals. Common to these efforts is the explicit or implicit definition of understanding of an idea as the representation of the idea and the appropriate connecting of that idea to other ideas in the person's memory.

In the extreme, students learn individual facts, definitions, or skills in isolation with almost no connections to anything. However, students can make connections among scientific ideas and still not have a sense of understanding them. Unless the ideas are related to other knowledge already possessed and to objects and events in the real world, the term "understanding" seems inappropriate. As formulated here, understanding of a scientific idea involves making connections between that concept and (1) the student's own prior knowledge, (2) objects and phenomena in the real world, and (3) other scientific ideas.

To illustrate, I will apply this criterion to the students in the force lesson described previously. A number of science educators (cf. Novak & Gowin,

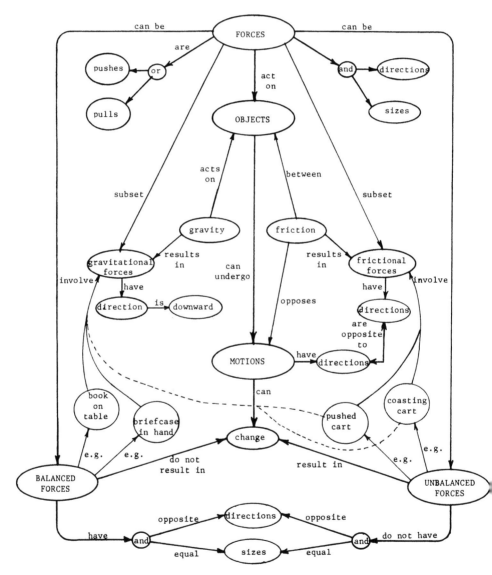

FIG. 3.2.   Concept map for the demonstration unit on force.

1984) have used a technique called "concept mapping" to represent the structure of students' knowledge. Fig. 3.2 is a concept map representing the inferred structure of the knowledge students developed in that lesson. Note that there are connections to students' prior knowledge (e.g., "push," "pull"), real-world objects (e.g., book, table), and other scientific concepts (e.g., friction, gravity). From the perspective of structure, it was in the working out of these connections that students came to understand, in an important way, the forces involved in the book-on-the-table problem.

The Problem of Conceptual Change

The criterion of connectedness as has been described makes learning sound deceptively simple. Students bring with them to the study of science a considerable amount of knowledge, which they have developed from their interactions with the natural world and the cultural milieu in which they live. However, learning science is usually not just a matter of adding information and making connections. Students' prior knowledge is often inconsistent with the scientific knowledge that they are expected to learn.

For example, in developing their understanding of the forces in the book-on-the-table problem, the students had to change an idea they had initially, that inanimate objects cannot exert forces (pushes or pulls). Understanding new scientific ideas frequently involves such changes. Understanding that plants make their own food in the process of photosynthesis requires that students change their conception of what constitutes food (Anderson & Smith, 1987). Understanding Newton's second law $(f = ma)$ requires that students change their conception of the relation between force and motion (Clement, 1982; Minstrell, 1984). This illustrates how the term "conceptual change" characterizes the view of learning presented in this chapter. Students' prior knowledge needs to undergo change for the new scientific ideas to fit. However, many studies of students' conceptions have demonstrated that science instruction often fails to bring about such changes. Students often demonstrate the same "naïve conceptions" or "alternative frameworks" after instruction that they did before. What makes this change problematical is, in part, the role played by prior knowledge. Learning is not simply a matter of adding new knowledge, nor a matter of correcting incorrect information. The prior knowledge includes the interpretive frameworks that the learner uses to make sense of the world and to communicate with other people. It is these interpretive frameworks that must change. As Carey (1986) points out, there is a paradox here. For, while understanding requires relating new information to prior knowledge, the prior knowledge—part of the sense-making apparatus itself—must change. This is what Toulmin (1972) refers to as "the problem of conceptual change."

Requirements for Conceptual Change

As illustrated in the force lesson described here, promoting conceptual change is not simply a matter of telling the student they are wrong and what the correct idea is. The students must become convinced. Posner and his colleagues (Posner, Strike, Henson, & Gertzog, 1982) presented a model of conceptual change in the form of a set of requirements—conditions that must be fulfilled for such change to take place.

- *Dissatisfaction* with the prior conception must develop.
- An *intelligible alternative* must be available.
- The alternative must be viewed as *plausible*.
- The alternative must be viewed as *fruitful* (more fruitful than the prior conception).

Dissatisfaction.   Students are not likely to give up commitment to a conception that they have held and used successfully unless they have reason to question it. In the book-on-the-table problem, dissatisfaction with the idea that the table (an inanimate object) could not push or exert a force on another object developed out of the comparison with the hand-on-the-table situation. If the hand pushed or exerted a force on the book to balance the force of gravity and keep the book stationary, must not the table be doing the same thing? Especially when the forces in the two situations were diagrammed, the argument that the two situations were essentially parallel was quite compelling. This seemed to lead most students at least to begin to question their initial assumption.

In some cases, observations of events promote dissatisfaction with a conception. Consider, for example, the idea that matter is destroyed or turned into energy in the process of burning. The observation that the "ashes" from a burning magnesium ribbon weigh more than the original ribbon may lead to some dissatisfaction with that idea (cf. Hesse & Anderson, 1990). It is a mistake, however, to assume that even such "discrepant events" (Hewson & Hewson, 1984; Nussbaum & Novick, 1982) by themselves are sufficient for conceptual change. Other conditions are also required.

Intelligible Alternative.   Without an alternative, an existing idea is more apt to be "repaired" or simply retained in spite of apparent problems. The idea of the table pushing on the book, introduced by the teacher in the initial question, was intelligible. Each of the terms was familiar and had no special meaning. However, for many of the students, the idea was initially implausible. Furthermore, they saw no particular advantage in ascribing such an ability to the table or other inanimate objects that are just sitting there.

When the term "force" was introduced, the students had little difficulty applying it to instances of pushes and pulls that were obvious to them. They could readily describe the direction, the object acted upon and the relative size of the force in the examples considered. Thus, it appears that the idea of the table, and other inanimate objects, exerting forces was intelligible to the students. In some cases it is more difficult to establish an intelligible alternative, as in situations where Newtonian explanation requires vector addition of forces or calculations of changes in momentum resulting from particular forces.

Plausibility. Even when an alternative idea is available and intelligible, a student is not likely to entertain it very long if it does not seem plausible. As we have indicated, the idea that the table was pushing on the book was counter-intuitive or implausible to some students. Although the analogy with the book on the hand created doubt about the inability of the table to exert a force, and seemed to convince some students of the necessity of changing their position, there remained several students who were not convinced. Even some of those who were convinced continued to express a sense of its implausibility.

There seemed to be specific sources of the implausibility. One aspect of the implausibility was the lack of a mechanism by which the table could exert a force. Another was how, if it did exert a force, that force would be just the right size to balance the force of the book pushing down (under the effect of gravity).

Both of these were addressed by the activity in which varying numbers of books were placed in a pile on the table. Clearly, if the table were exerting a force, the size of the force was changing, always matching the applied force in size and opposite in direction. The idea that the table was exerting a force in *reaction* to a force applied to it made the existence of that force more plausible. Others working on this problem (DiSessa, 1983; Minstrell, 1982) have used an analogy between the table and a spring to make the idea more plausible.

Fruitfulness. This requirement has to do with what is gained by using the new alternative rather than the original idea. In other words, what difference does it make? The new ways of thinking about pushes, pulls, and the interaction between stationary objects worked well and resolved the problems that had been identified. But why go through all this? What is to be gained from thinking this way? The accomplishment demonstrated in the discussion of the book-on-the-table problem was primarily providing a consistent explanation of why the book remains stationary, regardless of the kind of object (animate or inanimate) upon which it is placed.

While the students may appreciate this accomplishment, other accomplishments are needed to convince the students of the value of continuing to think this way. This requirement is addressed in other lessons in which similar problems are considered, such as:

- Why don't you fall over when you lean against a wall?
- In a tug-of-war with a large tree, why doesn't the rope move?
- Why doesn't a large table move even though someone pushes on it?

These contribute to the perceived fruitfulness of the new conception of force and the idea that inanimate objects can exert (reaction) forces.

Implications

The students' experience in the demonstration lesson was unusual or unique for them not only because they felt that they understood, but also because of what they were and were not doing. Rather than simply receiving and remembering information, they engaged in a process in which they drew on their own knowledge, reasoned and argued, inferred and concluded. During this process they became convinced of the plausibility and value of thinking about phenomena in a new and, not only different, but initially counterintuitive way. Such a process is frequently required for learning science with understanding.

However, when teachers rely primarily on explaining the ideas and connections, the explanations don't make sense to many of the students because they do not go through a process of conceptual change. Even when teachers use experiments and demonstrations, students tend to interpret them in terms of their own prior conceptions or find that they don't make much sense either (Anderson & Smith, 1987; Smith & Anderson, 1984).

With conventional methods of science teaching, a minority of students seem to engage spontaneously in a "conceptual change sense-making" approach to learning. The majority, however, tend to memorize and recall to meet the demands of instruction (Anderson & Roth, 1989). This need not be the case. With the kind of support illustrated in the demonstration lesson, a substantial majority of students are capable of this kind of intellectual activity and learning with understanding (cf. Minstrell, 1984; Roth, 1984; Anderson & Smith, 1987; Berkheimer, Anderson, & Blakeslee, 1990). But, what is the nature of this support?

Cognitive theories of comprehension and knowledge structures, studies contrasting students' naïve conceptions to scientific alternatives, and the model of conceptual change described here in are useful in characterizing what cognitive changes need to happen for learning with understanding. They are less helpful, however, in characterizing how the process of conceptual change can be promoted. In order to think about these instructional issues, it is necessary to consider how people use scientific knowledge in social contexts.

The demonstration lesson illustrated a complex social context in which the students were actively engaged in a variety of activities through which they were constructing and reconstructing their own knowledge. Further, the teacher played several different critical roles, and the interactions among the students were important as well. The next section of this chapter will describe a social constructivist perspective that explicitly incorporates many of these features.

UNDERSTANDING AS USEFULNESS IN A SOCIAL CONTEXT

Cognitive psychology, including the conceptual change view that has been described, has treated knowledge and learning from the standpoint of the individual learner. Social constructivist psychologists, however, have developed a perspective in which development of knowledge by the individual is intimately related to the participation of that individual in social contexts. In this view, understanding can be considered as competent performance of tasks valued by the group in the social context where they normally occur. Furthermore, learning occurs through a form of "cognitive apprenticeship" (cf. Collins, Brown, & Newman, 1989) in which expert performance is modeled and learners are coached in cooperative performance of the tasks. Responsibility for task performance is gradually transferred to the learners until they are able to carry out the tasks independently.

By bringing the behavior of the teacher and the students as well as the knowledge students acquire into the same framework, this perspective is useful in analyzing the nature of the support for learning illustrated in the demonstration lesson. Furthermore, it expands the view of what is learned in important ways. First, it raises the issue of the uses or functions of scientific knowledge, the structure of which is the focus of the cognitive perspective. It also raises the issue of other kinds of knowledge that may be required to carry out those functions.

Functions of Scientific Knowledge

A large body of research has attempted to describe the structure of students' knowledge of various science topics. The standard method for developing such descriptions has been the use of interviews in which students are presented with tasks to perform. Observed responses serve as data for inferences about the structure of students' knowledge. Following Piaget's "modified clinical interview" (1965), most such research asked students to predict and explain relevant phenomena (cf. Nussbaum & Novak, 1979). Similar tasks have been employed in studies in which written responses from larger numbers of students have been obtained and analyzed. Thus, the structural criterion of connectedness implicitly involved the criterion of being able to *use* the concepts.

The student conceptions research used task performance primarily to infer the structure of the students' knowledge. From a social constructivist perspective, however, knowledge should be understood as consisting of patterns of language and action shared by subcultures or "knowledge communities," not simply as cognitive patterns within individuals (cf. Brufee, 1982; Toulmin, 1972, pp. 159–160). Anderson (1989; Anderson, Belt, Gamalski, & Greminger, 1987) identified *description, explanation, prediction*, and *control* as important activities for which scientifically literate people use scientific knowledge. Following an analogy with structure–function reasoning in biology, he described these activities as *functions* of scientific knowledge. This is more than a semantic argument. Emphasis on the functions of knowledge raises the question of what it can be used for and why it is worth learning. Attention to this issue increases the likelihood that students will learn to use their knowledge in ways that are useful to them both immediately and in the future.

Performance in a Social Context

Toulmin and others have argued that science is a social activity as well as a logical one.

> To begin with, then: Considered as an entire human enterprise, a science is neither a compendium of ideas and arguments alone, nor a population of individual scientists alone, nor a system of institutions and proceedings alone. At one point or another, the intellectual history of a scientific discipline, the institutional history of a scientific profession, and the individual biographies of the scientists involved evidently touch, interact, and merge. (Toulmin, 1972, p. 308)

Despite these developments in philosophy of science, most psychological conceptions of what it means to learn and understand science, including the conceptual change view characterized herein, tend to focus on the knowledge and/or behavior of individuals. Resnick (1987) has contrasted school tasks, which tend to be assigned to individuals in isolation, to those in the workplace, which tend to be collaborative.

Social constructivists have advanced a view of learning as developing the ability to participate in the activities of a community that shares common knowledge, language, purposes, and values. Understanding, in this view, implies development of knowledge sharing a common structure and the ability to carry out the tasks or functions of knowledge valued and carried out by members of that community. It thus subsumes or interrelates the structure and function perspectives described here. However, it also conceptualizes aspects of understanding ignored by those perspectives, including ways that members of a community share a common language (not just vocabulary), values, and purposes.

From this perspective, the force demonstration lesson given earlier can be viewed as attempts to socialize students into a community of scientifically literate adults. This socialization process involves not only the development of conceptual understanding, but also the introduction of students to *linguistic conventions* (such as the use of force diagrams), to understandings of important *purposes* of science (such as describing and explaining natural phenomena), and to *values* shared by members of scientific communities (such as the language, purposes, and the preference for internal consistency and parsimony). While such values can be thought of as held by individuals, it is in the social context that they operate.

In addition to these contributions to what it means to understand, the social constructivist perspective has unique contributions concerning how learning with understanding takes place. These implications derive from insights into how learning in nonschool settings takes place, such as language learning in young children, and from the applicability of the same perspective to the *classroom* as a community where values, norms, and purposes develop.

Learning in this social constructivist perspective is viewed as occurring in a social context or "culture of expert practice," which, according to Collins et al. (1989) "refers to the creation of a learning environment in which the participants actively communicate about and engage in the skills involved in expertise, where expertise is understood as the practice of solving problems and carrying out tasks in a domain."

Cognitive Apprenticeship

Prominent in the social constructivist work on learning are the attention to expert modeling of performance and various forms of assistance and feedback to learners in the context of task performance. Collins, et al. use the term "cognitive apprenticeship" to describe a set of elements that are common to successful programs in mathematics, writing, and reading comprehension. The core of their approach consists of modeling and coaching, which are gradually "faded" as responsibility for performance is transferred more completely to students.

Modeling involves showing an expert carrying out a task so that students can observe and build a conceptual model of the processes that are required to nplish the task. In cognitive domains, this requires the externalization of lly internal (cognitive) processes and activities.

Coaching consists of observing students while they carry out a task and offering hints, scaffolding, feedback, modeling, reminders, and new tasks aimed at bringing their performance closer to expert performance.

Scaffolding refers to the supports the teacher provides to help the student carry out a task. These can take the forms of suggestions or help. . .or of physical support, as with the cue cards in Scardamalia et al.'s (1984) procedural facilitation of writing. . .

Anderson and Roth (1989) described an adaptation of cognitive apprenticeship designed to promote conceptual change and meaningful understanding of science. They characterize three kinds of activities occurring in classrooms that function most successfully as "scientific learning communities." These are "establishing problems that engage students in scientific reasoning, modeling and coaching through scaffolded dialogue, and student work that leads to independent use of scientific knowledge and integration with other scientific knowledge."

Although there is much commonality between this formulation and that of Collins, et al. (1989), Anderson and Roth elaborate on Collins, Brown, and Newman's ideas in some important respects. The most obvious elaboration is Anderson and Roth's first stage, establishing a problem. The explicit inclusion of this stage is a response to specific problems in the teaching and learning of science for understanding, most notably the problem of conceptual change. This stage is critical in bridging the gap between the teacher's scientific perspective and those of the learners.

Students not only have their own alternative conceptions, but

Are not aware that the scientific knowledge is useful for any purpose that is real to them, or that is "about" anything that is familiar to them. In addition, teachers are often unfamiliar with their students' reasoning about topics that they are preparing to teach. (Anderson & Roth, 1989)

Beginning instruction on a topic with questions that elicit students' reasoning "activates students' prior knowledge and helps make them aware of its limitations, serves an important diagnostic function for the teacher, and engages teacher and students in dialogue about commonly understood issues." Such questions and problems should "tend to focus on objects and ideas that are familiar to the students, and on the scientific functions of description, explanation, prediction and control" (Anderson & Roth, 1989). Other elaborations on Collins, Brown, and Newman's ideas in Anderson and Roth's formulation lie in the tactics suggested for conducting the modeling and coaching. These are designed to promote the process of conceptual change necessary for students to integrate the new scientific knowledge with their own prior knowledge. Such tactics include, for example, modeling that explicitly connects or contrasts scientific ideas with the ideas that students have expressed and coaching students to compare their answers to key questions at different points in time and write about how their ideas have changed.

Features of Anderson and Roth's formulation are illustrated in the next section, in which their formulation is used to describe an example unit on force that incorporates the demonstration lesson described at the beginning of the chapter.

AN ILLUSTRATION OF A UNIT BASED ON ANDERSON AND ROTH'S FORMULATION

The unit is built around a set of objectives, generic tasks which students should become proficient in through participation in the unit. The five objectives are briefly defined in Table 3.1. As illustrated in the table, during the course of the unit students encounter several instances of each objective, in the context of activities that provide opportunities to establish problems, model and coach performance, and gradually fade support.

Notice how the activities of the demonstration lesson are represented in the table. The book on the table and hand activity established a problem related to the description of forces on objects, bringing out students' naïve conceptions and their limitations in the process. A more adequate way of describing forces was modeled in the briefcase activity. Students were coached in describing the forces in the book on the table problem as part of the strategy to promote conceptual change. Scaffolding for the description of forces includes providing partly completed diagrams and suggestions for completing and, for verbal descriptions, reminders of the features to be included in a complete description. This support is gradually faded during the remaining activities in the unit. The description of forces on objects plays a key role in performance of the other objectives and in promoting important conceptual changes.

Important features of Anderson and Roth's formulation are illustrated in the activities summarized in Table 3.2. A problem is established in the context of a force (push) being exerted on a heavy table. Why doesn't the table move? While not an obvious question (it doesn't seem like a problematical issue), without the concept of a force resulting from friction, it is an apparent instance of an unbalanced force without resulting change in motion. Description of the forces involved results in the need for a balancing force and prepares the context for the introduction of the concept of a force resulting from friction. As part of the modeling, the teacher explains the preciseness

TABLE 3.1
Force Unit Instructional Approach

Activities	Objectives				
	1 Describe forces Acting on objects	*2* Explain constant Motion or at-rest Condition of objects	*3* Explain changes In objects' motion	*4* Predict changes in objects' motion	*5* Design ways to control Objects' motion
Book on table and on hand —Part 1	E				
Briefcase, etc. ("force")	M				
Book on table and on hand—Part 2	C				
Lean on wall	C	C			
Push on stationary table (friction)	C	E			
Push on cart	F	MC	EM		
Coasting cart	F		EM	E	
Friction sled	F	C	C	C	
Oiling wagon wheels	F		C	C	
Toy car on rough and smooth surfaces	F		F	F	EMC
Tug-of-war	F	F			F
Car on icy and on dry road	F	F	F	F	F

E = Establish a problem

M = Model

C = Coach

F = Fade

58

Example Activities from the Force Unit

Activity	Objectives	Key questions & ideas	Expected responses and interpretations
Push on table (no motion)	1 2 3 4 5 C E	Why doesn't the table move when I push on it?	Establishes a problem that can be resolved well with the invention of the idea of force of friction Responses will probably include: • Because you aren't pushing hard enough. • Because it's too heavy. • Because of friction.
		What forces are acting on the table?	Students will probably identify: • Force of gravity downward • Force from the floor upward, equal to gravity (may need coaching). • Force from the hands pushing (horizontal).
		A force of friction exerted by the floor balances the pushing force so the table did not start to move.	Without a horizontal force opposing the push, there appears to be an unbalanced force without any change in motion. This should be a problem for most students. It can be resolved by using a force of friction exerted on the table by the floor, which is introduced at this point.
Push on cart	1 2 3 4 5 C ME	Why did the cart start to move?	Likely responses: • Because you pushed it. • Because you pushed it hard enough. • Because you exerted a big enough force.
		Describe the forces acting on the cart as it starts to move.	Students will probably identify: • Force of gravity downward balanced by the floor. • Force of the hands pushing. • Force of friction (not as large as push).
		The push was greater than the force of friction so the cart started to move.	

of the idea of a force resulting from friction, compared with a simple appeal to friction as an explanation. With the concept of a force resulting from friction, the students and teacher can cooperatively construct an explanation in terms of balanced forces on the table.

Also to be addressed in this activity is the implausibility of the floor exerting a force in the horizontal direction. Appeal to the necessity of this force to have balanced forces (and thus no change in motion) and an explanation of friction as a reaction force (parallel to the arguments in the demonstration lesson) are useful for this purpose. The fruitfulness of the concept of a frictional force becomes more apparent as it is used in the other activities in the unit. The coaching of students to consider it is faded over the course of those activities.

Anderson and Roth (1989) stress the importance and nature of the dialogues that occur during the various stages of instruction. The typical responses to the question about why the table doesn't move (see Table 3.2) are significant in several ways. First, none of them is very complete. The teacher coaches the students to elaborate. However, elaboration of the first response (such as adding, "If you pushed harder, it would start moving") doesn't add much. It is essentially a circular argument that reiterates that which is to be explained.

The teacher explains this in feedback to the class. While this may seem harsh, it need not be.

> Teachers can also support their students by fostering dialogue in which they and their students listen carefully to each other and respond to each other, sometimes critically but in ways that reflect serious and respectful attention to the ideas of the speaker. (Anderson & Roth, 1989)

This is the kind of dialogue that occurs among scientifically literate adults engaged in discourse about phenomena. Students need modeling and coaching if they are to develop the ability to participate in such discourse.

The second response adds the observation that the table is heavy. This does represent a form of explanation. However, it is less complete than one based on identification of the balanced forces on the table. Such an explanation illustrates an "explanatory ideal" (Hesse & Anderson, in press; Toulmin, 1961) for Newtonian reasoning. That is, apart from any purely logical criteria, a good Newtonian explanation of motion appeals to the forces acting on the object and whether or not they are balanced.

The valuing of explanations that appeal to the forces acting on an object is implicit in the teacher's question or suggestion that the students consider the forces acting on the table. It should at some point also be made explicit. Such a rationale is part of sound modeling. A similar dialogue about the quality of explanations is coached in the next activity in which unbalanced forces (the pushing force is greater than the frictional force) are used to explain why a cart begins to move.

Changes in standards for what constitutes a good explanation represent something in addition to conceptions per se that needs to change in conceptual change learning (Smith, 1987). The foregoing examples illustrate how this and other values such as parsimony and internal consistency can be addressed through modeling and coaching in the context of dialogues in classrooms functioning as scientific learning communities.

CONCLUSION

I will conclude with a personal note about my own conceptual changes as I have worked in the synthesis of the conceptual change and social constructivist perspectives. I began writing this chapter with a simple division in mind: Conceptual change ideas help me to *convince* the students of the usefulness of Newtonian concepts while cognitive apprenticeship ideas help them to *master the application* of those concepts. However, I have come to understand that the relationship between these theoretical frameworks is more complex. At a deeper level, convincing is a form of modeling. In convincing my students that it makes sense to say that the table exerts an upward force, I model a form of discourse in which concepts are defined precisely and applied carefully, and in which reasoned judgment is the norm. In inviting my students to join in the discourse, I engage them in coaching and scaffolded dialogue. Thus the conceptual change framework, rather than being separate and dealing with different problems, provides a set of conceptual tools that help me to understand certain critically important features of scientific discourse.

This perspective also implies that science and learning science aren't as much a matter of logical reasoning from data plus "invention" (Atkin & Karplus, 1962) as traditional epistemology in science education (and my own) has implied. The social aspects, language, conventions, and values are also a part of the expert knowledge or competence that must be developed. One has to learn how to participate in a "culture." The social constructivist epistemology and view of learning better fits the Kuhn and Toulmin view of science and the conceptual change nature of learning.

A question that arose for me was: How do you know whether students are really being *convinced*? Are they just learning to do certain kinds of reasoning in order to pass a course, mimicking at some level? It may not matter. Someone who can "mimic" Newtonian analyses of motion demonstrates a greater understanding than most current students. So what is conceptual change besides successful mimicry? Sometimes I think that the criteria are partly affective. Students who have successfully undergone conceptual change choose to pursue the issues that arise, in a group context, because they are interested. But this definition also leaves me with doubts. While this is a worthy goal for teaching science, I hardly expect everyone to choose such a path. (I don't expect everyone to take up music or sports with a passion, either.)

So in the end, my definition of conceptual change does not necessarily involve conviction or affect. A student may give the Newtonian description and explanations while continuing to believe that tables don't "really" push. It is critical, though, that students *use* scientific ideas for new tasks in different contexts. Even if they begin the process without conviction, by working through new tasks in different contexts students may come to appreciate the fruitfulness of a new idea or way of reasoning.

ACKNOWLEDGMENTS

I wish to acknowledge the contributions of others to the arguments made here. The work of George Posner, Ken Strike, and Peter Hewson in conceptual change was very influential in my own conceptual change and development. I especially want to acknowledge both the intellectual and editorial contributions of Charles (Andy) Anderson, whose pioneering work in applying the social constructivist perspective to science teaching and learning has strongly influenced my own thinking, as reflected in this chapter.

REFERENCES

Anderson, C. W. (1989). The role of education in the academic disciplines in the graduate preparation of teachers. In A. E. Woolfolk (Ed.), *Research perspectives on the graduate preparation of teachers*. Englewood Cliffs, NJ: Prentice Hall, pp. 88–107.

Anderson, C. W., Belt, B. L., Gamalski, J. M., & Greminger, J. (1987). A social constructivist analysis of science classroom teaching. In J. Novak (Ed.), *Proceedings of the Second International Seminar on Misconceptions and Educational Strategies in Science and Mathematics* (Vol. 1). Ithaca, NY: Cornell University.

Anderson, C. W., & Roth, K. J. (1989). Teaching for meaningful and self-regulated learning of science. In J. Brophy (Ed.), *Advances in research on teaching: Vol. 1. Teaching for meaningful understanding and self-regulated learning*. Greenwich, CN: JAI Press.

Anderson, C. W., & Smith, E. L. (1987). Teaching science. In V. Richardson-Koehler (Ed.), *The educator's handbook: A research perspective*. New York: Longman.

Atkin, M., & Karplus, R. (September, 1962). Discovery or invention? *The Science Teacher, 29*, 45–51.

Ausubel, D. S. (1968). *Educational psychology: A cognitive View*. New York: Holt, Rinehart, & Winston.

Berkheimer, G. D., Anderson, C. W., & Blakeslee, T. D. (1990). Using a new model of curriculum development to write a matter and molecules teaching unit. Research Series No. 196, Institute for Research on Teaching, Michigan State University, East Lansing, MI.

Bruffee, K. A. (1982). Liberal education and the social justification of belief. *Liberal Education*, *68*, 95–114.

Bruner, J. S. (1960). *The process of education*. New York: Random House.

Carey, S. (1986, April). Cognitive science and science education. *American Psychologist, 41*(10), 1123–1130.

Clement, J. (1982). Students' preconceptions in introductory physics. *American Journal of Physics*, *50*(1), 66–71.

Collins, A., Brown, J. S., & Newman, S. E. (1989). Cognitive apprenticeship: Teaching the craft of reading, writing, and mathematics. In L. B. Resnick (Ed.), *Knowing, learning, and instruction: Essays in honor of Robert Glaser*. Hillsdale, NJ.: Lawrence Erlbaum Associates, pp. 453–494.

DiSessa, A. (1983). Phenomenology and the evolution of intuition. In D. Gentner & A. L. Stevens (Eds.), *Mental models*. Hillsdale, NJ: Lawrence Erlbaum Associates.

Hesse, J. J., & Anderson, C. W. (1990, April). A case study of conceptual teaching: *Teaching the necessity of conservation in physical and chemical changes*. Paper presented at the annual meeting of the National Association for Research in Science Teaching, Atlanta.

Hesse, J. J., & Anderson, C. W. (in press). Students' conceptions of chemical change. *Journal of Research in Science Teaching*.

Hewson, P. W., & Hewson, M. G. A. (1984). The role of conceptual conflict in conceptual change and the design of science instruction. *Instructional Science, 13*, 1–13.

Minstrell, J. (1984). Teaching for the development of understanding of ideas. Forces on moving object. In C. W. Anderson (Ed.), *Observing science classrooms: Perspectives from research and practice*, Yearbook of the Association for the Education of Teachers in Science.

Minstrell, J. (January 1982). Explaining the "at rest" condition of an object. *The Physics Teacher*, *20*, 10–14.

Novak, J. D., & Gowin, D. B. (1984). *Learning how to learn*. New York: Cambridge University Press.

Nussbaum, J., & Novak, J. D. (1979). An assessment of children's concepts of the earth utilizing structured interviews. *Science Education, 60*, 535–550.

Nussbaum, J., & Novick, S. (1982). Alternative frameworks, conceptual conflict, and accommodation. Toward a principled teaching strategy. *Instructional Science, 11*(3), 183–200.

Piaget, J. (1965). *The child's conception of the world*. Totowa, NJ: Littlefield, Adams.

Posner, J., Strike, K., Hewson, P., & Gertzog, W. (1982). Accommodation of a scientific conception: Toward a theory of conceptual change. *Science Education, 66*, 211–227.

Resnick, L. (1987). Learning in school and out. *Educational Researcher, 16*(9) 13–20.

Roth, K. J. (1984). Using classroom observations to improve science teaching and curriculum materials. In C. W. Anderson (Ed.), *Observing science classrooms. Perspectives from research and practice*. Yearbook of the Association for the Education of Teachers in Science. Columbus, OH: ERIC/SMEAC, pp. 77–102.

Scardamalia, M., Bereiter, C. & Steinbach, R. (1984). Teachability of reflective processes in written composition. *Cognitive Science, 8*, 173–190.

Schwab, J. J. (1964). The structure of the natural sciences. In G. W. Ford & L. Pugno (Eds.), *The structure of knowledge and the curriculum*. Chicago: Rand McNally.

Smith, E. L. (1987). What besides conceptions needs to change in conceptual change learning? In J. D. Novak (Ed.), *Proceedings of the second international seminar on Misconceptions and Teaching Strategies in Science and Mathematics*. Cornell University, Ithaca, NY.

Smith, E. L., & Anderson, C. W. (1984). *The planning and teaching intermediate science study: Final report*. (Research Series No. 147). East Lansing, MI: Institute for Research on Teaching, Michigan State University.

Toulmin, S. (1961). *Foresight and understanding*. Bloomington: Indiana University Press.

Toulmin, S. (1972). *Human understanding*. Princeton, NJ: Princeton University Press.

4 Students' Conceptual Frameworks: Consequences for Learning Science

Reinders Duit
IPN—Institute for Science Education at the University of Kiel

Much research on the role of students' preinstructional conceptual frameworks in learning science has been carried out during the past 10 to 15 years. This research reveals a disappointing situation, namely that science instruction very often has rather limited success, that attempts to guide students from their preinstructional conceptual frameworks to those of science very often fail—this is true worldwide. This sad situation is one of the main challenges to science education today. The problems revealed in the many studies available are basically the same in rather different school systems. This inevitably leads to the conclusion that the problems are inherent in the "nature" of science knowledge *and* the (traditional) way science is taught worldwide. My position is that the problems caused by the specific nature of science knowledge can only be addressed implicitly in science instruction. We cannot change the nature of science. I therefore, consider that learning science is a difficult task for students and will be a difficult and demanding one in the future. But the many research results available and the many new lines of thought about science instruction initiated by the "sad" situation referred to provide a profound basis for changes in science instruction. They provide the key to an adequate consideration of the problems of learning science inherent in the nature of science knowledge, and hence to make science instruction more fruitful and pleasing for students as well as for teachers.

In short, research on students' conceptual frameworks in science offers a basis for progress in teaching and learning science—on the basis of a realistic view of the difficulties inherent in learning science. The present chapter sets out to provide an overview of what research in this field has to offer school practice at the moment. Major approaches, findings and trends are reviewed in the following sections.

A BRIEF PORTRAIT OF THE RESEARCH AREA DEALING WITH STUDENTS' CONCEPTUAL FRAMEWORKS

There has been a boom in research on the role of students' preinstructional conceptual frameworks in learning science in the past 10 to 15 years, and research is still flourishing and developing. Bibliographies provide overviews on the range and amount of work done. Pfundt and Duit's (1991) bibliography, which is continually updated, currently contains some 2,000 entries. Reviews further ease access to the many research papers (see, e.g., Driver & Erickson, 1983; Gilbert & Watts, 1983; Hashweh, 1986; Duit, 1987).

At the outset (i.e., in the mid-1970s) the emphasis was on detecting students' conceptions on science topics such as heat, light, energy, combustion, chemical reactions, photosynthesis and genetics (for the number of studies available in different areas of science see Table 4.1, p. 71). Quite often, this research also looked for conceptual change during (mostly traditional) instruction. However, studies on the effects of instruction specifically designed to bring about conceptual change followed a little later.

Research and development activities mentioned so far are based upon the assumption that students' preinstructional conceptions of science topics (i.e., their conceptions on a content level) guide their learning considerably. Research findings confirm this, but the constructivistic view of learning suggests that many other conceptions guide students' learning. The constructivistic view has widened the focus of research in science education.

VARIETY AND CONCURRENCE—MANY POSITIONS WITHIN THIS RESEARCH AREA

The researchers dealing with students' conceptual frameworks are by no means a homogeneous group. Another chapter would be necessary to do justice to the variety of opinions which exist in this field. Only a few remarks can be made here.

The plethora of terms that has been used so far in this chapter to refer to what has been called students' conceptions or students' conceptual frameworks is an indication of the many different perspectives that are taken (for discussions of these terms see Gauld, 1987; Abimbola, 1988; Hills, 1989). Only some of the many terms will be discussed here.

Conceptual Framework.   This term stands for the view that students' conceptions of natural phenomena are not usually specific, isolated conceptions but that they mostly form a framework which is broader in nature. This view is substantially supported by the research findings available. Students' conceptions are not usually a collection of "fuzzy" ideas but are surprisingly coherent (see, e.g., Engel-Clough & Driver, 1986; Rhöneck & Grob, 1988), though their range may be regarded as limited from a science point of view.

Alternative Framework.   This term has been coined by Driver and Easley (1978). It stands for a view that is supported by most of the researchers in our field. Students' conceptual frameworks are viewed as frameworks in their own right, providing students with valuable guidance in most everyday situations. In such situations, these frameworks really are alternatives to the science taught in schools.

Misconceptions.   This is a misleading term. Some 10 years ago it stood for the position that was opposed to the "alternative frameworks" point of view. According to the misconception position, students' conceptual frameworks are viewed solely from a science standpoint. What is not in accordance with this view is seen as an error, as a mistake, as false. It stood, therefore, for the position that scientific conceptions are the only ones that can be tolerated. There still appear to be some facets of this meaning of misconception left even in the work of researchers who view themselves as members of the alternative frameworks party.   Some members of this party explicitly use the term misconception but in a different sense from the one outlined herein. They refer to misconceptions as incorrect conceptions (seen from the science point of view), which have been formed by science instruction itself (see Hills, 1989).

Children's Science.   In the work of many researchers in our field, we find the metaphor of the "child as a scientist" (see Gauld, 1988). Kelly (1955) used the idea of "man-the-scientist," that is, the idea that the mental constructions of human beings are in principle comparable with the constructions of scientists. This idea became quite popular in research on students' conceptual frameworks. Children are widely viewed as scientists in their endeavor to make sense of natural phenomena, though of course only within the limited range of their stage of development (see, e.g., Gilbert, Osborne, & Fensham, 1982). The term "children's science" is, therefore, another attempt to take students' conceptions seriously, to attach dignity to them.

Minitheory.   Claxton's (n.d.) term primarily emphasizes the idea of the student as a scientist, too: "theory" stands for this. But it further points out that the range of students' theories is limited. Minitheories are content- and context-specific; that is, students hold many of these theories, each of them valid only in small content and context areas. There are also overlaps of minitheories, that is, content and context areas where more than one minitheory is held by a single person.

This brief survey of some of the terms used in our research area indicates both variety and similarities. Today, most of the researchers basically follow the position of "alternative frameworks"; that is, they admit that students' conceptions form some sort of conceptual framework that is of great use in most everyday situations and must, therefore, be taken seriously in science instruction.

THEORETICAL BACKGROUND OF RESEARCH—THE CONSTRUCTIVISTIC VIEW

The preceding paragraph was an attempt to indicate that, despite the many considerable differences, there are major correspondences among the views of researchers in our field. These correspondences are represented within the constructivistic view of learning.

Although there is much valuable potential in the constructivistic view, some reservation about the use of the term "constructivistic" in research is necessary. In some ways it became fashionable to be a constructivist. In other words, the label constructivistic became a matter of identification as member of a group dealing with students' learning difficulties. Quite frequently the acceptance of the new label did not change views and research focuses in any substantial way (see, for instance, the critical note on the constructivistic view by Strike, 1987).

In brief, the constructivistic view holds that human learning is a very active construction process. Learning is not seen as a process of simply storing pieces of knowledge provided, for instance, by the teacher. On the contrary, it is seen as a process of active construction of knowledge on the part of the learners themselves on the basis of their already existing conceptions.

It is important to mention that the constructivistic view integrated influential contemporary lines of thought that take counterpositions to traditional empiristic and positivistic ones. The constructivistic view became so popular and influential within research on students' conceptual frameworks because it fit into the mainstream of alternative (versus traditional) thoughts.

"The most important single factor influencing learning is what the learner already knows. Ascertain this and teach him accordingly" (Ausubel, 1968). Ausubel's dictum is undoubtedly the most-cited one in articles on students' conceptual frameworks. Ausubel's position in general has been very influential on research in our field.

Piaget, the outstanding epistemologist of this century, also influenced research very much but in a way different from Ausubel's. On the one hand

Piaget's research method of clinical interviews has been widely used. It is certainly no overstatement that this and related methods are still used most often. Furthermore, some aspects of Piaget's theory were adopted (e.g., to view children's learning as an active construction process). But research on students' conceptual frameworks was also viewed explicitly as a counterposition to Piaget's. The focus on general operations of thought is seen as a limitation. It became apparent that students' conceptions of natural phenomena are very content- and context-dependent. It is interesting to note that two partly rival schools developed into the "Piagetians" and the "alternative frameworkers." Recently there appear to be attempts to unite the rival positions (see, e.g., the proceedings of a conference organized by Adey, 1989).

Piaget's position may be viewed as constructivistic (see, e.g., Glasersfeld, 1983). Other constructivistic traditions have also been adopted, especially those of Kelly (1955) and Vygotsky (1962, 1978). For the significance of Kelly's position in science education see, for instance, Pope (1985). Vygotsky's social constructivism is discussed, for instance, by Anderson (1987).

Philosophies of science as developed by Hanson, T. S. Kuhn, Feyerabend, Lakatos, and others, that is, "new philosophies of science" (Brown, 1977), have been most influential in research on students' conceptual frameworks. Above all, the idea that perception and development of new theories is considerably guided by "old" theories met the main assumption of researchers in our field that learning is guided by students' preinstructional conceptions.

Cognitive science and information-processing theories have had significant impact. Close connections between research in these areas and research on students' conceptual frameworks frequently led to very fruitful cooperation (see, e.g., Jung, 1985; Carey, 1986).

The radical constructivism (see, e.g., Glasersfeld, 1983; Watzlawik, 1981) in some way became a major reference point for the constructivistic view in our field. Radical constructivism adopted the positions already mentioned here plus others. Among these we find the approaches of self-organizing systems. Their main paradigm supports the constructivistic view in that inner structures of systems determine the development of processes such as learning.

As has already been mentioned, the constructivistic view is an alternative position to the traditional empiristic and positivistic positions. It is, therefore, no surprise that old positions of a similar kind have been rediscovered. German hermeneutics and phenomenological traditions dating back to Dilthey (1877–1911) and Husserl (1877–1908) have been adopted above all in the discussion about adequate research methods (namely "qualitative" methods) from a constructivistic perspective (see e.g., Erickson, 1986). They result in interpretive studies of an ethnographic kind, for example, and in action research activities (see, e.g., Fensham, 1989).

This very brief survey of the main theoretical backgrounds to research on students' conceptual frameworks only points to major approaches. It may give the impression that research in this area is part of a mainstream of contemporary thought in many areas. It is necessary to emphasize that the constructivistic view is not a well-elaborated theory like those of Piaget or Ausubel. It is more a "view," a framework used to conceptualize pedagogical events in science learning. But it is a very powerful one as will be explained later in this chapter.

OVERVIEW OF STUDENTS' CONCEPTUAL FRAMEWORKS IN DIFFERENT CONTENT AREAS

As has already been mentioned, empirical research started investigating students' conceptions before instruction as well as the change of these conceptions during instruction, mainly in "traditional" instructional settings. Only a little later did studies follow on the impact of specifically developed teaching materials, teaching strategies, and the like designed to bring about conceptual change. In the bibliography of Pfundt and Duit (1991), studies of the first kind still predominate. About four times as many of these as of those of the second kind are available. Table 4.1 provides an overview of the number of studies of the first kind. It shows the areas for which research results on students' conceptual frameworks are available. It shows that the focus is on physics topics. It is surprising that studies on biology, and especially chemistry, are comparably small in number and that many areas of science instruction are totally missing or are only represented by a few studies. Sound and magnetism belong to the elementary areas where only a few studies are available. Further research is necessary to provide teachers and curriculum developers with information about students' most important conceptual frameworks in science instruction topics.

SOME FINDINGS ON THE ROLE OF STUDENT'S CONCEPTUAL FRAMEWORKS IN TRADITIONAL EDUCATIONAL SETTINGS

It has already been said that most students' conceptual frameworks are not just "fuzzy ideas" but often form surprisingly coherent frameworks that guide and determine learning considerably. In the following sections main findings will briefly be summarized.

Conceptions Guide Observations.   Demonstration experiments play a very important role in science instruction for several good reasons. They are quite often used to illustrate science concepts and principles. However, research

TABLE 4.1
Studies on Students' Conceptions in Different Areas

Mechanics	281	Force and motion/work, power, energy/speed, acceleration/gravity/pressure/density/floating, sinking
Electricity	146	Simple, branched circuits/topological and geometrical structure/models of current flow/current, voltage, resistance/electrostatics/electromagnetism/danger of electricity
Heat	68	Heat and temperature/heat transfer/expansion by heating/change of state, boiling, freezing/explanation of heat phenomena in the particle model
Optics	69	Light/light propagation/vision/color
Particles	60	Structure of matter/explanation of phenomena (e.g., heat, states of matter)/conceptions of the atom/radioactivity
Energy	69	Energy transformation/energy conservation/energy degradation
Astronomy	36	Shape of the earth/characteristics of gravitational attraction/satellites
"Modern Physics"	11	Quantum physics/special relativity
Chemistry	132	Combustion, oxidation/chemical reactions/ transformation of substances/chemical equilibrium/symbols, formula/mole concept
Biology	208	Plant nutrition/photosynthesis/osmosis/life/origin of life/evolution/human circulatory system/genetics/health/growth

The figures give the number of articles contained in the bibliography by Pfundt & Duit (1991) in a certain area.

has shown that students very often do not even observe what is seemingly so obvious from the science point of view. Students' conceptual frameworks guide observations. It is not too much of an overstatement to say that students (as do humans in general) tend to see what they want to see. This is a common everyday experience. Every judge knows how different the "observations" of witnesses may be. Only one example from research on student conceptions will be presented here. Fig. 4.1 portrays an experiment used by Gunstone and White (1981). A bucket of sand and a weight are in equilibrium. A small spoonful of sand is added to the bucket. It is so small that no movement is caused. But college students who have the idea that the bucket will sink "observe" this (well, it sinks just a little). Then so much sand is added that an

FIG. 4.1.   An experiment used by Gunstone and White (1981).

accelerated movement of the bucket results. Students are asked to observe the speeds of the bucket at two positions. Students who believe that uniform speed will occur, "observe" it. There are several further findings supporting the issue highlighted here that conceptions guide observation.

Empirical Evidence Does not Necessarily Convince Students that Their Conceptions Are not Adequate.   It is a very popular strategy among science teachers to arrange a cognitive conflict by using conflicting empirical evidence. Gunstone and White (1981) had an apparatus like that in Fig. 4.1. First, bucket and weight are at equilibrium and at the same height. Then the bucket is pulled down, the weight lifted accordingly. The experimenter holds the bucket in this position. Students are asked to predict what will happen if the bucket is released. A number of students are of the opinion that the system will return to the initial state. The empirical evidence—there is no movement of the bucket and the weight, of course—does not convince a couple of students that their conceptions were wrong. They try to get rid of the unexpected empirical evidence by all sorts of arguments concerning specific circumstances. There are many other findings of this kind. So, empirical evidence does not necessarily convince students that their conceptions are not adequate. It is interesting to note that similar "behavior" is well known in the history of science. One single counterexample does not usually shake an accepted science paradigm (see Kuhn, 1970). Many pieces of evidence *and* new conceptual frameworks are necessary to bring about "conceptual change."

There Is a Tendency to "Observe" Only the Aspects of Experiments that Support One's own Views.   Human beings in general tend to accept only evidence in favor of an argument and to reject or simply ignore counterevidence (see Hashweh, 1986, for more details). Baird, Fensham, Gunstone, & White (1987), for instance, found during interviews with student teachers that many did not observe the processes presented to them carefully. They concentrated only on the aspects that supported their views.

Conceptions Guide the Information Provided by the Teacher, the Textbook, and so on.   Understanding of information is guided and even determined by the conceptions that the students hold. Many learning problems in science classes are due to such misunderstandings. According to the constructivistic view, information is always interpreted on the basis of one's own views. The following is a simple example of this from biology teaching. The biology teacher speaks about fruit and means the part of the plant containing the seeds. The students have something quite different in mind when they hear the word fruit. They may think of fruit as a dessert, such as pineapples and cherries. There are numerous misunderstandings of this kind reported in the literature, misunderstandings caused by different meanings of scientific terms in everyday usage. In general, research provides ample evidence that teachers should not assume that the information they (and the textbook, etc.) provide is interpreted by the students in the manner intended (Fig. 4.2 shows an example of a similar misunderstanding from a chemistry lesson).

FIG. 4.2.   Images in the classroom. From Kleinman, Griffin, & Konigsberg Kerner, (1987). Images in chemistry. *Journal of Chemical Education, 64,* 766. Reprinted by permission.

Instruction Very Often Fails to Guide Students from their Own Conceptions to the Science Ones. This sad outcome of science instruction has already been mentioned. Frequently, students do not have confidence in the usefulness of science knowledge when explaining phenomena and processes. Students use science concepts and principles if they resemble what has been dealt with in science instruction. But as soon as it becomes a little more difficult or if the phenomena and processes are unfamiliar to the students, they do not seem to trust their science knowledge, but use everyday explanations. Under a thin surface layer of superficially learned science knowledge, students' preinstructional conceptual frameworks appear to be mainly unchanged. There are other interesting outcomes besides the "unchanged" one (see, e.g., Gilbert, et al., 1982). It can happen, for instance, that the science viewpoint is not really accepted but memorized (by heart) to please the teacher and to pass exams. Sometimes there are interesting attempts by students to amalgamate their views and the science ones. A very disappointing outcome quite often occurs: Instruction supports—unwittingly, of course—students' preinstructional frameworks.

SOURCES OF STUDENTS' CONCEPTUAL FRAMEWORKS

Research on the sources of students' conceptions is not very well developed, but the main sources are known.

Sensual Impression. Everyday experiences involving sensual impressions encountered in natural phenomena, such as heat, sound, light, force and motion, combustion, the growing of plants and animals, and many others, are undoubtedly a major source of conceptions.

Everyday Language. This is the other major source of "everyday" conceptions. Our everyday language conserves many conceptions that have often been outdated in science for centuries. "The sun rises," for instance, leads to the idea of the sun's path in the heavens and not to the "modern" one of the earth revolving toward the sun. On the other hand, the grammatical structure of the language guides thought because in some way it mirrors logical structures.

It has to be kept in mind that the two sources mentioned so far lead to very deep-rooted conceptions. The everyday conceptions are supported continuously in everyday experiences *and* they are generally quite successful when everyday situations are concerned. They appear to be the ones that are most stable, which are very difficult to change in science instruction.

Innate Structures of the Brain. I shall briefly refer to a fascinating thought.

Preece (1984) introduced the idea that students' conceptions may be "triggered" by innate structures of the brain and that they are not (merely) learned. This idea stems from evolutionary epistemology, which claims that the structures of our brain have developed during evolution in a way that is best fitted to our everyday needs. If this view holds, it would offer another explanation as to why many students' conceptions are rather resistant to attempts to change them.

Learning in Students' Social Environments. In everyday communication with friends, parents, and others, students pick up both pieces of science knowledge and alternative conceptions. Further sources of information such as mass media, also provide science knowledge that is not always correct from a science point of view. It is probable that these sources are more influential than science instruction in school because only a small number of hours is dedicated to science instruction, whereas the rest of the time students encounter the other sources.

Instruction. It has already been mentioned that instruction quite often causes new "misconceptions" or supports "old" students' conceptual frameworks. Several pieces of evidence in support of this are reported in the literature. "Misconceptions" may be due to false information provided by the teacher (or the textbook) or misinterpretation of basically correct information, as will be explained shortly.

STARTING FROM STUDENTS' CONCEPTIONS?

Starting from the students' conceptions and experiences is a quite popular strategy in science instruction. This is basically a valuable strategy. But it may be dangerous to support students' everyday conceptions and hence raise the

	NEWTONIAN VIEW	EVERYDAYLIFE VIEW
A body remains in uniform motion, if ...	... no force is acting on the body.	... a constant force is acting on the body.
If a force is acting on a body ...	... it changes velocity into the direction of the acting force: $F \sim a$	... it moves into the direction of the acting force: $F \sim v$

FIG. 4.3. Newtonian and everyday views of relations between force and motion.

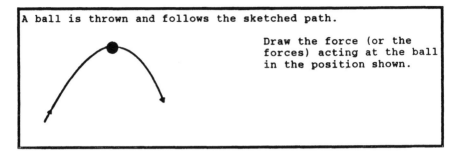

FIG. 4.4.   A task frequently used to investigate students' conceptions on the relations between force and motion.

barrier between students' views and science views as the two sources are often contradictory. This is widely known in the area where most research is available, the concept of force in physics. Fig. 4.3 contrasts the everyday view and the Newtonian, that is, the physics view. A task frequently used in research in this field (Fig. 4.4) illustrates this a little further. The ball in Fig. 4.4 is affected—if we neglect friction—by one single force only, namely the downwards-acting gravitational force. No other forces are needed, from the Newtonian point of view. Readers who are not familiar with this view may think that there should also be a horizontal force acting that pulls the ball into the actual direction of movement. This is exactly what many students think— up to university level. Our daily experiences with pulling and pushing of bodies support the idea that whenever a body has to be kept in motion a force in the direction of motion is needed. However, this is not true from the Newtonian point of view. Fig. 4.3 therefore emphasizes that learning Newtonian physics means learning a totally new way of viewing mechanical processes. A huge mental step is necessary. Comparable steps (though not always of equal magnitude) are necessary in many fields of science. If this is neglected, then an approach starting from the students' conceptions and experiences will definitely fail.

PARALLELS BETWEEN STUDENTS' CONCEPTUAL FRAMEWORKS AND HISTORICAL CONCEPTIONS

The everyday view of Fig. 4.3 will remind those who are familiar with the history of physics of the impetus theory positions of the Middle Ages or of Aristotelian physics (see, e.g., Saltiel & Viennot, 1985). In fact, many students' conceptions are reminiscent of historical conceptions and it is fascinating to see how often this is the case. It is not possible to discuss this issue here in any length. I only want to make the following comments, which throw some light on general aspects of the nature of science and learning science.

Fig. 4.3 indicates that most students and laypersons have not followed the revolution of modern physics provided by Galileo, Newton, and others. They are, in some way, still medieval thinkers. At least their general way of making sense of complex phenomena appears to be nearer to medieval thinking (namely more holistic), and not the analytical type of Galileo and Newton. The latter isolates ideal cases and reconstructs complexity by putting the pieces together again.

Parallels between students' conceptual frameworks and ideas in the history of science are not restricted to similarities on the content level (i.e., regarding natural phenomena). The processes of development of science knowledge in history on the one hand and science learning by our students on the other hand show striking analogies. Our students' many difficulties concerning exchanging their everyday conceptions for the science ones are paralleled by conceptual change from old paradigms to new ones in the history of science (Kuhn, 1970).

STUDENTS' CONCEPTIONS OF THE PURPOSE OF SPECIFIC TEACHING EVENTS

The research discussed so far has dealt solely with students' conceptions on the content level, that is, with the "content topics" of science instruction. But there are several other "conceptions" guiding students' learning.

Some interesting research results are available concerning students' "awareness" of what they learn. Whereas teachers usually have a long-term perspective of the purpose of a particular teaching or learning event, say an experiment, such a perspective is usually missing among the students. They have only a rather limited idea as to why the particular experiment is carried out, which aspects already learned have to be employed, and where the results of the experiment will lead (see Gunstone & Northfield, 1986; Hallden, 1988).

STUDENTS' CONCEPTIONS OF THE NATURE OF THEIR LEARNING PROCESS—TOWARD METALEARNING

A key factor in learning has been given much attention in research on students' conceptions during the last few years. It became obvious that most students hold a very "traditional" view of what learning is. This view has already been contrasted to the constructivistic one. It is a passive one, the idea of filling prepacked "nuggets of truth" (Kelly's, 1955, term) into waiting stores. This view determines learning behavior considerably. It leads to allocating writing (notes and the like) more importance in learning than active elaboration of information. Accordingly, schoolwork for students is mainly associated with writing. Discussions in class on the adequate view of a phenomenon (which is a key method of "constructivistic" teaching) is not given the dignity of being work (Baird & Mitchell, 1986).

It is expected that a change in students' conceptions of learning will improve learning. Baird, Fensham, Gunstone, and White (1989) are, for instance, convinced that the rather limited success of many attempts to guide students from their conceptual frameworks to the science ones is due to the lack of adequate "metacognitive" skills. Glasersfeld (1983) employs an analogy to training in sports. He is of the opinion that this is the only area where new teaching and learning methods lead to spectacular results. He thinks the reason is the mental training widely used there, that is, the training that mentally represents a succession of motions in great detail. These inner representations control the motion. In much the same way, improvements of cognitive learning by conscious control of learning processes should be possible, as Glasersfeld argues.

Several attempts at metacognitive training have been made. These are attempts to train the "mental" muscles so to speak. Novak and Gowin's (1984) techniques of "concept maps" and "vee maps" can be classified as such. In fact, they appear to be valuable tools, controlling learning to some degree. From a Piagetian position, Adey and Shayer (1988) have presented strategies for metalearning. But there are approaches of much broader range. An example of this is furnished by studies carried out at Monash University in Melbourne (see Baird et al., 1989). Students are guided by teachers and worksheets to think about their learning processes; they are asked to ponder about what they have learned and how they did it. Suggestions as to how to change learning behavior are offered. Students further portray their learning in diaries. Action research studies integrate researchers, teachers, and students; that is, they develop the views of learning of all of these participants simultaneously.

The results of these attempts are quite encouraging. But it became apparent that the process of change is a long and painstaking one. Students— especially in the beginning—are not willing to change their views of learning. First, the new view is much more demanding than the old one. Second, there is no immediate payoff in a school system that rewards learning outcomes that can be achieved more easily with the old techniques.

ON THE ROLE OF TEACHERS' CONCEPTIONS

The constructivistic view—if taken seriously—demands not only taking a broad variety of students' conceptions into consideration but teachers' conceptions, too. A wide variety of teacher and student conceptions must be

TABLE 4.2
Variables of a Constructivistic View of Science Teaching and Learning

Media (e.g., Textbooks) used in instruction
(1) Conceptions of science topics (e.g., energy, chemical bonding, particles, photosynthesis)
(2) Conceptions of the nature and range of science

Student	*Teacher*
(1) conceptions of science topics	(1) conceptions of science topics
(2) conceptions of the nature and range of science	(2) conceptions of the nature and range of science
(3) conceptions of the purposes, the aims of science instruction	(3) conceptions of the purposes, the aims of science instruction
(4) conceptions of the purpose of particular teaching events	(4) conceptions of the purpose of particular teaching events
(5) conceptions of the nature of the learning process	(5) conceptions of the nature of the learning process
(6) attitudes to science, to specific topics of science, to learning science, to the science teacher, to being in school, to learning in general	(6) attitudes to science, to specific topics of science, to being a teacher, to the students
	(7) conceptions of students' conceptions (1) to (6)

Researcher
conceptions (1) to (6)
and conceptions of these conceptions

considered (see Table 4.2). It is noteworthy that the emphasis given to teachers' conceptions has led to closer cooperation between research on students' conceptual frameworks and research on "teachers' thinking" (concerning the latter see, e.g., Lowyck, 1986).

It is not surprising that many teachers hold similar (alternative) conceptions on the content level (e.g., concerning heat and combustions) as their students, especially if they have been inadequately trained.

However, teachers' conceptions of the learning process are undoubtedly more important. Teachers usually hold the traditional passive view. Research has revealed that it is as difficult to change this view as it is to change students' alternative conceptions (Gunstone & Northfield, 1986).

CONSTRUCTION OF CONSTRUCTION

The constructivistic view points to an issue of central importance. Teachers have to be aware that they can understand (interpret) all responses of the students (of whatever kind) only according to the conceptions that they possess. They can construct their knowledge about students' knowledge only on the ground of their own conceptions. Because students' responses are constructions on the ground of their own conceptions too, the teachers' constructions are constructions of constructions (compare Marton, 1981).

The construction of construction issue is also valid for researchers' knowledge of teachers' and students' conceptions. They, too, are only constructions of constructions on the ground of the researchers' conceptions. Of course, this insight is in some way self-evident for every piece of empirical research. But it appears that it is not always considered in interpretations. Claxton (1986), for instance, criticizes the fact that research in the field of students' conceptions often rests on assumptions about the aims of science teaching and the aims of research that are not explicitly stated.

CONSEQUENCES FOR SCIENCE TEACHING

Consequences for science teaching that rest upon research on students' conceptual frameworks have already been alluded to or explicitly stated several times. Here some further consequences will be summarized.

New Aims of Science Teaching.   It appears to be one of the fundamental laws of education that there is nothing really new. Therefore, quite often, what appears new or is called new is only a rediscovered old idea. There seems to be a never-ending switch of emphasis on different positions throughout the history of pedagogy and science education as well. In this sense, the discussion about changing the aims of science teaching in favor of "new" ones mainly serves to remind one of positions that are only given little emphasis in our schools today. It is difficult to summarize the different proposals to change the aims of science teaching on the ground of research on students' conceptual frameworks. Most science educators still give emphasis to traditional aims and most members of the alternative frameworks party do not question that it is valuable for students to learn science. Therefore, the new aims appear to be in keeping with the old ones to a considerable degree. Yet a constructivistic view does demand an important change of emphasis. A constructivistic science instruction must accentuate a relational view of science conceptions. Science instruction must accordingly convince students that both their everyday conceptions and the science ones are conceptions in their own right that are valid in specific contexts only. It must further emphasize that science conceptions are not eternal truths but are open to revision if new empirical evidence or theoretical insights demand this. A note on recent research findings is necessary here. Students have severe difficulties in gaining such a relational view of science. There is a strong aversion on the part of the students to "playing around" with different conceptions; they want to know the right or the "true" one (see Driver, 1986; Mitchell & Baird, 1986).

Conceptions of the Nature and Range of Science Must be Given More Emphasis. It is an "old" aim that students should not only learn science knowledge but also get an insight into the nature and range of science knowledge, that is, into metaknowledge. As has been argued this metaknowledge is essential from a constructivistic point of view. Students' views here seem to be quite restricted to simple and naïve positivistic positions. Therefore, it is necessary for teachers to change these views to more adequate ones. Such attempts are also necessary for conceptual change on the content level because an adequate understanding of science conceptions is only possible on the ground of adequate metaknowledge. Only a few attempts at research and development have been undertaken here so far (e.g., see Niedderer, 1989).

Changing the Content Structure of Instruction. It seems reasonable to change the content structure of instruction in order to avoid misunderstandings or to challenge conceptions. Many proposals for overcoming learning difficulties are of this kind. Feher and Rice (1985), for instance, challenge the children's conception that a shadow "comes out of the body" when it stands in the light, by using light sources producing shadows that are not similar to the body, but to the structure of the light source. Such light source demonstrations have not yet entered the curriculum.

New Teaching Aids. There is, of course, the expectation that new teaching aids may help to overcome problems. The computer in particular is seen as a promising tool (see, e.g., Klopfer, 1986). Several attempts have been made to employ computers as guides toward science conceptions. Only a few approaches can be mentioned here. Goldberg (1987), for instance, has developed a computer-controlled videodisk as a tool for investigating and facilitating students' understanding of optics. Linn (1986) employs computers as students' lab partners in teaching about heat concepts, for instance. Driver and Scanlon (1989) have designed a research program to facilitate conceptual change by the use of computer software tools. Another British program aimed at tools for exploratory learning (Bliss & Ogborn, 1989) leads in a similar direction.

Changing Teaching Strategies. This is an area that is given much emphasis. Several teaching strategies to guide students from their preconceptions toward the science ones have been developed and evaluated. Chapters in the present volume contain examples. The main idea is always some sort of negotiation phase in which students' views are discussed and contrasted to the science ones. Driver and Erickson (1983) have summarized the main strategies known at that time as well as research results concerning their success. They conclude that there are encouraging as well as discouraging findings; that in general a great "breakthrough" is not in sight. This conclusion appears still to be valid. A main reason seems to be that such "conceptual change strategies" may fail to convince the students that the science conceptions are more valuable than their old ones. Students are often quite pleased with their ideas; they do not see clearly enough how the new conceptions are more fruitful than the old ones. Indeed, science conceptions are quite often more abstract and more sophisticated than students' conceptions. That they are more fruitful is understandable only for those who are already very familiar with the science point of view (see, e.g., Mitchell & Baird, 1986; Driver, 1986).

Integrating Cognitive and Affective Aspects of Learning.   Research on the significance of new teaching strategies has strongly stressed that cognitive and affective aspects are interwoven in conceptual change learning. The change from a position held to be true for a long time to another one always implies admitting that one was in error. Therefore, conceptual change processes often have to overcome emotional resistance to the new (see Hashweh, 1986). There is also no doubt that attitudes of several kinds influence learning. There is much research available on students' attitudes (see, e.g., Gardner, 1985). But the efforts to bring together research findings in the area of students' attitudes and conceptions have so far been limited.

Employing Strategies of Metacognition.   Such attempts have already been discussed. They undoubtedly lead in a similar direction to the strategies that have just been referred to concerning the implementation of conceptual change. Usually strategies of metacognition are integrated in some kind of conceptual change approach.

Teaching Teachers Constructivistic Views.   This aspect has also already been dealt with. Several attempts of new models of teacher training are being developed (see, e.g., Driver 1989; Baird et al., 1989). They are of pivotal importance. However, it is also necessary to keep in mind that the teachers' courses themselves have to be organized in a constructivistic manner because *teachers teach* as *they are taught*, not *as they are taught to teach.*

CONCLUDING REMARKS

In this chapter I wanted to present an overview of what research on students' conceptual frameworks has to offer to school practice at the moment. It was not intended to provide practical hints for direct use by the teacher. Instead I tried to give an insight into the main areas of research that may be significant where school practice is concerned. I thought an appropriate way to do this would be to outline main approaches and main trends in the research area.

The trends are, in my view, really exciting. Research started from a very important, but nevertheless limited, emphasis on investigations of students' conceptual frameworks. The scope is now much broader. The constructivistic view of learning has been proven to be a powerful and valuable driving force of research. Table 4.2 summarizes "variables" that have to be regarded if the constructivistic view is to be taken seriously.

But there are warnings necessary at the end of this chapter. First, science learning will continue to be a difficult task for students in the future. Many problems are inherent in the "nature" of science knowledge. Learning science always means learning a totally new point of view. Secondly, constructivistic science instruction will not help teaching and learning in a simple way. On the contrary, teaching and learning are more demanding if this approach is taken; research is too. To illustrate these demands, consider the following quote of a student who took part in a program aimed at developing metacognitive skills (White, 1986): "I see now what you are trying to do. You're trying to help us think. Well, I don't want to do that."

REFERENCES

Abimbola, I. O. (1988). The problem of terminology in the study of students' conceptions in science. *Science Education, 18*, 175–184.

Adey, P. (Ed.). (1989). *Adolescent development and school science*. London: Falmer Press.

Adey, P., & Shayer, M. (1988). Strategies for meta-learning in physics. *Physics Education, 23*, 97–104.

Anderson, C. W. (1987). *Three perspectives on cognition and their implications for science teaching*. Paper presented at the annual meeting of the American Educational Research Association, Washington DC.

Ausubel, D. P. (1968). *Educational psychology: A cognitive view*. New York: Holt, Rinehart, & Winston.

Baird, J. R., Fensham, P. J., Gunstone, R. F., & White, R. T. (1987). Individual development during teacher training. *Research in Science Education, 17*, 182–191.

Baird, J. R., Fensham, P. J., Gunstone, R. F., & White, R. T. (1989). *A study of the importance of reflection for improving science teaching and learning*. Paper presented at the annual meeting of the National Association of Research in Science Teaching, San Francisco.

Baird, J. R. & Mitchell, I. (Eds.). (1986). *Improving the quality of teaching and learning–An Australian case study*. Melbourne, Australia: Monash University Printery.

Bliss, J., & Ogborn, J. (1989). Tools for exploratory learning. *Journal of Computer Assisted Learning, 5*, 37–50.

Brown, H. J. (1977). *Perception, theory and commitment–The new philosophy of science*. Chicago: Precedent.

Carey, S. (1986). Cognitive science and science education. *American Psychologist, 41*, 1123–1130.

Claxton, G. L. (undated). *Teaching and acquiring scientific knowledge*. Centre for Science and Mathematics Education. Kings' College. University of London.

Claxton, G. L. (1986). The alternative conceivers' conceptions. *Studies in Science Education, 13*, 123–130.

Driver, R. (1986). *Reconstructing the science curriculum: The approach of the Children's*

Learning in Science Project. Paper presented at the annual meeting of the American Educational Research Association, San Francisco.

Driver, R. (1989). Changing conceptions. In P. Adey, *Adolescent development and school science.* London: Falmer Press, pp. 79–99.

Driver, R., & Easley, J. (1978). Pupils and paradigms: a review of literature related to concept development in adolescent science students. *Studies in Science Education, 5,* 61–84.

Driver, R., & Erickson, G. (1983). Theories-in-action: Some theoretical and empirical issues in the study of students' conceptual frameworks in science. *Studies in Science Education, 10,* 37–60.

Driver, R., & Scanlon, E. (1989). Conceptual change in science. *Journal of Computer Assisted Learning, 5,* 25–36.

Duit, R. (1987). Research on students' alternative frameworks in science–topics, theoretical frameworks, consequences for science teaching. In J. Novak (Ed.). *Proceedings of the Second International Seminar Misconceptions and Educational Strategies in Science and Mathematics* (Vol. 1). Ithaca, NY: Cornell University, pp. 151–162.

Engel-Clough, E., & Driver, R. (1986). A study of consistency in the use of students' conceptual frameworks across different task contexts. *Science Education, 70,* 473–496.

Erickson, F. (1986). Qualitative methods in research on teaching. In M. Wittrock (Ed.), *Handbook of research on teaching (3rd ed.).* New York: Macmillan, 119–161.

Feher, E., & Rice, R. (1985). Development of scientific concepts through the use of interactive exhibits in a museum. *American Museum of Natural History, 28,* 35–46.

Fensham, P. (1989). Theory in practice: How to assist science teachers to teach constructively. In P. Adey (Ed.), *Adolescent development and school science.* London: Falmer Press, pp. 61–74.

Gardner, P. L. (1985). Students' interest in science and technology: An international overview. In M. Lehrke, L. Hoffmann,& P. Gardner (Eds.), *Interests in science and technology education.* Kiel, West Germany: IPN/UNESCO, pp. 15–34.

Gauld, C. (1987). Student beliefs and cognitive structure. *Research in Science Education, 17,* 87–93.

Gauld, C. (1988). The "pupil-as-scientist" metaphor in scientific education. *Research in Science Education, 18,* 35–41.

Gilbert, J., Osborne, R., & Fensham, P. (1982). Children's science and its consequences for teaching. *Science Education, 66,* 623–633.

Gilbert, J., & Watts, M. (1983). Concepts, misconceptions and alternative conceptions: changing perspectives in science education. *Studies in Science Education, 10,* 61–98.

Glasersfeld, E. V. (1983). Learning as a constructive activity. In J. C. Bergeron & N. Hevscovics (Eds.), *Proceedings of the fifth annual meeting of PME-NA.* Montreal.

Goldberg, F. (1987). Using an interactive videodisc as a tool for investigating and facilitating student understanding in geometrical optics. In J. Novak (Ed.), *Proceedings of the Second International Seminar Misconceptions and Educational Strategies in Science and Mathematics* (Vol. 3). Ithaca, NY: Cornell University, pp. 180–186.

Gunstone, R., & Northfield, D. J. (1986). *Learners-teachers-researchers: Consistency in implementing conceptual change.* Paper presented at the annual meeting of the American Educational Research Association, San Francisco.

Gunstone, R. F., & White, R. T. (1981). Understanding gravity. *Science Education, 65,* 291–299.

Hallden, O. (1988). The evolution of the species—Pupil perspectives and school perspective. In R. Duit & R. Säljö (Eds.), *Students' conceptions of subject matter content.* Kiel, West Germany: IPN Reports-in-Brief, pp. 21–55.

Hashweh, M. Z. (1986). Toward an explanation of conceptual change. *European Journal of Science Education, 8,* 229–249.

Hills, G. L. (1989). Students' "untutored" beliefs about natural phenomena: primitive science or common sense? *Science Education, 73,* 155–186.

Jung, W. (1985). *Uses of cognitive science to science education.* Paper presented to the ATEE Symposium on the Implications of Cognitive Science for the Education of Science Teachers, Kiel, West Germany.

Kelly, G. A. (1955). *The psychology of personal constructs* (Vol. 1, 2). New York: Norton.

Kleinman, R. W., Griffin, H. C., Konigsberg Kerner, N. (1987). Images in chemistry. *Journal of Chemical Education*, 64, 766–770.

Klopfer, L. E. (1986). Intelligent tutoring systems in science education: the coming generation of computer-based instructional programs. *Journal of Computers in Mathematics and Science Teaching*, 5, No. 4, 16–32.

Kuhn, T. S. (1970). *The structure of scientific revolutions.* Chicago: University of Chicago Press.

Linn, M. (1986). *Learning more with computers as lab partners.* Berkeley: University of California.

Lowyck, J. (1986). *Teacher thinking: A critical analysis of four studies.* Paper presented at the Annual Meeting of the American Educational Research Association, San Francisco.

Marton, F. (1981). Phenomenography—Describing conceptions of the world around us. *Instructional Science*, 10, 177–200.

Mitchell, J. & Baird, J. (1986). Teaching, learning and the curriculum: I. The influence of content in science. *Research in Science Education*, 16, 141–149.

Niedderer, H. (1989). *Qualitative and quantitative methods of investigating alternative frameworks of students—with results from atomic physics and other subject areas.* Paper presented at the annual meeting of the American Association of Physics Teachers, San Francisco.

Novak, J., & Gowin, D. B. (1984). *Learning how to learn.* New York: Cambridge University Press.

Pfundt, H., & Duit, R. (1991). *Bibliography: Students' alternative frameworks and science education.* (3rd ed.). Kiel, West Germany: IPN.

Pope, M. (1985). *Constructivist goggles: Implications for process in teaching and learning.* Paper presented at British Educational Research Association Conference, Sheffield, England.

Preece, P. (1984). Intuitive science: learned or triggered? *European Journal of Science Education*, 6, 7–10.

Rhöneck, C. V., & Grob, K. (1988). Representation and problem-solving in basic electricity—Predictors for successful learning. In R. Duit & R. Säljö (Eds.), *Students' conceptions of subject matter content.* Kiel, West Germany: IPN Reports-in-Brief, pp. 57–83.

Saltiel, E., & Viennot, L. (1985). What do we learn from similarities between historical ideas and the spontaneous reasoning of students? In P. L. Lijnse (Ed.), *The many faces of teaching and learning mechanics. Conference on Physics Education.* Utrecht, Netherlands: GIREP/SVO/UNESCO, 199–214.

Strike, R. A. (1987). Toward a coherent constructivism. In J. Novak (Ed.), *Proceedings of the Second International Seminar Misconceptions and Educational Strategies in Science and Mathematics* (Vol. 1). Ithaca, NY: Cornell University, pp. 481–489.

Vygotsky, L. S. (1962). *Thought and language.* Cambridge, MA: MIT Press.

Vygotsky, L. S. (1978). *Mind in society.* Cambridge, MA: Harvard University Press.

Watzlawick, P. (Ed.). (1981). *Die erfundene Wirklichkeit.* Munich: Piper.

White, R. T. (1986). Observations of a minor participant. In J. R. Baird & I. Mitchell (Eds.), *Improving the quality of teaching and learning—An Australian case study.* Melbourne, Australia: The Monash University Printery.

CONCEPTUAL DEVELOPMENT AND LEARNING SCIENCE

5

Developmental Patterns in Students' Understanding of Physics Concepts

Joseph Stepans
University of Wyoming

As children, my brothers and I would get excited when my father came home from the store announcing the arrival of a letter from abroad. Some of our relatives lived in Russia and a few others in America. When my father would say, "We got a letter today!", one of us would ask, "From whom?" Another brother would wonder, "How long did it take to get here?" My father would respond after looking at the date. Someone else would ask, "How did it come?" Again my father would look at the envelope and say by water, air, or land. The first time he responded, "By water," I took the envelope and looked at it. IT WAS DRY! I opened it, looked carefully at the writing—no indication of it being in water!

Being the eldest of five brothers, though still young, I was usually responsible for mailing family letters. The closest mailbox was a little one that hung on the wall outside a bookstore. I had envisioned that behind the mailbox there was a big hole that led to the rivers under the ground that eventually led to the big oceans. As I dropped the letter, I would put my ear to the mailbox trying to hear the letter hitting the water. Sometimes I thought I actually heard it hit the water, and I knew then it was on its way. Upon reaching the river, I imagined the letter was carried to the ocean where there were special winds at work. If the letter were to go to Russia, winds from a particular direction would carry the letter toward Russia, and if it were to go to America, there were other winds that were responsible for carrying it to its destination. I had imagined that my aunt or grandmother was waiting on the other side of the ocean for the letter, day after day. Finally, she would see it floating on the water, carried to her by the waves. She would scream with joy and run into the water to retrieve her letter. She would then stand in line to dry her letter.

I had envisioned a man who had opened a letter-drying business and charged people a certain amount of money to drop their letters in a large cylinder with holes in it and dry them by turning a crank. This is how I explained to myself why the letters were not wet.

If my father told us the letter came by air, I had much more difficulty visualizing how the letters were able to survive winds from different directions and still reach their destination.

One day, when I was a young boy, I was approaching the bookstore with the little mailbox outside it, and saw a uniformed man carrying a large bag. He walked up to the mailbox, took out a set of keys, unlocked it, removed a stack of letters, and placed them in the bag. In a way I was disappointed that there was no hole behind the box but what I saw partly explained how mail went from one place to another (Stepans, 1988).*

Nine years ago, when I joined the university faculty, I began to look for a direction to channel research efforts. Reflecting back on my own childhood, I felt a need to talk to students of all ages and listen to their views of the world and of how things work. I soon discovered that talking to learners was delightful and educational.

I began the work by posing such questions as:

What beliefs does the learner bring with him or her to the classroom?

How can we find out what these beliefs are?

Once we have determined those beliefs, what do we do with them?

How can we structure our classroom in order to bring about the desired change in learners?

As students move up the educational ladder, to what extent do they change their naive ideas in science?

In this chapter I will:

(I) Report on studies on the pattern of misconceptions in physics among learners of various age groups; the concepts include: (A) the sinking and floating phenomena of solids in liquids, (B) concepts associated with weather; and (C) structure and behavior of matter; (II) Discuss factors that may either contribute to students retaining their misconceptions related to various science concepts or cause confusion in them; (III) Discuss the implications of research findings related to students' misconceptions to the teaching/learning of science; (IV) Examine two teaching strategies used in teaching physics concepts; and (V) Elaborate on an innovative teaching model that has shown to be effective in helping students to remove their misconceptions in physics concepts.

---

*From: What are we learning from children about teaching and learning? *Teaching & Learning: The Journal of Natural Inquiry*, 2,(2), Winter 1988. Reprinted with permission.

I-A.   STUDENTS' VIEWS ON SINKING AND FLOATING

In an attempt to deal with the problem of misconception, a study was conducted to determine students' understanding of concepts related to how objects sink and float in water (Stepans, Beiswenger, & Dyche, 1986). For this research, 184 students were interviewed at the primary, intermediate, and junior high levels from public schools in Wyoming and at the college level from science content courses for elementary education majors at the University of Wyoming. The plan had two purposes: (1) to determine the patterns of change in students' conceptions at the four educational levels, and (2) to identify some of the underlying reasons for those patterns.

The clinical interview developed by Piaget was used since it is recognized as a superior method for detecting students' conceptions and conceptual change (Posner & Gertzog, 1982). During the interviews, items similar to those employed by Carpenter (1981) at the University of Nebraska were used: a small wooden cube, large wooden cube, small metal cube, looped wire, large metal cylinder, small metal cylinder, aluminum sheet, crumpled aluminum sheet, clay ball, clay pot, jar lid, and jar lid with holes. The objects enabled the researchers to evaluate how students related the factors of mass, volume, density, surface tension, water pressure, and buoyancy to sinking and floating.

Each interview began with "If I place this object in this much water, will it float or will it sink? Why?" Follow-up questions were formulated according to the student's response. If a student said, "This object will float because it is made of wood," the interviewer might ask, "Does wood always float?" If a student said, "This object will sink because it is heavy," the interviewer might ask, "Are all ships that float on water light?"

To organize the data, the responses were categorized as complete understanding (CU) when students were correct in their predictions and gave a completely correct explanation; as partial understanding (PU) when they gave partly correct explanations, although their predictions may have been correct or incorrect; and as no understanding (NU) when they gave incorrect predictions and incorrect explanations.

The percentages in Fig. 5.1 show that there is little difference in understanding of sink/float concepts among students at the various academic levels. This stands in contrast to theory: Students past age 11 or 12 should have developed the formal logical structures needed to understand density, according to Piaget. A large number of college students said that when a piece of aluminum is crumpled it becomes heavier. This response is similar to that given by some of the elementary school children.

If you compare the CU responses in Fig. 5.1, you will find that college students did slightly better than younger students on aluminum and clay objects and looped wire but that the differences are very small.   One distinguishing characteristic was identified, however. Students at the various

Object	Primary (K-3) N=36			Intermediate (4-6) N=40			Junior High (7-8) N=56			College N=52		
	CU	PU	NU	CU	PU	NU	CU	PU	NU	CU	PU	NU
Large wooden cube	0	62	38	0	78	22	2	84	14	2	70	28
Small wooden cube	0	88	12	0	90	10	4	91	5	2	78	20
Small metal cube	0	100	0	0	97	3	0	98	2	0	100	0
Looped wire	0	38	62	0	72	28	0	34	66	2	58	40
Large metal cylinder	0	100	0	0	97	3	0	87	13	0	98	2
Small metal cylinder	0	81	19	0	90	10	0	89	11	0	79	21
Aluminum sheet	0	88	12	0	85	15	0	82	18	4	83	13
Crumpled aluminum	0	65	35	0	45	55	0	43	57	2	71	27
Ball of clay	0	100	0	0	90	10	0	91	9	4	90	6
Pot of clay	0	89	11	0	70	30	0	73	27	6	79	15
Jar lid	0	88	12	0	88	12	0	93	7	2	98	0
Jar lid with holes	0	35	65	0	15	85	0	7	93	0	8	92

FIG. 5.1.   Percentage of students who understand concepts related to sink/float concepts.   Students display complete understanding (CU), partial understanding (PU), or no understanding (NU). Reprinted with permission from *Science Teacher*, September 1986. Copyright © 1986 by the National Science Teachers Association, 1742 Connecticut Ave., NW, Washington, DC 20009.

levels used significantly different language to describe concepts. Terms such as *light*, *heavy*, and *weight* used by the elementary students were replaced by *density*, *physical properties*, and *surface tension* at the junior high level.

Unfortunately, the junior high students' increase in sophisticated science vocabulary was not accompanied by increased understanding. In a similar pattern, the college students used the terms *surface tension*, *displacement*, *surface area*, *volume*, and *mass* but had little understanding of the concepts the terms described. Apparently, the elementary students were giving responses based on common sense and had not yet been encumbered with scientific terminology. On the other hand, many of the older students seemed to be so concerned with trying to fit the correct scientific terms into their explanations that they lost sight of the phenomena at hand.

I-B. STUDENTS' THINKING RELATED TO PHYSICS PHENOMENA ASSOCIATED WITH WEATHER

A study was conducted to examine the understanding of weather held by children in grades two and five (Stepans & Kuehn, 1985). The purpose of this study was to find out exactly how these children explained particular weather phenomena and to categorize the general level of their understanding about weather. Information was also sought to determine the degree to which responses given by second grade students would differ from those given by fifth graders. Topics were ones commonly discussed in elementary science textbooks: wind, clouds, thunder, lightning, rain, snow, and rainbows. The textbook series, *Concepts in Science*, by Brandwein et al. (1975), which was used in the school district studied, was analyzed to determine what weather topics the children included in this sample had been exposed to in grades one through five (see Table 5.1).

Students were selected for this study from four different classes- two

TABLE 5.1
Weather Phenomena Studied by Children in Test Group by Grade

First Grade	Water vapor and steam
	Clouds
	Rain
	Water cycle
	Hot and cold
Second Grade	Effects of temperature change on air
	Rainbows
Third Grade	Condensation and evaporation
	Changes of state
	Physical and chemical changes
Fourth Grade	Evaporation and condensation
	Clouds: how they are made, raindrops from, seeding rain, raindrops, rainfall
	Water cycle
	Snow
Fifth Grade	Effects of wind on land

second grades and two fifth grades—in two different schools. One second grade and one of the fifth grades used textbooks as a basis for instruction. The other two classes used Elementary Science Study (ESS) and other hands-on activities as their science programs. Fifteen students were randomly selected from each of the four classes.

Data were collected through an interview with each child and were recorded on tape. Interviews began with a general question—for example, "What is wind?" The next question depended on the answer that the child had given. Subsequent questions were also tailored to the child's responses and were designed to probe the child's understanding of the topic. The following sample interview with an 11-year-old shows that continued questioning sometimes uncovered misconceptions on what appeared to be a solid understanding of a concept:

Interviewer: What is rain?

Child: It's water that falls out of a cloud when the clouds evaporate.

Interviewer: What do you mean clouds evaporate?

Child: That means water goes up in the air and then it makes clouds and then, when it gets too heavy up there, then the water comes and they call it rain.

Interviewer: Does the water stay in the sky?

Child: Yes, and then it comes down when it rains. It gets too heavy.

Interviewer: Why does it get too heavy?

Child: 'Cause there's too much water up there.

Interviewer: Why does it rain?

Child: 'Cause the water gets too heavy and then it comes down.

Interviewer: Why doesn't the whole thing come down?

Child: Well, 'cause it comes down at little times like a salt shaker when you turn it upside down. It doesn't all come down at once 'cause there's little holes and it just comes out.

Interviewer: What are the little holes in the sky?

Child: Umm, holes in the clouds, letting the water out.

After the interview, each child's response was placed into one of five developmental categories based on the work of Piaget (1963) and on Fuson's (1976) later discussions of Piaget. These stages, called *feelings of participation, animism, artificialism, finalism,* and *true causality,* are briefly described herein. Each description includes a student response illustrating that particular stage:

1. *Feelings of participation.*   The child thinks that he or she participates in the actions of nature. Sometimes these feelings are accompanied by beliefs in magic.

   Interviewer: What makes the clouds move along?
   Ten-year-old: It's when you walk.

2. *Animism*:   The child attributes life and consciousness to inanimate objects.

   Interviewer: What is rain?
   Seven-year-old: Clouds think it's too hot, and one day they start sweating. I guess they start sweating and then the sweat falls on us.

3. *Artificialism*:   The child thinks that things happen for the good of human beings and other living things.

   Interviewer: Why does it rain?
   Eleven-year-old: To give us moisture and the better our crops grow.

4. *Finalism*:   The child thinks that there is an explanation for everything. (The explanation is not scientifically accurate, and it does not fall within the categories already mentioned.) Two major subgroups within this category were identified.

   a. *Religious finalism.*   In these explanations, the child refers to supernatural causes such as God and angels.

   Interviewer: What is thunder?
   Five-year-old: Thunder is when God becomes mad at all of the angels.
   Interviewer: What is lightning?
   Five-year-old: The noise that the angels make when they are crying after God has yelled at them, like Mom does to me.
   Interviewer: What is rain?
   Five-year-old: The tears of God and the angels crying after they have made friends again.

   b. *Nonreligious finalism*:   In these explanations the child makes no reference to the supernatural.

   Interviewer: What is snow?
   Seven-year-old: There are white mountains where white bears live and would cut out snowflakes and they would spread them all over.

5. *True causality*:   The child gives a fairly accurate explanation for the physical phenomenon.

> *Interviewer*:   Why does it rain?
>
> *Eight-year-old*: 'Cause water evaporated up in the sky and it forms that cloud, and the cloud gets too heavy and cannot hold the water anymore.

A given student's answers to questions about clouds, say, might fall into a different category from his or her answers about thunder, so a student's understanding of weather was generalized according to which developmental stage predominated. For example, a second grader from the class using the hands-on approach, gave religious finalistic responses to questions on thunder, artificialistic responses to questions on rain, and nonreligious finalistic responses to questions concerning wind, clouds, lightning, snow, and rainbows. Based on the frequency of responses, this student was identified as having a nonreligious finalistic view on the concept of weather.

The results, summarized in Table 5.2, showed that, while some students in the fifth grade had reached the stage of true causality, the majority of students in both grades were at the stage of nonreligious finalism. The data and analysis results provided support for the following statements:

- The only animistic views were given by second graders using textbooks.
- More second graders gave religious finalistic responses than fifth graders.

TABLE 5.2
Views of Children in Test Group by Developmental Stages

	Animism	Artificialism	Religious Finalism	Nonreligious Finalism	True Causality
Second Grade Textbook	14%		28%	58%	
Second Grade Hands-on			28%	72%	
Fifth Grade Textbook			7%	72%	21%
Fifth Grade Hands-on			7%	65%	28%

- More second graders using the hands-on approach gave nonreligious finalistic responses than second graders using textbooks.
- Although no second grader's understanding of weather had attained the true causality stage, nearly 25% of fifth graders had reached that stage.

Table 5.3 shows the percentages of students from each class who gave true causal responses for each of the seven phenomena. The following statements were supported by the data and the analysis:

- More second graders who were using the hands-on approach gave true causal responses to questions about wind and rain than second graders using textbooks.
- More fifth graders who were using the hands-on approach gave true cause responses to questions about clouds, snow, and rainbows than fifth graders using textbooks.
- More fifth graders using textbooks gave true causal responses to questions about rain than fifth graders using the hands-on approach.
- More fifth graders gave true causal responses than second graders on all topics except thunder.

TABLE 5.3
Children in Test Group Giving True Causal Responses

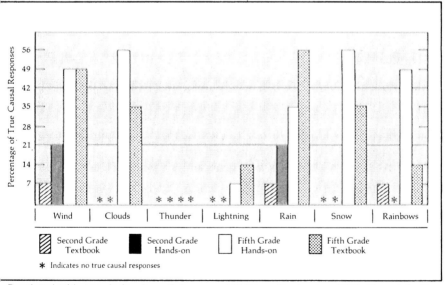

- No one gave a true causal response to questions about thunder.
- More students (in general) using the hands-on approach gave true causal responses to questions about wind, clouds, snow, and rain than students who were using textbooks.

I-C. STUDENTS' BELIEFS RELATED TO THE STRUCTURE AND BEHAVIOR OF MATTER

For more than a year, the author and other researchers have been talking to students in grades four through eight about their views of the structure and behavior of matter. Each student has been interviewed individually and follow-up questions have been used based on students' responses.

Included in this chapter are three of the items used in interviews with students on their ideas about matter. They include:

- The structure of a ball of clay versus that of a steel ball;
- The behavior of salt stirred in water versus that of corn starch;
- The behavior of ice when heated compared with that of dry ice.

In each situation the student was asked, "If you had a giant microscope and were able to see the smallest particle, what would you be seeing?" The student, in each case, was encouraged to give descriptions, draw pictures, build models, and elaborate.

Clay vs. Steel

Each student was shown a ball of clay and a steel ball of approximately the same size and asked, "Why am I able to squeeze the ball of clay and make it into a pancake, but no matter how hard I try I am not able to do it with a steel ball? If you were looking through a microscope, what would you be seeing as you view the ball of clay and the steel ball?"

Fourth graders' responses were generally limited. For example: "Steel is much harder than clay," or "Steel is made of steel but clay is made of mud (wax)."

Fifth graders gave a more detailed description and did not hesitate to draw pictures while elaborating. Some sample views included: "Clay particles are getting smashed, squished, flat or smooth down." Other views included: "Molecules of clay get warm and spread apart, but molecules of steel have a 'harder mass' and can't do this." Still others believed that steel "atoms" and "molecules" were harder than those of clay.

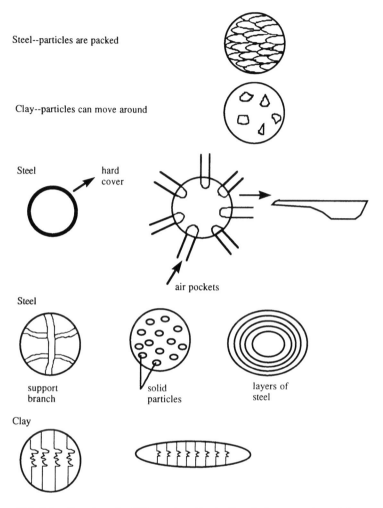

FIG. 5.2.   Drawings by fifth graders illustrating their perception of the difference between clay and steel at the particle level.

Fifth graders interviewed provided drawings similar to those given in Fig. 5.2.

Responses of seventh and eighth graders to the question were more sophisticated and included the following:

"Since atoms are flexible, they are being flattened and stretched, while atoms of steel are too strong and solid."

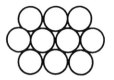

"Atoms of steel are not puffy like clay."
"The atoms change shape when you press down on clay."

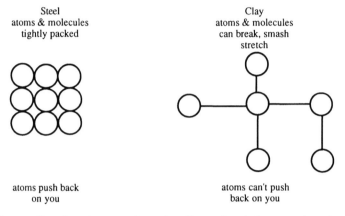

FIG. 5.3.   Drawings by seventh graders illustrating their perception of
the difference between clay and steel at the particle level.

"Atoms of the clay are not as compact. They are soft and will bend."

"Atoms are like rubber balls and are squishing together. Atoms of steel
are hard and tight."

"Atoms of clay are big and 'puffy' so when you squeeze the clay, atoms
change shape."

Students' drawings are given in Fig. 5.3.

Salt vs. Cornstarch

A teaspoon of salt was placed in a beaker of water and stirred until it was clear. In another beaker a teaspoon of cornstarch was stirred until "milky." The student again was asked the question as to what the difference was between the two situations.

Fig. 5.4 gives some of the views expressed by students in grades four, five, seven, and eight.

Ice Cube vs. Dry Ice

An ice cube was placed in a beaker and set on a hot plate. A piece of dry ice was placed in another beaker. The student again was asked, "If you had a giant microscope and could see the smallest particles, what would you be seeing?"

Some of the views expressed by students in grades four, five, seven, and eight are given in Fig. 5.5.

For most children in grades four through eight interviewed on the structure and behavior of matter undergoing physical changes (including smashing a ball of clay, dissolving salt in water and melting ice) the atoms are conceptualized as colored circles that can be smashed, stretched, or otherwise changed, and molecules are colored spheres joined together with sticks, rods, or springs.

What Are We Learning From Learners?

- That learners have no prior knowledge relative to a concept is not a valid assumption.
- Young learners have their own theories and views of the world and may be quite different from those of adults.
- Concepts are presented in a manner assuming that the learners will immediately understand and accept them.
- Many adults, in spite of being exposed to many years of science instruction, tend to retain their naive ideas.
- Children's naive ideas may be similar to those held by primitive humans and documented in the history of science.
- Instruction appears to be effective in bringing about conceptual changes with respect to some, but not all, science concepts.

II.   WHAT ARE SOME POSSIBLE SOURCES OF MISCONCEPTIONS

Students who come into a learning environment bring their own preconceptions of the world. These conceptions are not necessarily those of scientists that are accepted as "correct" by curriculum writers and teachers. Despite what teachers think about science concepts, many students maintain their early and erroneous concepts of the world for several years, even into adulthood.

Among possible sources responsible for students retaining their misconceptions or naive conceptions are the following:

Fourth Grade

Salt is seasoning
Salt blends in
    melts
    disappears

Starch is powder
Cornstarch is thicker

Fifth Grade

Salt disintegrates
Water eats the salt
Water chemicals attack
salt, make it disappear
Water is like acid,
turns salt to water
Stirring pressures salt
makes it melt

Starch bundles up
Starch has an outer protection
Starch chemicals attack water,
make them white
Starch has more white and takes
over water
Starch doesn't have as many grains

Eighth Grade

Salt atoms are there but
are skinny and clear, it
looks like nothing is there

Cornstarch atoms are thicker and
in chunks, not as clear

Salt crystals are pulled
apart

Starch molecules bond together
more tightly, not letting water pull
them apart

FIG. 5.4.   Views expressed by fourth, fifth, and eighth graders on the difference between salt and cornstarch.

A. Teachers lack of awareness and/or interest related to students' misconceptions;

B. Everyday language and metaphors;

C. Assumption that when something is taught it is immediately learned;

D. Assumption that words imply understanding;

E. Textbook presentation of concepts;

F. Overemphasis on lecture.

Salt is dissolving

because atoms are being
released in the particles
of salt

In salt you can see the molecules
and atoms moving around
Salt atoms dissolve
Salt pieces spread apart
Salt is weak, water will dissolve it

Cornstarch is not

dissolving because atoms are
remaining in the particles of
cornstarch

Starch is too thick so atoms can't
move around as easily
Cornstarch atoms don't
Starch clumps together in big pieces
Cornstarch is too strong

Responses from eighth graders

Salt melts, corrodes
Salt atoms are smaller than water,
they connect and dissolve
Salt disappears

Starch has many more atoms and
can't melt
Starch atoms are heavier, push the
water atoms to the middle
Starch has more mass, sticks
together

FIG. 5.4.   (Continued)

A. Butzow and Gable (1986) asked secondary science teachers to rate 25 research areas according to importance. Identifying and dealing with the misconceptions of students was rated as one of the lowest areas of interest by secondary science teachers.

When the author has raised the issue of identifying and addressing students' misconceptions in science, some teachers have been less than enthusiastic and have stated that there are many more important issues they need to address and therefore cannot afford spending time dealing with students' misconceptions.

B. In an unpublished study, this author asked science teachers of grades five through nine to write down how their students would predict outcomes to certain situations. The teachers also wrote down the reasons that the students would provide for their predictions. Later the teachers were asked to question their students and compare what they thought their students would say and what their students actually said. The teachers included in this study were amazed at the difference between what they thought the students would predict and what the students actually predicted.

Children develop preconceptions from the conceptual models they build for themselves, by reading children's stories, and from views presented to them by family members and adults they encounter in such places as day care

Responses Given by Fourth Graders

Heat melts the ice and steam comes out.
Ice is drops of water; dry ice is a chemical.
Dry ice evaporates faster; it doesn't have time to melt.
Dry ice is really dry water. Water, when heated, becomes steam. Ice is just water and will be a liquid.

Responses of Fifth Graders

Figure 5.5 illustrates fifth graders' ideas on ice, water, and gas.

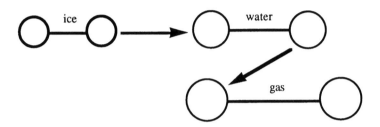

They stretch and become longer.
When ice atoms hit the side of the wall and when it starts to melt, atoms bump into each other.
When ice melts, gas atoms break down into smaller atoms and still smaller.
When they melt, they get bigger, spread out.
The following are typical responses given by seventh and eighth graders:
Ice will leave water and go up in steam. Dry ice will not leave water and a cloud like smoke will come.
Dry ice doesn't have water so it can't have vapor. You'll see little droplets of H and O linked together and in dry ice you'll see only one molecule of carbon dioxide or something.
When you heat ice it melts. The atoms aren't destroyed but they rise in the air. It is the same for dry ice.
Ice atoms get farther and farther apart until they are evaporated.
Dry ice atoms separate into gaseous form, which happens to be their natural state.
Ice gives clear vapor and only a few atoms coming out far apart. Dry ice has a lot of atoms close together.
Dry ice atoms are being pressured into the air and when it comes in contact with the air it forms a white cloud.

FIG. 5.5.   Views expressed by fourth and fifth graders on the difference between the phase change of ice and dry ice when heated.

centers and Sunday School classes or from the media. As an example, a bicycle has been called a "wind horse" in many cultures.

C. In relying heavily on lecture, reading, or standard experiments, science teachers assume that if a concept is covered (taught), it is immediately learned.

Wandersee (1986), in a study of plant nutrition concepts, questioned students from grades 5, 8, and 11, as well as college sophomores, about their beliefs. On some items, the majority of students selected the option which was believed to be true in 350 B.C. In the words of Arnold Arons (1981), "The Greeks did not resolve zero's paradoxes, and it took the human mind 2000 years to invent and clarify the concepts of kinematics as we now know them. It is necessary to allow our students to relive some of this conceptual development, and it should not be surprising that they have serious difficulty with the same subtleties which bewildered able minds in the past."

D. Stepans, Dyche, and Beiswenger (1988) determined that when college students were asked to identify factors affecting why objects sink or float in water, the majority gave words such as density, buoyancy, surface tension, mass, volume, surface area, and Archimedes's Principle. These terms usually imply understanding when used with typical means of evaluation. But during follow-up questioning, when asked to explain what these terms meant, very few showed understanding.

E. The language found in textbooks and used by teachers may either contribute to creating misconceptions or prove ineffective in removing naive conceptions. Examples will illustrate how written materials may bring about confusion in children.

A second-grade science book starts a discussion on "where does the water go?" by showing a child sailing a boat in a puddle. The next picture shows that the following day when the child returns, the puddle is gone. The teacher's guide suggests to the teacher to ask the children: "Where did the water go?" The teacher is to tell the students that water evaporated and went into the air. Looking at the second picture, one sees cracks in the ground. When second graders have been presented with the two pictures and asked where they thought the water went, most of them responded, "Into the cracks, of course! Because there were no cracks in the first picture!"

The ambiguity between what the words say to children, and/or suggest to teachers to tell the children, and what the visual representations accompanying those words seem to indicate apparently creates a state of confusion in children.

A fourth-grade science textbook starts a discussion on "Machines and Work" with an introduction on how scientists define such terms as work, force, and so on. The picture accompanying the definition shows a girl holding a large rock with the statement that, according to scientists, the girl is not doing any work. The discussion on machines begins with two pictures— one of a tilted board and the other of a bottle opener—as examples of simple machines. This page introduces machines as well as other terms, such as *slope*, *inclined plane*, *ramp*, and *slanted surface*. The objectives for the child consist primarily of naming these words. The following pages give staircases, screws, wedges, needles, forks, and nails as examples of simple machines. This type of presentation introduces a new and difficult concept in physics and, at the same time, holds the learner responsible for a complex set of new vocabulary words. It totally ignores what the learner brings to the learning environment. The child's conception of a machine is probably something that has wheels, an engine, and makes noise. The presentation of an inclined plane, a bottle opener, and a screw as machines may add to the learner's confusion. In introducing the terms in this way, the book holds the child responsible for concepts as defined by scientists rather than incorporating the new ideas into what the child already knows.

Most elementary science textbooks start introducing the topic of matter in grade three by discussing mass and weight and continue the concept by going on to states of matter, structure of atoms, molecules, elements, and compounds. By the eighth grade, textbooks cover balancing chemical equations and even nuclear fission and fusion. In textbooks, atoms are usually colored spheres, which keep changing color and size from one chapter to the next. Molecules are represented by washers and paper clips, nuts and bolts, or marshmallows joined by toothpicks

In justifying the use of models, textbook authors suggest that a scientific model explains something that is not familiar or cannot be seen in terms of something that is familiar or visible. In conversations with children, the researchers are finding that children, however, view matter as presented to them in textbooks. These results substantiate the belief of Renner and Marek (1988) who state, "In presenting concrete learners with abstract concepts such as models of atoms and molecules, what learners learn are the models rather than the concept they represent."

F. As science teachers, due to pressures of coverage, we spend most of our class time lecturing. Lecture, however, is often not an effective way of helping students remove their naive conceptions (Stepans et al., 1988). It does not provide students with the opportunity to reveal their own misconceptions, test their ideas, and try to bridge the gap between what they believe and what they observe.

Immediately after discussing Newton's Third Law, that is, for every action there is an equal and opposite reaction, prospective secondary teachers were given the following challenge: "Who can hit this piece of paper with a force of 50 lbs?" More than two-thirds raised their hands. What students believed and what they verbalized were quite different. It is evident that just telling students does not remove the mismatch between what they believe and what they are told.

III. IMPLICATIONS FOR LEARNING AND TEACHING RESEARCHERS TELL US THAT IN ORDER TO CREATE AN EFFECTIVE LEARNING ENVIRONMENT WE MUST LISTEN TO OUR STUDENTS AND ASK OURSELVES:

- Do we give the learner the opportunity to share his or her views in the learning process?

- Do we allow the learner to see that there are, in fact, other viewpoints on the same concept and the viewpoint of the book and the teacher is just another one?
- Are we in a hurry to correct a child's view and present, or impose on the child, the adult's, or scientist's view of things?

We try to teach by lecturing—telling, rather than providing the learners with more effective opportunities to correct their naive conceptions. All too often we spend considerable time teaching, and children waste too much of their energy trying to learn concepts in ways that are inefficient and inappropriate.

The student's inability to understand a concept and to apply information may stem from some of the following factors:

- The concept was introduced too early;
- The concept was not developed properly;
- No attention was given to what the child brought to the learning environment;
- The concept was introduced only verbally; no opportunity was provided to interact with ideas.

As educators we should take the time to talk to students, to find out how they view things, and to try to incorporate their way of looking at the world into the development of concepts. We should provide learners with some ownership in the development of the concept. We should give students the opportunity to see that it is perfectly acceptable to have different viewpoints on a given phenomenon or concept and create an atmosphere in which the learner is not afraid of being wrong. If we believe that a major purpose of education is to help our students to remove their misconceptions, we need to (1) identify the naive conceptions held by learners, and (2) decide on proper time and effective methods to remove those conceptions.

IV.   TWO TEACHING STRATEGIES

Fifty-two college students were equally divided between two sections of a science content course designed for elementary education majors (Stepans, Dyche, & Beiswenger, 1988). On the average, students entering this science class had completed 4 years of science since grade nine; some of them had as little as 1 year, while others had the equivalent of 8 years. A preliminary interview was done to:

- Determine the individual's understanding of the concepts of sinking and floating of solids and water;

- Enable the researchers to measure any future changes that might occur due to instruction;
- Compare the effectiveness of the two models of instruction: the expository and the learning cycle.

The expository teaching model consisted of teacher lectures, written problems given to the students, and teacher conducted demonstrations. Students were encouraged to take notes on all phases of the presentation. They were given the definitions to the following: mass, weight, volume, density, displacement, buoyancy, water pressure, surface tension, and Archimedes's Principle. The formula for determining density was given to the students. Problems related to density, volume, and mass were worked on the board. Other problems dealing with water pressure on objects submerged at various depths below the surface of different liquids were assigned and later discussed and worked in class. Given the dimensions and densities of certain objects, students were asked to predict whether those objects would sink or float in water and why. In addition to the lectures and assigned problems, a few demonstrations were also conducted by the instructor. These were done to illustrate the concepts of density, surface tension, and Archimedes's Principle.

To summarize the unit, factors that influence the sinking and floating of objects were discussed and student questions related to the concepts presented were answered. The learning cycle approach proceeded as follows:

The exploration phase—Students in teams of three and four were given several objects and asked to find out what they could concerning the floatability of the objects. The kit contains a variety of items made from different materials: wood, aluminum, acrylic, and polystyrene spheres, cylinders, and cubes. Care was taken not to include objects used in the pre- and postinterviews.

The invention phase—The instructor, using student ideas and observations, developed definitions for: mass, weight, volume, density, buoyancy, displacement, surface tension, and Archimedes's Principle.

The application phase—In this stage of the learning cycle, students tried to apply the terms defined in the invention phase to new situations. For example, students were supplied medicine droppers and three colored solutions of differing densities. They were asked to relate what they had observed to explain how submarines and life jackets work and why crocodiles swallow pounds of rocks and store them in their gizzards. The class members and instructor then discussed the results of all the activities and the instructor attempted to answer questions posed by the students concerning the concept. Every effort was made by the instructor not to favor one model over the other.

Table 5.4 summarizes the results for both groups. It compares the percentage of students giving correct responses on the initial interview with

TABLE 5.4
Percentage of Correct Responses and Percentage of Gain for
Expository and Learning-cycle Groups

Item	Expository Group			Learning Cycle Group		
	Pre-Interview % Correct	Post-Interview % Correct	% Gain	Pre-Interview % Correct	Post-Interview % Correct	% Gain
Small wooden cube	0	27	27	4	50	46
Metal cube	0	38	38	0	45	45
Large wooden cube	0	19	19	4	22	18
Aluminum foil sheet	4	23	19	0	27	27
Aluminum foil folded	4	23	19	0	27	27
Clay ball	4	27	23	4	23	19
Clay pot	0	31	31	12	36	24
Jar lid	0	34	34	4	36	32
Jar lid with holes	0	4	4	0	0	0
Summary: Factors influencing sinking/floating	34	50	16	31	64	33

From: Stepans, J. I., Dyche, S., & Beiswenger, R. The effects of two instructional models in bringing about a conceptual change in the understanding of science concepts by prospective elementary teachers. *Science Education, 72*(2), 185-195. Copyright © 1988. Reprinted by permission of John Wiley & Sons, Inc.

those on the final interview. In order for a response to be correct, an accurate prediction and explanation had to be given. The results also give the percentage gain in the correct category for each item for each group.

Only a small percentage of students in both groups gave responses that could be placed in the correct category during the initial interview. These results were similar to those of Shepherd and Renner (1982), who found that none of the high school students in their study exhibited a sound understanding of the concept of density of water as it related to turnover in lakes in the spring and fall. However, on the summary question in the initial interview, 34% of students in the expository group and 31% of those in the learning-cycle group were able to identify at least two factors that cause an object to float or sink.

The expository group actually showed a 7% *decline* in their understanding of water pressure on the posttest. This difference may not be significant, but it could point out that the lecture-recitation form of science teaching can, at times, confuse students about abstract concepts and that the memorization of terms, facts, and formulas does not result in real learning when students are concrete operational.

Examples of the appropriate uses of the terms related to sinking/floating given by students appear in Table 5.5. Table 5.6 provides examples of inappropriate uses of these terms.

It should be pointed out that in neither group did the number of correct responses exceed 50% for any of the objects used in the interview. One might question why the total number of responses was not higher. One possible explanation is that concrete operational students have difficulty learning formal concepts (Lawson & Renner, 1975). Preassessment studies of several sections of the science content courses that served as the source of subjects for the study revealed that about one half of these students are operating at the concrete transitional level. Another factor that may have been at play in this study was that of misconceptions held by students. Eaton, Anderson, and Smith (1983) found in their study that if students approach a topic without knowing anything about it, they may be willing to consider any information their teacher presents. However, if students already have ideas about a topic, these ideas can interfere with their ability to understand. The subjects of this study were college students and obviously many had previous ideas about the concepts.

Another comparison can be made between this study and others cited in the literature with respect to the improvement shown by the learning cycle group when compared with the expository group. For example, in the study of 10th-grade students' understanding of matter and density changes, Shepherd and Renner (1982) found a significant gain in favor of students at a concrete operational level who were taught through firsthand experiences, compared with students taught concrete concepts formally. Thus, the learning cycle may be preferable to expository because concrete instruction promotes superior cognitive development of concrete-level thinkers (Schneider & Renner, 1980).

Based upon postsession interviews, both groups showed gains in under-

TABLE 5.5
Examples of Student Comments Using Terms in the Appropriate
Context in the Pre- and Postinterview

Density—The wooden block floats because its density is less than that of water.
Water Pressure—The weight of the aluminum foil is spread out over a large area. It will lay on more water and the pressure from the water will help it to float.
Archimedes's Principle/Water Displacement—The clay ball will sink; it weighs more than the volume of water it is going to displace.
Surface tension—The aluminum sheet will float. The surface tension, something about the water molecules sticking together, might hold it up.

From: Stepans, J. I., Dyche, S., & Beiswenger, R. The effects of two instructional models in bringing about a conceptual change in the understanding of science concepts by prospective elementary teachers. *Science Education, 72*(2), 185-195. Copyright © 1988. Reprinted by permission of John Wiley & Sons, Inc.

TABLE 5.6
Inappropriate Use of Terms

Density—The aluminum sheet will float because of its weight, which is low, and its high density.
Water Pressure—The sheet of aluminum foil would float. It is covering a lot of area. Air would be trapped between the foil and water. The air wouldn't get pressed under the water and isn't very heavy.
Archimedes's Principle/Water Displacement—What determines whether an object will float or not is displacement. Density would determine that weight, how heavy an object is.
Surface Tension—The small metal cube will sink because of its surface tension.

From: Stepans, J. I., Dyche, S., & Beiswenger, R. The effects of two instructional models in bringing about a conceptual change in the understanding of science concepts by prospective elementary teachers. *Science Education, 72*(2), 185-195. Copyright © 1988. Reprinted by permission of John Wiley & Sons, Inc.

standing the concepts involved in sinking/floating. Except for one object (jar lid with holes) gains in the percentages of students giving correct responses ranged from 15% to 46%. The overall gains of the learning cycle group were slightly higher than those of the expository group. In two instances, the small wooden cube and the summary statement on factors influencing sink or float, the percentages of gains for the learning cycle group were considerably higher than those of the expository group.

The learning-cycle model generally yielded a higher percentage of correct responses than did the expository model. The differences between the groups were not tested for significance. The learning-cycle model provides for and incorporates factors that Wise and Okey (1983) consider necessary for effective science instruction. They found that in an effective science classroom, students have opportunities to interact physically with instructional materials and engage in varied activities. They also concluded that altering instructional procedures should occur when it is thought that such change might be related to increased impact. Rowell and Dawson (1977) also found that an approach emphasizing the use of physical materials and photographic slides to teach sink/float concepts was effective with 14 year-olds in Australia. Their approach was especially successful with students who were pretest conservers of volume. The nonconservers were less successful as a group, although some individuals achieved a sound understanding of the concepts.

Both teaching models in this study were effective in bringing about a change in students' understanding of concepts associated with sinking and floating when applied to most of the objects. However, neither model brought about a change in students' responses associated with the floating of jar lids with holes. (In neither group were objects with holes used in sink/float presentations.) This may be an example of learners holding on to their original conceptions regardless of the type of instruction they receive. This may be due either to the fact that learners were more influenced by their own perceptions than by their understanding of the concepts, or that the instruction did not adequately address the surface tension and its effect on floating and sinking. Serious consideration, particularly in the case of certain science concepts about which a large number of students exhibit misconceptions, should be given to the design and use of alternative models of instruction if we are to correct student misunderstandings.

V.   AN INNOVATIVE TEACHING MODEL

The hands-on approach, laboratory work, and the use of the traditional learning cycle (consisting of exploration, concept invention and application) have been shown to be superior to the routine lecture format. These approaches have helped learners to understand science concepts and to develop a more positive attitude toward science and the learning of science. However, the effects of these strategies have been minimal in bringing about a conceptual change in learners with respect to science. This can be concluded from the study discussed in Part IV, where only about one-half of those in the learning cycle group exhibited a conceptual change with respect to the sinking and floating of solids in water. Work by Smith and Anderson (1984) also shows that merely using a hands-on approach in the form of the traditional learning cycle, as proposed initially by Karplus and implemented in such programs as SCIS, is not effective in helping learners to overcome their naïve ideas. Just handling physical materials does not address the preconception the learner brings to the classroom.

Researchers such as Cohen (1981), Eaton et al. (1983), Nussbaum and Novick (1981), Smith and Anderson (1981), and Za'rour (1975) maintain that educators need to look at and start with the learner's view and conception of the topic at hand. These authors, among others, recommend that in order to bring about significant accommodations in the learner, the following steps should be taken when introducing a new science concept:

- Provide the learners with a challenging situation, which will bring to the surface students' preconceptions (a discrepant event, for example).
- Allow students to share their views on the situation with others in the learning environment.
- Present the "correct" view as just another view.
- Provide students with the opportunity to discuss the pros and cons of each view presented (including the "correct" view) and if appropriate, test the various views.

- Help students in their search for solutions and accommodations; do not continually provide "ready-made" knowledge.

These recommendations have been translated into an instructional model consisting of the following:

1. Students make personal predictions based on their preconceptions about various physical setups.
2. Students expose their beliefs by sharing predictions and explanations in small groups and then with the entire class.
3. Students test their predictions by working in small groups with physical setups.
4. Students resolve conflicts between their predictions based on misconceptions and their laboratory observations, by class discussion.
5. Students extend the concepts learned from the physical setups in the laboratory to other situations.

Much valuable work has been done in implementing these suggestions in the teaching of physics concepts. Fehr and Rice (1986) used this approach in the teaching of optics. Clement (1987) and Veath (1988) have applied it in the teaching of kinematics. The strategy can also effectively be used with the concept of sinking and floating of solids in liquids. One can proceed as follows:

Students in groups of three or four are provided with an empty plastic container and several objects (similar to those described earlier in the chapter). The members of each group are asked to predict whether each object will float or sink when placed in the plastic container full of water and provide explanations for their predictions. The students are reminded that all opinions given are equally important and encouraged. This allows each member to become aware of his or her own preconceptions with respect to the sinking and floating phenomena. Each group will have a member recording all predictions and explanations on a large piece of paper to be presented to the entire class. The sharing phase of the activity provides students with the opportunity to expose their views and to listen to the ideas given by other students. They find out that students have different opinions related to the concept.

The teacher tallies the predictions on the board and writes summaries of the explanations given without making judgments whether they are scientifically sound. Following this phase, the students place the objects in water to test their predictions and make revisions of the explanations if they choose to. Here the students have the opportunity to discover that the best answers come by working with materials and that they can, in fact, pose questions, formulate ideas and test them.

The students have the opportunity to test their ideas and discuss the discrepancies, if any, between their ideas and their observations. The teacher then poses appropriate questions and helps students to bridge the gap between what they thought and what they saw. This assists the students in developing such concepts as density, buoyancy, Archimedes's Principle, and other, as appropriate. Following these steps, the teacher helps students to make a connection between the concept discussed and situations familiar to the students. Finally, in order to continue the process of wonder and questioning, the teacher encourages the students to think of additional questions and problems related to the concept that they would like to pursue.

REFERENCES

Arons, A. (1981). Thinking, reasoning and understanding in introductory physics courses. *Physics Teacher, 19*(3), 166–172.

Bradwein, P., et al. (1975). *Concepts in science.* New York: Harcourt Brace.

Butzow J. W., & Gabel, D. (1986). We should all be researchers. *Science Teacher, 53*(1), 34–37.

Carpenter, E. T. (1981). Piagetian interviews of college students. In R. G. Fuller (Ed.), *Piagetian programs in higher education.* Lincoln: University of Nebraska.

Clement, J. (1987). Overcoming students' misconceptions in physics: The role of anchoring intuitions and analogical validity. *Proceedings of the second international seminar: Misconceptions and educational strategies in science and mathematics, 3,* 84–97.

Cohen, M. (1981). *How can sunlight hit the moon if we are in the dark?: Teachers concepts of phases of the moon.* Paper presented at the Seventh Annual Henry Lester Smith Conference of Educational Research, Bloomington, IN.

Eaton, J. F., Anderson, C. W., & Smith, E. L. (1983). When students don't know they don't know. *Science and Children, 20*(7), 7–9.

Fehr, E., & Rice, K. (1986). Shadow Shapes. *Science and Children, 24*(2), 6–9.

Fuson, J. (1976). Piagetian stages in causality: Children's answers to why? *Elementary School Journal, 72*(2), 150–157.

Lawson, A. E., & Renner, J. W. (1975). Piagetian theory and biology teaching. *American Biology Teacher, 37*(6), 336–343.

Nussbaum, J., & Novick, S. (1981). *Creating cognitive dissonance between students' preconceptions to encourage individual cognitive accommodation and a group cooperative construction of a scientific model.* Paper presented at the AERA Annual Convention, Los Angeles, CA.

Piaget, J. (1969). *The child's conception of the world.* Totowa, NJ: Littlefield, Adams.

Posner, G. J., & Gertzog, W. A. (1982). The clinical interview and the measurement of concept changes. *Science Education, 66*(2), 195–200.

Renner, J. W., & Marek, E. A. (1988). *The learning cycle and elementary school science teaching.* Portsmouth, NH: Heinemann Educational Books.

Rowell, J. A., & Dawson, C. J. (1977). Teaching about floating and sinking: Further studies toward closing the gap between cognitive psychology and classroom practice. *Science Education, 61*(4), 527–540.

Shepherd, D. L., & Renner, J. W. (1982). Student understandings and misunderstandings of states of matter and density changes. *School Science and Mathematics, 82*(8), 650–665.

Smith, E. L., & Anderson, C. W. (1981). *Planning and teaching intermediate science: Progress report.* National Science Foundation Grant, Michigan State University.

Smith, E. L., & Anderson, C. W. (1984). *The planning and teaching intermediate science study:*

Final report. Research Series No. 147. East Lansing, Michigan, Michigan State University, Institute of Research on Teaching.

Stepans, J. I. (1988). What are we learning from children about teaching and learning. *Teaching and Learning—Journal of Natural Inquiry, 2*(2), 9–18.

Stepans, J. I., Beiswenger, R. E., & Dyche, S. (1986). Misconceptions die hard. *Science Teacher, 53*(6), 65–69.

Stepans, J. I., Dyche S., & Beiswenger, R. (1988). The effect of two instructional models in bringing about a conceptual change in the understanding of science concepts by prospective elementary teachers. *Science Education, 72*(2), 185–195.

Stepans, J. I., & Kuehn, C. (1985). Children's conceptions of weather. *Science and Children, 23*(1), 44–47.

Veath, M. L. (1988). Comparing the effects of different laboratory approaches in bringing about a conceptual change in the understanding of physics by university students. Doctoral dissertation, University of Wyoming, Laramie.

Wandersee, J. H. (1986). Can the history of science help science educators anticipate students' misconceptions? *Journal of Research in Science Teaching, 23*(7), 581–597.

Wise, K. C., & Okey, J. R. (1983). A meta analysis of the effects of various science teaching strategies on achievement. *Journal of Research in Science Teaching, 20*(5), 419–436.

Za'rour, G. I. (1975). Science misconceptions among certain groups of students in Lebanon. *Journal of Research in Science Teaching, 12*(4), 385–392

6

Developing Students' Understanding of Chemical Concepts

Joseph S. Krajcik
University of Michigan

INTRODUCTION

An understanding of chemistry requires students to integrate and link fundamental chemical concepts such as chemical and physical change. Do students develop these understandings in secondary school chemistry? Studies reveal that even after a year of chemistry instruction, secondary students lack conceptual understanding of basic chemical concepts (Andersson, 1986; Ben-Zvi, Eylon, & Silberstein, 1982, 1987; Hesse & Anderson, 1988; Osborne & Cosgrove, 1983; Yarroch, 1985). Students learn factual information; however, they do not develop a conceptual framework that helps them understand other chemical concepts and phenomena. Although students will not develop the integrated understanding that a PhD in chemistry has developed, students should develop an understanding that serves as a foundation for learning other related chemical and scientific concepts. Chemical and physical change, the particulate nature of matter, kinetic molecular theory, and the interactive and dynamic aspects of chemical reactions are fundamental to the understanding of chemistry. An understanding of other chemical concepts depends on students developing an integrated understanding of these concepts.

Students must conceptually integrate their personal knowledge with scientific knowledge to develop integrated understanding (Anderson, 1987; Anderson & Roth, 1988; Pines & West, 1986). Pines and West refer to "personal knowledge" as "spontaneous knowledge." They describe spontaneous knowledge as a person's creative and personal attempt to make sense of the world. An individual constructs personal knowledge as he or she interacts with individuals and the environment. Parents, friends, teachers, books, television, movies, and cultural customs all impact on the construction

117

of personal knowledge. Pines and West (1986) refer to "scientific knowledge" as "formal knowledge" or "school knowledge." They describe formal knowledge as someone else's interpretation of the world, and for most students it is a product of planned instruction in school settings. It is what we find in textbooks.

Most students learn scientific knowledge distinct from their personal knowledge and, as a result, fail to develop integrated conceptual understandings of fundamental scientific concepts. This includes fundamental chemical concepts. As a result of instruction, chemical concepts often become a list of memorized facts that students recall for examinations. As I will describe in this chapter, a student's personal understanding of fundamental chemical concepts often clashes with chemical knowledge making it difficult to develop an integrated understanding.

I present two examples to illustrate the foregoing comments. When we ask students to explain chemical and physical phenomena, they exhibit a variety of understandings that differ from scientific explanations. When students observe water boiling in a beaker and condensing on a cool surface, such as an evaporating dish suspended above the beaker, they might use the terms evaporate, condense, and boil to describe and explain what they observe. However, if we use probe questions to elicit from them a more in-depth explanation of the phenomena, we find that many of them have understandings that differ from how a scientist would explain the phenomena (Osborne & Cosgrove, 1983). In their explanation of boiling, some students would say that the bubbles in the water are made of air or hydrogen and oxygen gas! Others would say that evaporation is occurring but could not give a molecular explanation of the phenomena. This example illustrates that although the students use scientific terms, they do not have a conceptual understanding of the fundamental concepts. Students who have a conceptual understanding of the process of boiling might say that the bubbles are filled with water molecules in the gaseous phase.

This example illustrates that students' underlying conceptual understanding of physical change differs from that of chemists. Many students' understandings of chemical change also differ from that of chemists. If students observe a piece of steel wool burning in air, many would say that a chemical reaction has occurred. However, they would not predict that the substance remaining after burning would have an increased mass. If we question the students to explain the increase in mass, some would say that the steel wool turned into carbon, which is heavier than steel wool (Andersson, 1986). The students lack understanding of combustion, a substance chemically combining with oxygen to form a new substance.

These examples illustrate that when we ask students to explain physical and chemical phenomena qualitatively, students typically use words such as evaporation, condensation, or reaction; but they cannot explain the underlying physical or chemical concepts (Ben-Zvi et al., 1982, 1987; Eichinger & Lee,

1988; Osborne & Cosgrove, 1983). Students use the "correct" words and apply formulas to obtain correct answers but lack understanding of the underlying chemical and physical concepts. I have found that qualitative explanations of chemical and physical phenomena are a challenge not only for many middle and high school students, but also for many undergraduate and graduate students. I have used the foregoing examples in science teaching methods and in graduate courses and have found that even students with backgrounds in science have a difficult time giving qualitative explanations for the examples seen here. Many of these students are surprised that the residue has more mass than the steel wool, even though they successfully completed introductory college chemistry.

Students' lack of integrated understanding exists in many fields of science (Eylon & Lynn, 1988; Osborne & Freyberg, 1985). In this chapter, I focus on students' understanding of chemical phenomena. I will explore the conceptual development students need to understand chemical reactions, explore students' understanding of other fundamental chemical concepts, make recommendations for the improvement of the teaching of chemistry, and discuss implications for curriculum development and teacher education in chemistry.

UNDERSTANDING CHEMICAL REACTIONS

Most chemistry students do not develop an understanding of chemical reactions similar to that of chemists (Andersson, 1986; Ben-Zvi et al., 1987; Yarroch, 1985). Most students master the technique of balancing a chemical equation by picturing a chemical equation as a mathematical puzzle in which the number of atoms on each side of the equation has to equal each other. Unfortunately, many chemistry teachers, through the lecture method, often model this puzzle-balancing act of chemical equations. Seldom are students challenged to explain the chemical process expressed in the equation. Although challenging, many high school chemistry students could balance the chemical equation representing the combustion of iron: $4Fe_{(s)} + 3O_{2(g)} \rightarrow 2Fe_2O_{3(s)}$. Yet when probed to give explanations of the underlying process, most students could not give a molecular explanation of the reaction. Few students would describe that the chemical bonds between the oxygen molecules broke and re-formed to form new chemical bonds with the iron. If students observe steel wool burning in air, many would predict that the mass of the remaining material would be the same or less (Furio Mas, Perez, & Harris, 1987) than the steel wool with which they started.[1] Few students would

---

[1]The equation $4Fe_{(s)} + 3O_{2(g)} \rightarrow 2Fe_2O_{3(s)}$ does not completely represent the oxidation of steel wool in air. Other oxides besides Fe_2O_3 would form because of incomplete oxidation. In a pure oxygen environment, however, the reaction should go to completion. Steel wool also contains a small percentage of carbon which is not represented in the above equation but which is oxidized in the process. Even with incomplete combustion and the oxidation of the carbon, the mass of the residue is heavier than the starting material.

predict that the gray, brittle material that remains after burning has more mass than the steel wool, even though the increased mass is reflected in the chemical equation that they correctly balanced. Moreover, many students would not be able to explain the observed increase in mass (Andersson, 1986).

Understanding the underlying chemical concepts represented in elementary chemical equations requires students to have an integrated understanding of chemical concepts. Although not sufficient, students must have experiences to link with the chemical concepts. Students typically develop "chemistry knowledge" separate from experiences that would help them build meaning. For instance, balancing the equation that represents the combustion of steel wool becomes a meaningless chemical algebra exercise unless students relate the equation to the phenomena. Chemistry teachers can also help students build meaning by having students predict what will happen to the mass of steel wool when it burns in air, perform the activity, and explain and debate the observations to each other.

Chemists' Understanding of Chemical Reactions

Chemists' understanding of chemical reactions are embedded in a conceptual framework that has been developed from their active integration and structuring of concepts about the nature of matter and chemical change that they developed over time through a variety of experiences. I use "conceptual framework" to refer to the concepts and the interconnections between the concepts that an individual has developed. Experts in a discipline develop more concepts and more interconnections between the concepts than novices. As a result, experts have finely integrated conceptual frameworks. Some cognitive psychologists have referred to an individual's conceptual framework as a "conceptual ecology" (Anderson, 1987; Hesse & Anderson, 1988; Posner, Strike, Hewson, & Gertzog, 1982). Relating "conceptual ecology" to an ecology system will help to clarify this notion. In an ecological system the animals, plants, and other aspects of the environment are interconnected and dependent on each other. Similarly, in a conceptual ecology, a learner's concepts are interconnected and dependent on each other.

When a chemist sees a chemical equation, the symbolic representation of a chemical reaction, it triggers a wealth of integrated understanding that includes both mental models and physical phenomena and not just written symbols on paper or a chalkboard. Even an understanding of simple chemical reactions such as the combustion of iron, $4Fe_{(s)} + 3O_{2(g)} \rightarrow 2Fe_2O_{3(s)}$, or the combustion of hydrogen, $2H_{2(g)} + O_{2(g)} \rightarrow 2H_2O_{(g)}$, involve an integrated understanding of a variety of chemical principles and concepts.

Ben-Zvi et al. (1987) present a task analysis describing the wealth of integrated understanding necessary to have meaning for a relatively simple chemical equation such as $2H_{2(g)} + O_{2(g)} -> 2H_2O_{(g)}$. When a chemist sees the equation for the combustion of hydrogen, the following understanding would probably be activated:[2]

1. *The structural aspects of a chemical reaction.*
   The chemist's understanding that the chemical symbols represent molecular species is triggered. In the example just given, the symbols O_2 and H_2 each represent a molecule of an element in which two atoms of the same element are chemically bonded together and the symbol H_2O represents a molecule of a compound with two O–H bonds. A chemist's understanding that the symbol (g) represents that the elements and molecular compounds are in the gaseous state and consist of many particles in constant, linear, random motion is also activated.

2. *The interactive aspects of a chemical reaction.*
   The chemist's understanding that a chemical reaction is a process of bond breaking and bond formation is activated. In the reaction described, the bonds in each molecule of H_2 and O_2 must break and new bonds between the O and H must form.

3. *The dynamic aspects of a chemical reaction.*
   The chemist's understanding that a chemical reaction is a time-dependent process involving a dynamic interaction of many particles is activated.

4. *The quantitative aspects of a chemical reaction.*
   The chemist's understanding of the quantitative aspects of a chemical reaction is activated. In the reaction, two moles of H_2 react with one mole of O_2 to form two moles of H_2O.

A chemist's understanding of the energy aspects of the chemical reaction would also probably be activated. Hydrogen (H_2) and oxygen (O_2) are at a high energy level and will release energy when the atoms recombine to form water (H_2O). Some chemists would also visualize the kinetic components of the reaction. The physical properties of the reactants and products are also integrated into the chemist's understanding of the reaction.

Although this analysis of the understanding a chemist draws upon to construct meaning from a chemical equation appears detailed, it contains some implicit understanding not described. The analysis assumes that the chemist has an understanding of the particulate nature of matter and kinetic molecular theory. The analysis involves an understanding of both microscopic and multimolecular aspects of the chemical reaction (Ben-Zvi, et al.,

_____

[2]The following analysis was described by Ben-Zvi, Eylon, & Silberstein (1987, p. 117).

1982, 1987). A chemist visualizes bonds breaking in individual molecular species but also visualizes that many molecules take part in the reaction. An understanding of the reaction $2H_{2(g)} + O_{2(g)} \rightarrow 2H_2O_{(g)}$ also involves understanding the language unique to the chemist. The coefficient in front of H_2O refers to either two separate molecules of H_2O or to two moles of H_2O, whereas the two as a subscript in H_2 means two atoms of hydrogen chemically bonded together in one molecule of hydrogen.

This analysis of the understandings a chemist uses to construct meaning, even of a simple chemical equation, demonstrates the integrated conceptual framework that a chemist develops and applies when describing and explaining a chemical reaction.

Students' Understanding of Chemical Reactions

Although the chemical equation triggers a wealth of chemical understanding in chemists, when students see a chemical equation such as $2H_{2(g)} + O_{2(g)} \rightarrow 2H_2O_{(g)}$, what is triggered? Does the chemical equation also serve as a vehicle that triggers a wealth of integrated understanding?

The work of Ben-Zvi, et al. (1982, 1987) indicates that 15-year-old students, even after 7 months of studying elementary chemistry, hold alternative conceptions with regard to the structural aspects and the interactive nature of chemical reactions. Their work with 337 students indicates that many students have an additive model of chemical reactions rather than an interactive model. Students do not visualize chemical reactions as a process involving bond breaking and bond formation; rather, students visualize chemical reactions as the reactants adding together to form the products. For instance, when H_2 reacts with O_2, the O_2 adds to the H_2. Bond breaking in H_2 does not occur.

The work of Yarroch (1985) supports the findings of Ben-Zvi, Eylon, and Silberstein. Yarroch interviewed 14 high school chemistry students on how to balance simple chemical equations and the knowledge they used to balance them. The students had studied balancing chemical equations and were receiving good grades in chemistry. Although all the students could successfully balance the equations, 9 of the students demonstrated little understanding of what they were doing. They did not understand the meaning of the subscripts and the coefficients and believed that the reaction arrow was little more than an equal sign. When asked to draw diagrams that represented the equations they balanced, they could not draw appropriate representations. Of the 14 high school students he interviewed, only 5 were able to represent by drawing the correct linkage of atoms in molecules. For example, in the equation, $N_2 + 3H_2 \rightarrow 2NH_3$, students did not differentiate between $3H_2$ as three separate diatomic molecules with each molecule consisting of two hydrogen atoms bonded together and six independent particles.

Although students can correctly balance chemical equations, the work of Ben-Zvi, et al. and Yarroch suggests that for students chemical equations do not activate similar integrated understanding that they do for chemists. Rather than symbolizing a dynamic and interactive process, some students visualize a chemical equation as a mathematical puzzle.

Andersson (1986) synthesized several studies related to students' understanding of chemical reactions and developed a classification scheme to describe how students explain chemical change: (1) it is just that way, (2) displacement, (3) modification, (4) transmutation, and (5) chemical interaction. Andersson's synthesis indicates that very few students, even after some instruction in chemistry, use the concepts of atom and molecule in their reasoning about chemical reactions. Andersson stated:

> Of those who do, some treat the atomic world as an extrapolation of the macroscopic one. That which applies in the macroscopic world also applies in the atomic one. If wood burns up, the wood molecules also burn up. The students do not seem to have understood that the two worlds differ qualitatively, i.e., that the concept of the atom is part of a model invented in order to explain and predict what takes place in the macroscopic world. (1986, p. 553).

In this section I have examined students' understanding of chemical reactions and have contrasted these to those of chemists. Students do not visualize chemical reactions in ways consistent with a chemist's understanding. After studying high school chemistry, we should not expect students to develop the conceptual framework of a chemist regarding chemical equations; however, they should develop a conceptual framework that they can use as a foundation to understand real world phenomena and for future learning. In the next section, I explore the understandings students hold of other foundational chemical concepts.

STUDENTS' UNDERSTANDING OF CHEMICAL CONCEPTS

Students' Understanding of the Particulate Nature of Matter

The particulate nature of matter provides a foundation for understanding other chemistry concepts. To explain and predict chemical reactions, changes in state, pressure and volume relationships of gases, the dissolving of solutes in solution, as well as other chemical concepts, students must have an integrated understanding of the particulate nature of matter. However, prior to the study of chemistry in high school, many students hold an alternative conception of the structure of matter; many hold a continuous model of matter. As students progress through school, some appear to switch to a particulate model of matter; however, even then they lack a kinetic molecular model.

Krajcik (1989), as part of a study to examine the influence of an interactive computer simulation containing dynamic computer visuals, interviewed 17 ninth-grade biology students at the end of the school year and asked them to draw and describe what they would see if they had very powerful magnifying glasses that would allow them to see the air contained in a flask. The students read on grade level, had studied seventh-grade life science and eighth-grade physical science, and had studied introductory chemical concepts at the beginning of the ninth grade biology course. Of the 17 students interviewed, 14 initially held a continuous view of the air represented by a cloud model or vapor model. Fig. 6.1 illustrates the various models held by students.

Several quotes taken from the interview part of the study will help clarify the various models. The first quote helps illustrate the vapor model.

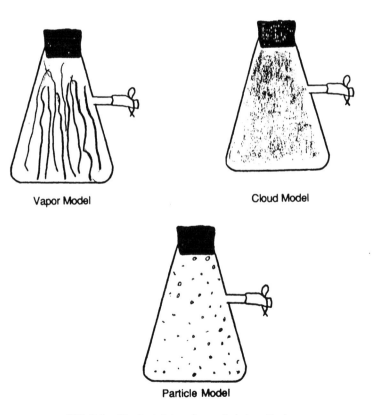

Vapor Model

Cloud Model

Particle Model

FIG. 6.1. Students' drawings of air in a flask.

Interviewer: If you could see the air in the flask, draw what you think you would see.

Student 1:   (Student drew his model and then stated) Like air just floating around.

Interviewer: Just air, just floating around?

Student 1:   Yeah.

Interviewer: You drew continuous lines there. What do those continuous lines represent?

Student 1:   Just air.

The next quote helps illustrate the cloud model.

Interviewer: Could you also explain what you drew there?

Student 2:   Drawing the air that I would see in the flask.

Interviewer: And what would you say it looked like.

Student 2:   Like a squiggly cloud.

The final quote helps illustrate the particulate model.

Interviewer: If you could see the air in the flask, draw what you think you would see.

Student 3:   (Student drew her model and stated) The little particles would be moving up and down.

Novick and Nussbaum (1978, 1981), Osborne and Schullum (1983) and Gabel, Samuel, and Hunn (1987) also found students holding a continuous model of matter but with the particulate model becoming more pervasive as students continued through school. However, many students who drew a particulate model, when asked what existed between the particles they drew in the flask, answered "more air particles," indicating that they retained their continuous model of matter even though they initially appeared to hold a particulate model of matter. Eichinger and Lee (1988) found that sixth-grade students who had a particulate model did not have a kinetic model.

Students also hold a continuous model of matter with respect to objects in the solid and liquid states. Many students do not make any distinction between the properties of the substance and the properties assigned to a single, isolated atom (Andersson, 1986; Ben-Zvi, Eylon, & Silberstein, 1986; Griffiths & Preston, 1989). For example, students believe that an isolated atom of copper has the same properties as a piece of copper wire and that both the atom and the wire conduct an electrical current and are malleable.

Students in the Griffiths and Preston (1989) study believed that water molecules in ice touch each other continuously, leaving no space. These findings suggest that students retain a continuous model even though they use some of the language of the particulate model.

It should not be surprising that students have developed a personal model of matter that is continuous and resistant to change. Our daily experiences support the construction of a continuous model of matter. A piece of copper looks continuous, even though the chemist would say that it is made up of copper atoms. All other solid and liquid materials also look continuous. The language and experiences we use in daily life to describe the gaseous phase also support the construction of a continuous medium. Individuals frequently describe a cloud in the sky as gas, or smoke from a fire as gas. Neither of these phenomena is an example of the gaseous phase but they are referred to as such in everyday life and both look to be a continuous medium. These experiences lead children to construct a continuous view of matter before they enter school.

How do students reconcile their personal continuous model with the scientific particulate model they learn in school? Ben-Zvi et al., (1986) argue that the students interpret the "particles" of a substance, called atoms or molecules, as very small parts of the continuous substance. Such a model incorporates the new terms memorized in school with the students' intuitive model. Hence, the particulate model is not at odds with their personal continuous model.

Students' Understanding of Heat and Temperature

An understanding of temperature and heat energy provides a foundation for understanding exothermic and endothermic reactions, heats of formation, heats of reaction, heats of fusion, heats of solution, and heats of vaporization—central concepts in understanding energy changes in chemical and physical processes. Unfortunately, many secondary students do not differentiate between heat energy and temperature (Erickson, 1979, 1980; Linn & Songer, 1988; Wiser & Kipman, 1988). Many students see these two concepts as similar, holding one thermal concept for both heat and temperature (Eylon & Linn, 1988). They believe that temperature measures heat energy. The following example illustrates how many students respond to questions involving heat energy and temperature. Many students, when asked if 100 mL of 80°C or if 40 mL of 80°C would lose more heat energy as it cooled to room temperature, respond that both beakers lose the same amount of heat energy. These students focus on the starting temperature of both samples of water. Others respond that the 40 mL would lose more heat energy. They focus on the rate at which the quantities of water cool. Few students respond that the

100 mL will lose more heat energy because it has the greater mass, even though it undergoes the same temperature change as the 40 mL of water.

To develop an understanding of heats of reaction, students must have an understanding of heat energy and temperature. Although research describing students' understanding of heats of reaction and heats of fusion does not exist, one must wonder what understanding students develop of these concepts when their personal understanding of the underlying concepts do not agree with the scientist. Wiser and Kipman (1988) argue that the conceptual understanding of students differs substantially from those of scientists. To develop understandings similar to scientists, students will have to change their personal, undifferentiated understanding of heat energy and temperature.

Students' Understanding of Advanced Chemical Concepts

The literature contains only a few studies that examine students' understanding of more advanced topics in chemistry, such as acid and base chemistry. This is not surprising because a majority of the work investigating students' conceptual understanding has been conducted since the mid 1980s. In this section, I examine students' understanding of acid and base chemistry, covalent bonds, and equilibrium concepts.

Nakhleh (1990) interviewed students regarding their understanding of acid and base chemistry and videotaped students as they thought aloud during titration exercises. Students had a grade point average of B or better, were at the end of first-year high school chemistry and had studied acid and base chemistry. Analysis of the data indicates that even though the students could solve word problems related to acid and base chemistry (e.g., calculate the molarity of a solution that results from 10 grams of NaOH to make 1 liter of solution), they could not describe what was occurring on the molecular level when titrating a strong acid with a strong base. Nakhleh's work demonstrates that, although students learn to solve word problems, they lack understanding of the underlying chemical concepts.

Peterson and Treagust (1989) designed a paper-and-pencil instrument to probe students' understanding of covalent bonding and structure. They found that even in a sample of 12th-grade students who had studied chemistry, a large number of students held alternative understandings related to basic bonding and structural concepts such as bond polarity and the shape of molecules. Even after studying chemistry, 39% of the students could not ascertain the correct position of the shared pair of electrons in the hydrogen fluoride bond and select an appropriate explanation for the bond location.

Gorodetshy and Gussarsky (1986, 1990) reported that students who studied chemistry, including equilibrium concepts, had difficulty understanding the dynamic nature of chemical equilibrium. Rather than viewing chemical equilibrium as a dynamic process in which forward and reverse reactions continuously occur at equal rates, students viewed chemical equilibrium as a balanced condition with no further reactions occurring. Kozma and Johnston (1990) found introductory college chemistry students to also hold this model of chemical equilibrium. In both of these studies, students viewed chemical equilibrium as a balanced condition with no further reaction occurring. Given the alternative models students hold in regard to chemical reactions, it is not surprising that these students do not construct a dynamic model of chemical equilibrium. Kozma and Johnston also identified students who held a qualitative, dynamic model of chemical equilibrium that was sufficient for further learning. Although these college students held rudimentary understandings, Kozma and Johnston concluded that their understanding was sufficient for further learning.

NEW APPROACHES TO TEACHING CHEMISTRY

The literature cited here indicates that students (1) do not understand fundamental chemical concepts, (2) do not relate chemical concepts to chemical phenomena, (3) memorize chemistry terms without understanding, and (4) memorize how to solve problems. Students learn bits of factual information; however, they do not develop an integrated conceptual framework that helps them understand other chemical concepts and phenomena. Chemical and physical change, the particulate nature of matter, kinetic molecular theory, and the interactive and dynamic aspects of chemical reactions are fundamental to the understanding of chemistry. An understanding of more advanced chemical concepts depends on students developing an integrated, conceptual understanding of these fundamental concepts. How can secondary chemistry teachers help students develop an integrated understanding of foundational chemical concepts?

In this section, I discuss new approaches to the teaching of chemistry that hold promise in helping students develop integrated understanding of chemical concepts. In particular I look at conceptual change teaching strategies and the role that new technologies can play in helping students develop understanding of fundamental chemical concepts. I also discuss some promising instructional techniques.

Conceptual Change Strategies

The personal understanding that students bring with them to the chemistry classroom often interferes with their developing understanding of chemical concepts similar to those of chemists. Their personal understanding of the structure of matter as continuous clashes with their development of the particulate model of chemists. Students' additive model of chemical reactions hinders their development of an interactive model. Ignoring the personal understanding that students bring with them to the chemistry classroom and "telling" students the chemist's models leads to students memorizing "school knowledge" without the development of integrated understandings. For some, memorization leads to success on classroom and standardized examinations; however, memorization does not lead to students applying chemical concepts.

Science education researchers, cognitive psychologists, and science curriculum developers have proposed various models of conceptual change teaching to help students integrate their personal knowledge with scientific knowledge (Anderson & Roth; 1988; BouJaoude, 1989; Driver & Oldham, 1986; Hesse & Anderson, 1988; Lewis & Linn, 1989; Nussbaum & Novick, 1982; Osborne & Freyberg, 1985; Pines & West, 1986). These models rest on the same theoretical foundation and have similar underlying components. Based on these models, I conceive conceptual change teaching as a dynamic and recursive process consisting of four major components: students describe their understanding, restructure their understanding, apply their new understanding, and compare their new understanding with their previous understanding. Teachers can use exposing events, concept maps, and predictions to help students describe their understanding. Restructuring of students' understanding consists of three phases: clarification and discussion of students' and teachers' understandings, exposing students to conflicting situations by using discrepant events, and students constructing new understanding.[3] Fig. 6.2 contains a model of conceptual change teaching. As the figure illustrates, conceptual change teaching is a dynamic and recursive process. Although a teaching sequence will start with students describing their understanding, the various segments may be re-entered. For instance, during the application phase, the restructuring phase may be re-entered to aid students in developing new connections.

Conceptual change teaching assumes that the existing ideas that students bring to the classroom have a major impact on students developing an understanding of concepts consistent with those of scientists. Chemistry teachers must recognize that these existing ideas often interfere with students developing understanding consistent with those of chemists. To develop a foundation of concepts that will allow students to develop similar understandings to chemists, students must restructure their current understanding (Posner et al., 1982; Vosniadou & Brewer, 1987). Conceptual change teaching recognizes the importance of students expressing their ideas and understandings to explain phenomena, even if these differ from scientists.

---

[3]I modified this conceptual change teaching sequence from Driver and Oldham, (1986).

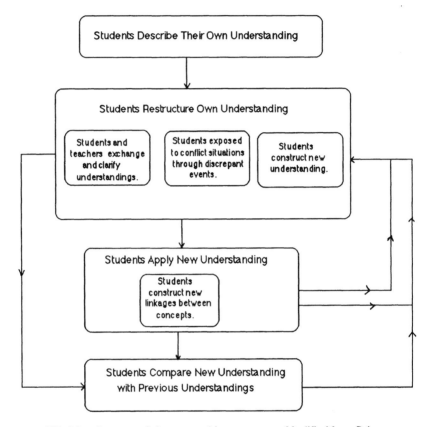

FIG. 6.2. Conceptual change teaching sequence. Modified from Driver and Oldham (1986).

Conceptual change teaching also requires that learners question their current understanding. The students must recognize that their current understandings do not explain a phenomenon and are inadequate. However, before students will give up their present inadequate conceptions, they must be shown another model that they understand and find useful to explain and predict phenomena.

Nussbaum and Novick (1982) presented a detailed description of a conceptual change teaching lesson for helping 11- to 13-year-olds change their understandings of the structure of matter. First, students drew and explained what they imagined air would look like if they could see the air in a flask, using a powerful magnifying glass. Next, the students drew and explained what they imagined the air in the flask would look like if it were partly evacuated. Nussbaum and Novick refer to these teaching techniques as exposing events because they encourage students to reveal their understanding. Third, students described their models to other students in the class and debated the pros and cons of the different models. Fourth, students observed a related phenomenon and explained it, based on their own model. For instance, to show that a gas must consist of particles rather than a continuous medium, a syringe can be filled with a gas (air) and then the cylinder compressed. Students debate if a continuous model of air or a particulate model is supported by the cylinder being able to be compressed. Next, students redrew and explained their models based on their new understanding. This lesson on introducing the particulate model of matter took two class periods. The typical presentation of this material lasts only 5 minutes.

To create dissatisfaction in students' current conceptual understanding and have them question this understanding, curriculum developers have used discrepant events. The students observe a phenomenon that is unexpected and that they cannot explain using their current understanding. Discrepant events aid students in asking "What is going on?" When students try to explain a discrepant event, they may form new linkages between concepts creating new understanding. This may also cause students to restructure their understanding. A teaching sequence might consist of students describing their understanding of a concept, using their understanding to make predictions, observing the discrepant event, and explaining how their observations confirm or refute their initial understanding. One example is the combustion of steel wool. As described earlier in this chapter, many students predict that the mass of the solid residue would be less than the steel wool; however, the residue has more mass. This experience does not match the personal experiences of most students. Although the total mass of the reactants must equal the total mass of the products, the residue of most combustion reactants is less than the combustible material. For example, when wood burns the remaining ash has less mass than the wood, although the total mass of the wood and oxygen must equal the total mass of the ash, carbon dioxide, and water vapor. The discrepancy that students observe when steel wool burns causes them to question their understanding of the combustion process.

Other curriculum developers have used predictions to help students focus on and question their initial understanding (Linn & Songer, 1988). Although discrepant events and predictions can aid students in questioning their understanding, they are not sufficient to help students construct or restructure new models. Students must also be shown scientific models. But more importantly, they must come to recognize that the scientific model explains and predicts all that their previous model could explain and predict. Students must also be given immediate opportunity to apply the scientific models to explain and predict other phenomena that their prior models could not.

Conceptual change is a slow and difficult process. Students must constantly re-examine their understanding and experience new applications of

Students' ideas of burning prior to conceptual change teaching:

R: "What is your definition of burning?"

S1: "Well, you apply heat, the string ignites and carbon and gases are released. It is like how when heat is supplied to an object, how some of it is changed into gas or energy or maybe some of it changes into gas." (page 8)

S2: "An object that changes by heat."

R: "What do you mean by changes?"

S2: "The form changes and sometimes the chemicals change."

Students' understanding of burning after conceptual change teaching:
S1: "It (burning) is when oxygen reacts with a substance and a new substance is formed and sometimes substances are released like new stuff."

S2: "....burning is taking a fuel and having it react with oxygen and it does usually give things.....It reacts with something to form something else, not necessarily a gas."

Notes: R = researcher; S1 = student one; S2 = student 2

FIG. 6.3. Students' understanding of burning before and after conceptual change teaching.

scientific models to restructure their understandings gradually and build new linkages. Conceptual change teaching rests on a strong theoretical foundation and several studies support the use of conceptual change teaching (BouJaoude, 1989; Lewis & Linn, 1989). Still, chemical educators and educational researchers need to investigate its effectiveness thoroughly.

BouJaoude (1989) applied conceptual change teaching to help students restructure their understanding of combustion. He presented a detailed report on the understandings of three students. Prior to employing conceptual change teaching, these students' understandings of combustion differed from chemists. They did not understand the role that oxygen played in burning (e.g., oxygen helps burning but is not consumed), believed that a chemical change did not occur during a chemical reaction, and believed that physical and chemical change were interchangeable concepts.[4] After instruction, two of the three students formed more acceptable understandings of burning. Quotes taken from BouJaoude's study and presented in Fig. 6.3 illustrate the changes students underwent.

Use of New Technologies

The development of new technologies offers promising new tools to use in chemistry instruction. These tools include microcomputer-based laboratories (MBL), graphing packages, microcomputer simulations of microworlds,

---

[4]Ben-Zvi, Eylon, and Silberstein (1987) report similar findings.

telecommunications, and interactive videodisks. These tools allow students to perform activities not possible in the past. Instructional microcomputer tools should enable students to perform activities that complement, not simply replace, elements of traditional chemistry instruction. For instance, dynamic interactive simulations allow students to explore microworlds of molecules, atoms, and electrons.

Although these tools hold promise in helping students learn science concepts, these tools in themselves will not necessarily help develop student understanding. The instructional components that surround the use of these tools appear essential to student learning. Combined with conceptual change teaching strategies these new tools hold promise.

Microcomputer-based Laboratories and Graphing Packages

MBL allow students to use the microcomputer as a laboratory tool by interfacing electronic probes to the microcomputer. These probes detect temperature, voltage, light intensity, or pH while the microcomputer directly records and graphs the data. MBL provides immediate information about the experiment in progress. Using MBL, students observe the graph being produced as the experiment is being performed, obtaining immediate graphical results of their data. Immediate graphical results allow students to see trends in their data that allow them to focus on the concepts they are exploring and ask new questions related to the experiment. Using traditional approaches, the student would collect the data while the experiment is being performed, but would not obtain a graph of the data until much later, possibly that evening as homework or the next day in class.

MBL has many applications for chemistry instruction. Students can use temperature probes to study heats of reactions and heats of formation. A heat pulser, an electronic device that adds a given quantity of heat energy to water or a nonvolatile solution, allows students to explore heats of freezing and vaporization. Using a pH probe, students can obtain a titration curve, observing the pH changing while conducting the titration.

Fig. 6.4 shows a screen printing from the software package *Heat and Temperature* (Human Resources Media, 1987). The graph shows the evaporative cooling graph of water and alcohol. The graph was produced by placing one temperature probe in room temperature water and another in room-temperature alcohol. Both probes where removed from the liquids at about 20 seconds. As the liquids on the probes evaporated, the computer recorded and graphed the temperatures of the probes. The darker of the two lines represents the evaporative cooling of water. Although this is an interesting graph to examine, it does not compare with the sense of wonderment that learners experience as they observe the graph being produced on the computer screen. Obtaining immediate graphical results causes students to

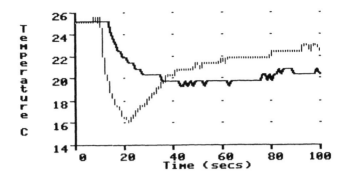

EVAPORATIVE COOLING

FIG. 6.4. A MBL graph of temperature versus time for water and alcohol.

question what happens in other situations. The evaporative cooling graph leads students to question what happens if other substances, such as oil, are used instead of water or alcohol.

MBL has several advantages over conventional laboratory tools. These include providing immediate information on the value of a variable at any given point in time, displaying the data as a graph on the monitor, providing a time history of the variable under study, and linking the concrete experience of data gathering with an instantaneous symbolic representation. These advantages suggest that MBL holds promise in helping students learn chemistry concepts, as well as other science concepts and graphing skills. Although some research indicates that MBL can help students learn physical science concepts and graphing skills (Lewis & Linn 1989; Linn & Songer, 1988; Mokros & Tinker, 1987), other research indicates that MBL does not help students restructure their understanding (Wiser & Kipman, 1988). More research exploring the understanding that students develop as a result of using MBL is needed. The work of Linn (Lewis & Linn, 1989; Linn & Songer, 1988) and Krajcik and Layman (1989) strongly suggests that the effectiveness of MBL is connected to the instructional sequence surrounding the MBL activity.

Microcomputer Simulations of Microworlds

Interactive microcomputer simulations allow students to interact with a model that can help them learn about some aspect of the world. Vosniadou and Brewer (1987) predict that physical models are one way to help students restructure their conceptual understanding. Interactive computer models present a method for students to see and test alternative models, helping students restructure their understanding. Such models can help students develop understanding consistent with the model, providing the conceptual foundation that students need to develop their conceptual understanding. Appropriate simulations can help students learn about the natural world by having them see and interact with underlying scientific models that are not readily inferred from firsthand observations. Students can explore models safely and efficiently. Frequently, the models are simplified by omitting nonessential details and either speedup or slowdown time. By interacting with the microcomputer simulation, students may build their own knowledge of the world.

The "Model of a Gas" lesson in the *Molecular Velocities* disk (Krajcik & Peters, 1989) presents a dynamic display of a particle animation representing gas molecules. In this program students develop a mental image of an ideal gas through observing and interacting with the particle animation. Fig. 6.5 presents a screen from *Molecular Velocities*. As shown in Fig. 6.5, students increase and decrease the temperature of the gas and observe the subsequent change in the movement of simulated gas particles. The program allows students to obtain primary information from interacting with the dynamic visual. The linear movements of the animated particles in these programs are consistent with the Boltzmann equation with some particles moving slowly, some moving fast, but most moving at intermediate speeds. These dynamic, computer visuals may facilitate conceptual learning that is difficult to achieve with conventional instructional materials and methods.

Krajcik (1989) studied the effectiveness of interactive visual microcomputer simulations. Seventeen ninth-grade biology students used one of the

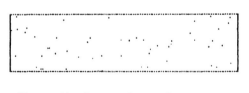

Change the temperature of our
ideal gas sample and watch how the
speeds of the gas molecules
change.

TEMP = 25°C

[RAISE T] LOWER T   GO ON

FIG. 6.5. Screen display from *Molecular Velocities*, illustrating the particle model.

following versions of computer software designed to teach concepts related to the kinetic molecular theory. Version one included tutorial dialogue (nonvisual software) and version two added the interactive, dynamic visuals in the form of particle animations presented in *Molecular Velocities*[5] (visual software). Both versions covered the same concepts; each was developed so that students needed to spend equal time to complete the program and was developed according to good software design. Pre- and posttreatment interviews probed students' understanding of the gaseous phase. Prior to the treatment, only one student in the visual group and one in the nonvisual group held a particulate model of the gaseous phase. The student in the visual group, however, did not visualize spaces between the particles. After interacting with the software containing the dynamic visuals, six of nine students held a particulate model of the gaseous phase consistent with kinetic molecular theory—small, rapidly, random-moving particles. After interacting with the non-visual software, two of eight students held a particulate model of the gaseous phase consistent with kinetic molecular theory. This represents, however, a change of only one student because one of the students held a consistent model prior to interacting with the software.

Wiser and Kipman (1988) also reported that interactive computer simulations help students restructure their understanding of heat energy and temperatures concepts. The work of Krajcik, and Wiser and Kipman appears consistent with the prediction of Vosniadou and Brewer (1987) that physical models help students restructure their conceptual understanding. Interactive simulations of microworlds hold promise in helping students construct or restructure their current understanding to form appropriate understanding of scientific concepts.

Videodisk Technologies

Interactive videodisk technology combines video pictures, animation, microcomputer graphics, and/or interactive computer-assisted instruction to present instructional lessons. These representations allow students to visualize chemical reactions and processes in real time, which otherwise would be too hazardous, time consuming, or expensive (Smith & Jones, 1988). Using interactive videodisk technology, students observe, in real time, the colorful but violent and noxious reaction between liquid bromine and aluminum foil. Or, they observe the explosive reaction of sodium with water. After observing the reactions, and the possibility of viewing the reaction several times, students can then write and balance the chemical equations. This instructional sequence allows students to link the observed phenomena with the

---

[5]I modified the program for research purposes; however, the particle animations were the same.

writing and balancing of the chemical equations. Linking the concrete phenomena with the writing and balancing of the chemical equation appears to be a more meaningful experience for many students than just balancing an equation presented in a textbook (Smith & Jones, 1988). Viewing chemical reactions using interactive video may provide one way for students to develop more meaningful understanding of chemical reactions.

Interactive video technology also offers other possibilities. For instance, students can observe and experiment with video images of various salt solutions to create their own table of solubilities. Although I do not suggest replacing laboratory experiences, combining interactive video with laboratory experiments appears promising. Using interactive video technology, students can repeat the experiments as many times as they like in a very short time. They are also not bound to the time constraints of a laboratory period, allowing them more time to make predictions and test results rather than just having enough to collect data.

Interactive videodisk technology allows students to visualize chemical reactions and other chemical processes that they otherwise could not have observed. However, we need to explore the understanding students develop as a result of using interactive videodisk lessons. Preliminary results from the University of Illinois (Smith & Jones, 1988) indicate that it may be an effective instructional media.

Other Promising Instructional Techniques in Chemistry Learning

Chemistry teachers can also use several powerful instructional techniques to help students develop understanding of chemical concepts, including: concept maps, redescription of chemical problems at the molecular level, and analogies. Although I will discuss each of these techniques, each has been described elsewhere and I encourage the reader to examine the references for an in-depth presentation.

Concept Mapping

Concept maps (Novak & Gowin, 1984) allow students to link to related ideas and concepts, helping them construct integrated understanding. Concept maps are a two-dimensional hierarchical diagrams that illustrate the connectedness between and among individual concepts. Links between concepts are shown in a hierarchical structure in which the lower concepts are subsumed beneath those which appear in higher levels and the superordinate concepts are more general than the subsumed concepts. The concepts are linked by verbs or connecting phrased to form propositions. For instance, the concept "chemical reaction" could be linked with the concept "interactive" by the verb "is." Figure 6.6 contains a concept map of the concepts and ideas

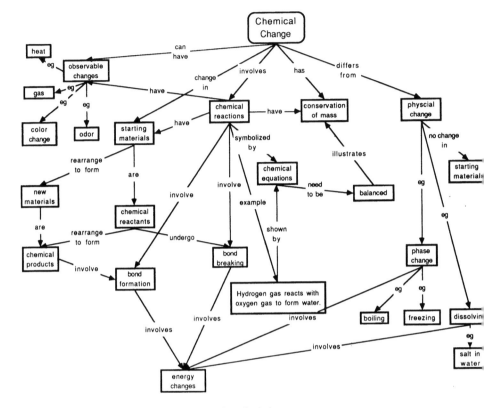

FIG. 6.6.   Concept map of chemical change.

related to chemical change. This concept map is the author's attempt at linking and representing the variety of ideas and concepts related to chemical change; other concept maps could also be constructed using this concept.

Concept maps can be applied in a variety of instructional settings. Chemistry teachers can have students make concept maps before instruction. This technique helps students elicit their understanding prior to instruction, giving an indication of students' initial understanding. As instruction continues, students make new concept maps, helping them form linkages between concepts. By comparing earlier versions of their concept maps with later versions, students see how their understanding has changed. Another useful approach would have students compare their concept maps with those of other students. This technique would allow them to see the connections formed by other students. Concept maps used at the end of an instructional unit help students tie together the concepts explored. Used in these ways, concept maps can be used as tools for negotiating meaning, making new and more powerful understanding possible.

A growing body of research supports the use of concept maps as instructional tools to help students develop science concepts (Novak, Gowin & Johansen, 1983; Pankratius, 1990; Stensvold & Wilson, 1990). Stensvold and Wilson found that low verbal ability, ninth-grade students, who constructed concept maps before and after a series of laboratory activities related to the reaction of chemical compounds, scored significantly higher on an achievement test than did low verbal ability students who did not. The construction of the concept maps, however, appeared to interfere with the learning of high verbal ability students. High verbal ability students who did not construct concept maps scored significantly higher than high verbal ability students who constructed concept maps. Although this result appears contradictory, it may be that the concept mapping activity interfered with the high verbal ability students' techniques of learning but enhanced the learning technique of the low verbal ability students by providing a structure. Studies that examine the impact of concept mapping over an extended period may be necessary to infer the potential learning outcomes for high verbal ability students.

Pankratius (1990) found that students who constructed concept maps before, during, and after a 3-week unit on energy and work scored significantly higher on an achievement test than students who constructed concept maps only after the unit or who did not construct maps. Also, students who constructed concept maps only after the unit scored significantly higher than students who did not construct maps. Although concept maps appear to be a viable instructional tool, further research is needed to explore the learning outcomes of this instructional tool and to determine the necessary instructional conditions to maximize learning outcomes.

Redescription of Chemical Problems at the Molecular level

Gabel (Gabel, Samuel, & Hunn, 1987; Gabel, Samuel, & Schrader, 1987) proposes that students redescribe chemistry problems at the molecular level before they attempt to solve the problems. Many students solve chemistry problems by using formulas and algorithms. They memorize how to solve mole–mole problems, mole–gram problems, and other stoichiometric problems; however, students do not understand the fundamental concepts underlying the problems. For instance, students may solve for the number of moles in 20 grams of potassium nitrate by memorizing that they divide by the molecular weight without having any understanding of why this technique works. Gabel proposes that if students could redescribe problems on the molecular level, then perhaps students would become better problem solvers and have a greater understanding of the problems and the underlying chemical concepts. This approach is consistent with how experts in chemistry and other areas solve problems (Eylon & Linn, 1988). Experts use time up front for planning and problem representation. Novice problem solvers spend little time in planning or problem representation. Redescribing chemical problems at the molecular level will help students with planning and problem representation.

Some research supports the use of this technique. Gabel, Samuel, and Schrader (1987) had teachers redefine chemistry problems during classroom instruction as often as possible by drawing pictures representing what occurs at the molecular level. Compared with a control group, students exposed to redescribing problems scored statistically higher on the *Particulate Nature of Matter Inventory*, an instrument that asks students to draw a new diagram after a chemical or physical change had occurred using circles and squares to represent atoms and molecules. No significant results where found on the *American Chemical Society—National Science Teacher High School Chemistry Examination* (ACS—NSTA). These results are not surprising. The teachers were not trained as experimenters and no consistent treatment was applied across the different settings. Also, the ACS—NSTA exam is a timed examination that would not allow students to redescribe problems. We also do not know how frequently students redescribed problems in classwork and homework. However, the results do indicate that students improve their solving of problems by redescribing chemistry problems at the molecular level before they attempt to solve the problem. This technique also points to another area in chemical education in need of further research.

Use of Analogies

Analogies provide a method for students to become actively involved in constructing meaningful knowledge by linking previous knowledge to new concepts. Vosniadou and Brewer (1987) suggest that analogies help students restructure their conceptual understanding. Chemical educators have encouraged chemistry teachers to use analogies in their teaching, especially in teaching the mole concept. When teaching the mole concept, the chemistry teacher introduces a familiar unit, such as the dozen, the ream, or the football team and links it to the unfamiliar unit of a mole (Herron, 1975).

Several studies indicate that the use of analogies interact with cognitive ability. A study by Gabel and Sherwood (1980) indicates that students who scored lower on a logical thinking test benefited more from analogies than did students who scored higher. A study by Sutula and Krajcik (1988) indicates that students with high cognitive scores benefited more from creating their own analogical connections than did students with low cognitive scores. However, the length of treatment was short and may not have allowed enough processing time for students with lower cognitive scores to construct the linkages. Further studies examining the learning outcomes with cognitive ability and with prior knowledge are needed.

IMPLICATIONS FOR HIGH SCHOOL CHEMISTRY CURRICULUM

High school chemistry textbooks present numerous chemical topics. A comparison of the table of contents with those of introductory college chemistry textbooks shows that the topics covered in most high school texts do not differ substantially. Unfortunately, in many classrooms, the textbook frequently becomes the curriculum, leading to the coverage of a great number of topics in a short period of time. To survive in the classroom, students revert to memorizing chemical terms and algorithms, which they use to solve chapter problems. If we want students to link and apply chemical concepts, and understand the importance of chemistry, then an integrated approach to the teaching of chemistry is needed. Rather than fleeting coverage of numerous topics, an integrated and in-depth approach to chemistry teaching calls for the coverage of a few central concepts, such as chemical and physical change, with emphasis on applications and problem solving. Using this approach, students would be able to link concepts to each other, construct and restructure their personal understanding, and build a foundation of chemical concepts necessary for developing other related understanding.

An in-depth approach would allow chemistry teachers to implement conceptual change teaching and other instructional techniques that are not compatible with the traditional curriculum. Teachers could encourage students to question their understanding by using exposing events and discrepant events. Rather than just being able to manipulate a chemical equation mathematically to balance it, students will have the opportunity to develop an integrated understanding of chemical reactions. In-depth coverage will allow students to develop conceptual understanding necessary to build and integrate other chemical concepts. A solid conceptual foundation will have been laid that will allow students to develop and attach other concepts.

The reduction of topics will allow chemistry teachers to spend more time on the integration of ideas and on the incorporation of applications, such as measuring the pH of natural waters and making nylon and other synthetic products, and the integration of the real-world experiences of students. Making interconnections between chemistry, the students' previous knowledge, applications and real-world experiences will help students internalize concepts. Covering "less" in the chemistry classroom will allow to student to learn "more."

ChemCom: Chemistry in the Community, a curriculum project developed by the American Chemical Society (1988), presents an integrated approach to learning chemistry through the use of societal problems. Using *ChemCom,* students apply knowledge, make decisions, and examine the interface among chemistry, societal issues, and other disciplines. For instance, Unit One begins with a newspaper article describing a polluted river that has influenced the water supply of a community. Around this issue, students are introduced to chemical concepts. Students are still introduced to laboratory techniques, such as filtering; however, in *ChemCom* the techniques are introduced for a purpose, in this case, for filtering and cleaning water. The approach presented in *ChemCom* can help students see the application of chemistry and how chemistry is related to their lives.

An in-depth coverage of a few central concepts clashes with the traditional way that high school chemistry has been taught. Some high school chemistry teachers and chemical educators argue that traditional high school chemistry, which presents a simplified version of college chemistry, is essential for successful completion of college chemistry. Some teachers argue that students must be drilled in quantitative procedures. Evidence suggest, however, that motivated students who have not had traditional high school chemistry are as likely to succeed in college chemistry as students who have studied high school chemistry (Yager, Snider, & Krajcik, 1988). This is not surprising, because most college courses also stress the memorization of chemical facts rather than the understanding of chemical principles. I have proposed that an integrated understanding of a few central concepts provides a conceptual foundation for attaching more advanced topics.

Closely related to an in-depth coverage of a few central concepts is the linking of concepts across and through the curriculum. Some central chemical concepts should be introduced early in the students' education but in ways that promote meaningful understanding. These conceptual understandings can be further developed and enriched as students continue their education. Novak and Musonda (1990) present convincing longitudinal evidence that students who are introduced to chemical concepts in elementary school develop conceptual understandings that are more consistent with those of chemists than students who do not. Fundamental chemical concepts and the application of chemistry must also be integrated into the study of other disciplines.

IMPLICATION FOR TEACHER EDUCATION

The research reviewed in this chapter suggests that chemistry teachers do not transform the subject matter of chemistry into instructional units that will help students develop a complex and integrated knowledge base of fundamental chemical concepts. Even students who have studied high school chemistry and who perform well on standardized examinations do not necessarily develop understandings consistent with those of chemists. Conceptual change teaching strategies, the use of new technologies, powerful instructional techniques (including redescribing chemical problems on the molecular level, concept mapping and analogies), in-depth coverage of central concepts, and applications of chemistry, hold promise in helping students develop an in-depth and integrated conceptual foundation. Ben-Zvi et al. (1987) developed a textbook that illustrates the dynamic nature of chemical reactions to help secondary students develop understanding consistent with those of chemists. Still, students had difficulties developing appropriate understanding.

For these new approaches to succeed, chemistry teachers need to change their view of chemistry teaching and learn how to use these new instructional approaches and tools in ways consistent with students' developing concepts. Unfortunately, too often teachers believe that a divergence from a traditional curriculum will not prepare students for success in advanced high school chemistry courses or college chemistry. This thinking is faulty on several grounds; chiefly, most students never enroll in an advanced chemistry course or college chemistry.

The work of Anderson (Anderson & Roth, 1988; Hesse & Anderson, 1988), Krajcik and Layman (1989), and Linn (Lewis & Linn, 1989; Linn & Songer, 1988) indicates the important role played by science teachers in transforming the subject matter into instructional units that help students develop integrated understanding. Chemistry teachers need to have a strong understanding of chemistry, but they must also have a strong understanding of how students learn and know how to transform the subject matter into meaningful instructional units. Using new technologies to present more information will not help students develop more integrated understanding. Chemistry teachers need to learn how to use the technology to explore concepts and solve problems. Chemistry teachers must take advantage of the new tools to help students develop understanding consistent with those of chemists. Chemistry teachers, and science teachers in general, will have to change their view of learning from one of information giving to one that helps students develop integrated understanding of concepts. To reach a majority of chemistry students, changes in the preparation of chemistry teachers must occur.

Preservice and in-service chemistry teachers must become aware of the crucial importance that the understandings students bring with them to the classroom has a major influence on learning and of the importance of not separating personal knowledge from school knowledge. They must appreciate that to understand chemistry is not merely the learning of isolated pieces of information but rather the learning of integrated knowledge. They must also understand that for an integrated and complex understanding of chemistry, concepts that are foundational for more advanced study must occur in greater depth. Teaching then becomes a process of helping students construct appropriate understanding rather than topic presentation.

Hewson and Hewson (1987) argue that for science teachers to develop an understanding of teaching as a process of helping students construct or restructure their understanding, teachers themselves will have to undergo a process of conceptual change, a restructuring of their view of teaching. Teachers' view of chemistry teaching as topic coverage will have to change to one of concept development. However, changes in the beliefs and understanding of teaching that preservice and in-service chemistry teachers hold will only occur if schools of education and the subject matter disciplines change their methods of instruction.

CONCLUSION

The literature in chemical education suggests that even though students who have studied chemistry use the words of chemists, solve chemical problems and balance chemical equations, they do not have an integrated and complex understanding of fundamental chemical concepts. Students' lack of integrated understanding is revealed when they are asked to explain phenomena qualitatively. Asking students to give qualitative explanations of physical processes (such as the dissolving of salt in water) or chemical changes (such as the burning of sugar) reveals that students know how to use words but lack conceptual understanding.

Conceptual change teaching that focuses on students' personal understanding and stresses students questioning their own understanding appears promising in helping students develop a conceptual foundation more consistent with chemists. Chemistry teachers can help students question their own understanding by using exposing events, discrepant events, and predictions. Other instructional techniques, such as redescribing problems on the molecular level, concept mapping, analogies, and the use of new technologies, also appear promising. However, further research in each of the areas is needed to substantiate the claims.

I have strongly suggested that students develop integrated understanding of a few central chemical concepts. This entails that what occurs in the chemistry classroom must be different than what has occurred traditionally. The traditional approach of covering numerous topics clashes conceptually with covering a few central topics in depth. For the changes suggested in this chapter to occur, both preservice and in-service teachers must change their view of teaching from topic coverage to one of facilitating students toward development of an integrated understanding of concepts, a process involving conceptual change.

We need to examine more closely the understanding that students develop as the result of incorporating more powerful teaching strategies and techniques in chemistry teaching, such as conceptual change teaching. We also need to examine students' understanding related to more advanced chemical topics, such as acids and bases and equilibrium.

ACKNOWLEDGMENTS

I thank Ann Novak for her helpful and insightful suggestions in preparing this chapter.

I wrote portions of this chapter while at the University of Maryland, College Park.

REFERENCES

American Chemical Society. (1988). *ChemCom: Chemistry in the community.* Dubuque, IA: Kendall/Hunt.

Anderson, C. W. (1987). *Incorporating recent research on learning into the process of science curriculum development.* Unpublished manuscript, Biological Science Curriculum Study, Colorado Springs, CO.

Anderson, C. W., & Roth, K. J. (1988). *Teaching for meaningful and self-regulated learning of science.* Unpublished manuscript, Michigan State University, Institute for Research on Teaching, East Lansing.

Andersson, B. (1986). Pupils' explanations of some aspects of chemical reactions. *Science Education, 70*(5), 549–563.

Ben-Zvi, R., Eylon, B., & Silberstein, J. (1982). *Students vs. Chemistry: A study of student conceptions of structure and process.* Unpublished manuscript, Weizmann Institute of Science, Department of Science Education, Rehovot, Israel.

Ben-Zvi, R., Eylon, B., & Silberstein, J. (1986). Is an atom of copper malleable? *Journal of Chemical Education, 63*(1), 64–66.

Ben-Zvi, R., Eylon, B., & Silberstein, J. (1987, July). Students' visualization of a chemical reaction. *Education in Chemistry,* pp. 117–120.

BouJaoude, S. (1989, April). *A study of conceptual change in junior high school science students during instruction about the concept of burning.* Paper presented at the annual meeting of the National Association for Research in Science Teaching, San Francisco.

Driver, R., & Oldham, V., (1986). A constructionist approach to curriculum development in science. *Studies in Science Education, 13*, 105–122.

Eichinger, D. C., & Lee, O. (1988, April). *Alternative student conceptions of the kinetic molecular theory.* Paper presented at the annual meeting of the National Association for Research in Science Teaching, Lake Ozark, MO.

Erickson, G. L. (1979). Children's concepts of heat and temperature. *Science Education, 63*(2), 221–230.

Erickson, G. L. (1980). Children's viewpoints about heat: A second look. *Science Education, 64*(3), 323–336.

Eylon, B., & Linn, M. C. (1988). Learning and instruction: An examination of four research perspectives in science education. *Review of Educational Research, 58*(3), 251–302.

Furio Mas, C. J., Perez, J. H., & Harris, H. H. (1987). Parallels between adolescents' conception of gases and the history of chemistry. *Journal of Chemical Education, 64*(7), 616–618.

Gabel, D. L., Samuel, K. V., & Hunn, D. (1987). Understanding the particulate nature of matter. *Journal of Chemical Education, 64*(8), 695–697.

Gabel, D. L., Samuel, K. V., & Schrader, C. (1987, April). *The particle nature of matter approach: Its effectiveness on chemistry achievement.* Paper presented at the annual meeting of the National Association for Research in Science Teaching, Washington, DC.

Gabel, D. L., & Sherwood, R. (1980). Effect of using analogies on chemistry achievement according to Piagetian levels. *Science Education, 64,* 709–716.

Gorodetsky, M., & Gussarsky, E. (1986). Misconceptualization of chemical equilibrium concept as revealed by different evaluation methods. *European Journal of Science Education, 8*(4), 427–441.

Gussarsky, E., & Gorodetsky, M. (1990). On the concept "chemical equilibrium": The associative framework. *Journal of Research in Science Teaching, 27*(3), 197–204.

Griffiths, A. K., & Preston, K. R. (1989, March). *An investigation of grade 12 students' misconceptions relating to fundamental characteristics of molecules and atoms.* Paper presented at the 62nd conference of the National Association for Research in Science Teaching, San Francisco.

Herron, J. (1975). The mole concept. *Journal of Chemical Education, 52*(11), 725–726.

Hesse, J. J., & Anderson, C. W. (1988, April). Students' conceptions of chemical change. In *Conceptual Models of Science Learning and Science Instruction.* Symposium conducted at the annual meeting of the American Educational Research Association, New Orleans.

Hewson, P. W., & Hewson, M. G. (1987). Science teachers' conceptions of teaching: Implications for teacher education. *International Journal of Science Education, 9*(4), 425–440.

Human Resource Media. (1987). *Heat and temperature* [Computer software]. Bridgeport, CT: Queue.

Kozma, R. B., & Johnston, J. (April, 1990). *College students' conceptions of chemical equilibrium.* Paper presented at the annual meeting of the American Educational Research Association, Boston.

Krajcik, J. S. (1989, November). Students' interactions with science software containing dynamic visuals. In M. Eisenhart & J. G. Goetz (Chairs), *Meanings of science and technology in schools and communities.* Symposium conducted at the 88th annual meeting of the American Anthropological Association, Washington, DC.

Krajcik, J. S., & Layman, J. W. (1989, March). *Middle school teachers' conceptions of heat and temperature: Personal and teaching knowledge.* Paper presented at the 62nd annual meeting of the National Association for Research in Science Teaching, San Francisco.

Krajcik, J. S., & Peters, H. (1989). *Molecular velocities* [Microcomputer program]. Oakdale, IA: Conduit, University of Iowa.

Lewis, E. L., & Linn, M. C. (1989, April). *Heat energy and temperature concepts of adolescents and experts: Implications for curricular improvement.* Paper presented at the 62nd conference of the National Association for Research in Science Teaching, San Francisco.

Linn M. C., & Songer, N. B. (1988, April). Curriculum reformulation: Incorporating technology into the science instruction. In *Conceptual models of science learning and science instruction.* Symposium conducted at the annual meeting of the American Educational Research Association, New Orleans.

Mokros, J. R., & Tinker, R. F. (1987). The impact of microcomputer-based labs on children's ability to interpret graphs. *Journal of Research in Science Teaching, 24*(4), 369–383.

Nakhleh, M. B. (1990). *A study of students' thought processes and understanding of acid/base concepts during the performance of instrument-based titrations.* Ph.D. Dissertation, University of Maryland.

Novak, J. D., & Gowin, D. B. (1984). *Learning how to learn.* Cambridge, England: Cambridge University Press.

Novak, J. D., Gowin, D. B., & Johansen, G. T. (1983). The use of concept mapping and knowledge vee mapping with junior high school science students. *Science Education, 67*(5), 625–645.

Novak, J. D., & Musonda, D. (1990). A twelve-year longitudinal study of science concept learning, *American Educational Research Journal,* in press.

Novick, S., & Nussbaum, J. (1978). Junior high school pupils' understanding of the particulate nature of matter: An interview study. *Science Education, 62*(3), 273–282.

Novick, S., & Nussbaum, J. (1981). Pupils' understanding of the particulate nature of matter: A cross-age study. *Science Education, 65*(2), 187–196.

Nussbaum, J., & Novick, S. (1982). Alternative frameworks, conceptual conflict and accommodation: Toward a principled teaching strategy. *Instructional Science 11*, 183–200.

Osborne, R. J., & Cosgrove, M. M. (1983). Children's conceptions of the changes of state of water. *Journal of Research in Science Teaching, 20*(9), 825–838.

Osborne, R., & Freyberg, P. (1985). *Learning in science: The implications of children's science.* London: Heinemann.

Osborne, R., & Schullum, B. (1983). Coping in chemistry. *Australian Science Teachers Journal, 29*(1),13–24.

Pankratius, W. J. (1990). Building an organized knowledge-base: Concept mapping and achievement in secondary school physics. *Journal of Research in Science Teaching, 27*(4), 315–333.

Peterson, R. F., & Treagust, D. F. (1989). Grade-12 students' misconceptions of covalent bonding and structure. *Journal of Chemical Education, 66*(6), 459–460.

Pines, A. L., & West, L. H. T. (1986). Conceptual understanding and science learning: An interpretation of research within a sources-of-knowledge framework. *Science Education, 70*(5), 583–604.

Posner, G. J., Strike K. A., Hewson, P. W., & Gertzog, W. A. (1982). Accommodation of a scientist conception: Toward a theory of conceptual change. *Science Education, 66*(2), 211–227.

Smith, S. G., & Jones L. L. (1988). Images, imagination, and chemical reality. *Journal of Chemical Education, 66*(1), 8–11.

Stensvold, M. S., & Wilson, J. T. (1990). The interaction of verbal ability with concept mapping in learning from a chemistry laboratory activity. *Science Education, 74*(4), 473–489.

Sutula, V. D., & Krajcik, J. S. (1988, April). *The effective use of analogies on mole problems in high school chemistry classes.* Paper presented at the annual meeting of the National Association for Research in Science Teaching, St. Louis.

Vosniadou, S., & Brewer, W. F. (1987). Theories and knowledge restructuring in development. *Review of Educational Research, 57*(1), 51–67.

Wiser, M., & Kipman, D. (1988, April). *The differentiation of heat and temperature: An evaluation of the effect of microcomputer models on students' misconceptions.* Paper presented at the annual meeting of the American Educational Research Association, New Orleans.

Yager, R. E., Snider, B., & Krajcik, J. (1988). Relative success in college chemistry for students who experienced a high-school course in chemistry and those who had not. *Journal of Research in Science Teaching, 25*(5), 387–396.

Yarroch, W. L. (1985). Student understanding of chemical equation balancing. *Journal of Research in Science Teaching, 22*(5), 449–559.

7 Conceptual Development in Astronomy

Stella Vosniadou
University of Illinois at Urbana-Champaign, and
Aristotelian University of Thessaloniki, Greece

My purpose in this chapter is to describe the process of conceptual development in the domain of astronomy and to discuss the kinds of instructional practices that can foster this development. I will argue that children form an intuitive understanding of the world according to which the earth is flat, stationary, and located in the middle of the universe; the sun and the moon move in an up/down or east/west direction and cause the day/night cycle; the stars are small objects; and gravity operates in an up/down gradient. These ideas change as children become exposed to current scientific views. The process of restructuring intuitive knowledge is a slow and gradual one and is characterized by the emergence of various misconceptions of scientific explanations. An analysis of students' misconceptions reveals that intuitive knowledge consists of a number of fundamental experiential beliefs and that understanding a scientific theory requires replacing these beliefs with a different explanatory framework. For instruction to be effective in bringing about conceptual change, we need to identify these experiential beliefs, to provide students with enough reasons to question them, and to offer a different explanatory framework to replace the one they already have.

In the following pages, I will start by discussing some of the reasons why science concepts are so difficult to learn. I will continue with a description of the research my colleagues and I have conducted in the area of astronomy and of some of the important findings of this research. I will then present an analysis of the process of conceptual development in astronomy and conclude with a discussion of the implications of this analysis for instruction.

THE PROBLEM OF LEARNING SCIENCE

Research in science education has shown that while students can memorize formulas and pass science courses, their understanding of science is superficial and full of misconceptions (e.g., Clement, 1982; diSessa, 1982; Driver & Easley, 1978; McCloskey, 1983; Novak, 1977; Osborne & Wittrock, 1983; Viennot, 1979). For example, even after a few years of high school physics, or after taking a university physics course, adults do not seem to understand Newtonian principles of motion but rather interpret motion phenomena using principles more appropriate to a theory of a motion, which is closer to everyday experience (diSessa, 1982; White, 1983). Why are science concepts so hard to learn?

One of the reasons that science concepts are difficult to learn can be found in the incompatibility that exists between students' intuitive explanations of natural phenomena and the scientific ones. Science-naïve individuals construct an intuitive understanding of the natural world that is based on their everyday experience. This intuitive knowledge provides explanations of everyday phenomena that are very different from the scientific explanations. Thus, unlike other areas of learning where students' prior knowledge can facilitate the acquisition of new information, in science learning, prior knowledge can act as an impediment to learning. In the process of learning science students must restructure their intuitive knowledge to make it conform with the currently accepted scientific knowledge. This process of conceptual re-structuring is difficult to achieve and can lead to misconceptions (see Vosniadou & Brewer, 1987, for a more detailed discussion of this issue).

Let us examine for instance, children's ideas about the shape of the earth. Young children seem to believe that the earth is flat and find it difficult to accept the notion of a spherical earth. The view that the earth is a sphere is counterintuitive and contradicts people's everyday experience. In the development of astronomy as a science, the idea that the earth is a sphere was often attacked by proponents of the flat–earth view on the ground that people on the other side of the spherical earth would fall off (Kuhn, 1957, p. 108).

In the process of changing from a flat-earth to a spherical-earth view, children form a number of misconceptions. For example, Piaget (1929) reports the case of a child who had developed the view that America was a flat piece of land located under Europe and that at night the sun dropped through the European layer and illuminated the lower American layer! Research by Nussbaum (1979), Nussbaum and Novak (1976), Sneider and Pulos (1983) and Mali and Howe (1979) has identified some children who believe that the earth is spherical but that there is ground below it. Others believe that the earth is a huge ball consisting of two hemispheres: an upper hemisphere made up of "air" or sky" and a lower hemisphere consisting of the ground where people live.

My colleagues and I are in the process of carrying out a systematic investigation of children's acquisition of knowledge about the shape, size, motion, distance, location, and composition of the earth, the sun, the moon, and the stars, and their explanations of phenomena such as the day/night cycle, the seasons, and the phases of the moon. The purpose of this research is to find out whether it is indeed the case that children form initial cosmological models that are based on their everyday experience and whether the process of restructuring these models leads to the formation of misconceptions. Some preliminary results from this investigation will follow.

INTUITIVE VS. SCIENTIFIC MODELS IN ASTRONOMY

Although experience with astronomical phenomena is not as direct as the behavior of objects in the physical world, it is nevertheless more than enough to create strong beliefs about the size, shape, composition, and movement of the earth, the sun, the moon, and the stars, and to give rise to certain explanations of natural phenomena, such as the day/night cycle, the seasons, and the phases of the moon. My colleagues and I hypothesized that children would create an intuitive understanding of astronomy based on their everyday experience, which would consist of the "commonsense" view that the earth is flat and motionless; that the sun and the moon move and that their movement causes the day/night cycle; that the earth is located in the center of our solar system and that it is bigger than the sun and stars; and that gravity pulls things down rather than toward the middle of the spherical earth. Such a view of the cosmos is of course very different from the currently accepted scientific view. Scientifically literate adults in our society believe that the earth is a sphere that rotates around its axis and revolves around the sun, that gravity operates toward the center of the earth; that the day/night cycle is caused by the earth's axis rotation; that stars are huge objects; and that the sun, not the earth, is located in the middle of our solar system. Table 7.1 shows this contrast between the intuitive and scientific understanding of astronomy.

TABLE 7.1
Differences in the Intuitive and Scientific Understanding of
Astronomy

	Intuitive understanding	Scientific understanding
Size of solar objects	earth > sun/moon > stars	stars/sun >earth > moon
Shape of earth	flat	spherical
Movement of earth	stationary	axis rotation and revolution around sun
Movement of sun	up/down or east/west	axis rotation
Solar system	geocentric	heliocentric
Day/night cycle	movement of sun and moon	rotation of earth
Gravity	up/down	toward the center of the spherical earth

If we assume that children's cosmologies change from a model based on a flat, stationary earth, a moving sun and moon, and a geocentric solar system, to a model based on a spherical earth that rotates around its axis and revolves around the sun in a heliocentric solar system, how does this change come about?

In order to answer this question, my colleagues and I have conducted a series of experiments investigating children's and adults' knowledge of astronomy. These studies have been conducted in the United States, India, Samoa, and Greece (Brewer, Hendrich, & Vosniadou, 1987; Vosniadou, 1987, 1988, 1989a; Vosniadou & Brewer, 1990, submitted).

Children's knowledge of astronomy has been examined using a 207-item questionnaire that included questions about the shape, size, composition, location, distance, and movement of the earth, the sun and the moon, and about the phenomena of the day/night cycle, the seasons, the phases of the moon, and the eclipses of the sun and the moon. The questionnaire was developed through extensive pilot work with a broad range of subjects. It consisted of two sections: In the first, the children were asked questions that they answered verbally; In the second, they constructed clay models and selected among a variety of styrofoam models of the earth, sun, moon, and stars. The children were seen individually in interviews, which lasted from 30 to 45 minutes. Follow-up questions and confrontation questions were used throughout the interview or at the end of the interview to clarify ambiguous responses and to obtain as accurate a picture of children's beliefs as possible. Here is an example of the questioning procedure followed.

Renae (grade 1)

Experimenter: If you walked and walked for many days in a straight line, where would you end up?

Child: You'd end up ...

Experimenter: Where?

Child: You'd end up somewhere, where you lost yourself.

Experimenter: What if you kept walking?

Child: If you turned around you'd be lost.

Experimenter: Would you ever reach the end or edge of the earth?

Child: Yes.

Experimenter: Could you fall off the edge of the earth?

Child: No.

Experimenter: Why not?

Child: Because once you fall off, you can't get back.

Experimenter: Well, would you ever fall off though?

Child: No.

Experimenter: But there is an edge to the earth?

Child: Yes.

Experimenter: What if you could get back on, do you think you could fall off then?

Child: Yes . . . and if you took to the edge of the thing, and you had one hand on it, you could fall off easier.

Children's beliefs were identified from their responses to many questions tapping each concept. Crucial to our approach was the distinction between *factual* and *generative* questions. Factual questions were designed to provide information about children's exposure to certain theoretically important facts. Examples of such questions are "What is the shape of the earth?" and "Does the earth move?" Children exposed to scientific information were expected to answer the factual questions correctly, for these questions require the simple repetition of facts. Otherwise, their responses would reveal the intuitive understanding that they had constructed on the basis of their experience.

Generative questions were questions about phenomena that children could not directly observe and about which they were unlikely to have direct instruction. These questions had the potential of uncovering children's intuitive understanding and of finding out whether this understanding had been affected by instruction. Examples of generative questions are "If you were to walk for many days would you ever reach the edge of the earth?" and "Is there an edge to the earth?"

Generative questions cannot be answered by the simple repetition of facts. They require the creation of a generative model. The degree of agreement or disagreement between children's responses to the factual and generative questions was used as a base from which to infer the extent to which the children had assimilated into their underlying conceptual structures the scientific information to which they had been exposed.

CHILDREN'S COSMOLOGICAL BELIEFS

For many of the concepts investigated we did not have to go beyond factual questions to confirm the hypothesis that children start by constucting a naïve understanding of the world consistent with their phenomenal experience and that later they change this understanding to conform with culturally accepted beliefs. In other cases, many factual and generative questions had to be used to understand the mental models children used generatively. In this section, I will describe the developmental changes that take place in children's understanding of the movement, relative size and location of the earth, sun, and moon, their explanations of the phenomenon of the day/night cycle, and their beliefs about the shape of the earth and about gravity.

The Movement of the Earth, Sun, and Moon

Table 7.2 shows the responses of elementary-school children from the United States and from Greece (Vosniadou & Brewer, 1990) to the question "Does the Earth move?" We see that in both samples there is a clear developmental shift from the predicted initial response that the earth is stationary (see Table 7.2, Response No. 2) to the currently accepted view that the earth rotates around its axis and revolves around the sun (Response No. 6), or that it moves in an unspecified way (Response No. 3).

Table 7.3 shows the responses of elementary-school children from the United States to the questions "Does the moon move?" and "Show me how" from our second elementary school study (Vosniadou & Brewer, in preparation). Again, we observe the expected shift from the naïve response that the moon moves up/down or east/west (Response No. 3) to the culturally accepted response that the moon revolves around the earth (Response No. 5). Surprisingly, a large percentage of third and fifth grade children believe that the moon does not move at all (Response No. 2).

TABLE 7.2
Percentage of Responses to the Question "Does the Earth Move?"

	American sample			Greek sample		
	Grade			Grade		
Responses	1	3	5	K	3	6
1. Do not know/No response	5	0	0	0	0	0
2. No	25	20	0	46.7	6.6	0
3. Yes, motion unspecified	40	55	40	33.3	76.7	80
4. Yes, axis rotation	10	20	15	0	0	3.3
5. Revolution	0	5	15	0	16.7	0
6. Both axis rotation and revolution	0	0	30	0	0	13.4
7. Nonrotational movement (earthquake, mythical)	5	0	0	16.7	0	0
8. Assimilatory movement (e.g., revolves around the moon, linear movement of the earth toward the sun, etc.)	15	0	0	3.3	0	3.3

TABLE 7.3
Percentage of Responses to the Question "Does the Moon Move?
Show Me How It Happens."

Responses	Grade		
	1	3	5
1. Don't know	6.25	6.67	0.00
2. It does not move	0.00	20.00	37.50
3. Up/down or east/west	50.00	13.33	0.00
4. Sideways	6.25	0.00	6.25
5. Revolution around the earth	18.75	26.67	43.75
6. Axis rotation	6.25	6.67	6.25
7. Both revolution and axis rotation	0.00	6.67	0.00
8. Motion unspecified	0.00	13.32	0.00
9. Revolves around sun	0.00	6.67	6.25
10. Other	12.50	0.00	0.00

The following are some examples from children's responses to the questions investigating their beliefs about the motion of the moon.

Steven (Grade 1)

Experimenter: Does the moon move?

Child: Yes.

Experimenter: How does it move? Show me how it happens.

Child: (Shows moon moving from left to right)

Experimenter: Why does the moon move?

Child: So it can be dark in the other places.

Experimenter: Does the moon move during the night while you are asleep in bed?

Child: Yes.

Experimenter: Does the moon move during the day?

Child: No.

Steven believes that the moon moves from left to right but that this happens only during the night. He thinks that the moon moves in order to cause the day/night cycle.

Niki (Grade 5)

Experimenter: Does the moon move?

Child: Yes.

Experimenter: How does the moon move? Show me how it happens.

Child: (Shows moon revolving around earth)

Experimenter: Why does the moon move?

Child: Whenever it's nighttime so that it can go in place of the sun so that we can still have a little light.

Experimenter: Does the moon move during the night while you are asleep?

Child: Yes.

Experimenter: Does the moon move during the day?

Child: Yes.

Niki knows that the moon revolves around the earth but still attributes human-like intentionality to the movement of the moon when she says that the moon moves so that we can have a little light at night.

Children's responses to the questions "Does the sun move?" and "Show me how it happens" are shown in Table 7.4. We observe the same developmental shift from the naive belief in a sun moving up/down or east/west (Response No. 2) to the belief that the sun rotates around its axis (Response No. 4), or that it does not move (Response No. 8). Many children have the erroneous belief that the sun revolves around the earth (Response No. 3).

The following are some excerpts from the protocols of Shaquita and Elissa when they answer the questions about the movement of the sun.

Shaquita (grade 1)

Experimenter: Does the sun move?

TABLE 7.4
Percentage of Responses to the Question "Does the Sun Move?
Show Me How It Happens."

Responses	Grade		
	1	3	5
1. Don't know	6.25	6.67	0.00
2. Up/down, east/west	31.25	20.00	6.25
3. Revolution around the earth	18.75	20.00	37.50
4. Axis rotation	0.00	6.67	0.00
5. Linear movement outward from the center of the universe (due to expansion/big bang, etc.)	0.00	0.00	6.25
6. Revolution around universe/galaxy	0.00	6.67	6.25
7. God makes it move, magic, etc.	6.25	0.00	0.00
8. It does not move	18.75	33.33	43.75
9. Believes that apparent motion is real	18.75	6.67	0.00

Child: Yes.

Experimenter: How does the sun move? Show me how it happens.

Child: (shows east/west type of movement)

Experimenter: Why does the sun move?

Child: So it can go to different places.

Experimenter: Does the sun move during the day while you are at school?

Child: Yes.

Experimenter: Does the sun move during the night?

Child: No.

Elissa (grade 5)

Experimenter: Does the sun move?

Child: No.

Experimenter: Does the sun move during the day while you are at school?

Child: No.

Experimenter: Does the sun move during the night?

Child: No.

The Day/Night Cycle

Table 7.5 presents children's responses to the question "How does it happen?" in relation to the day/night cycle. The younger children provided mostly intuitive explanations of the day/night cycle. For example, they said that clouds or night cover the sun, or that the sun goes down behind the mountains (Response No. 2). The Greek kindergartners gave a number of explanations that Piaget (1929) has called animistic and artificialistic (Response No. 4). These children used words such as "the sun hides" or "sleeps" to describe the disappearance of the sun during the night or said that night happens so that people can sleep. Nonexplanatory responses (e.g., it is light during the day and dark during the night were also used). (Response No. 5). Although these responses were not found in the first-grade American data, similar types of responses have been obtained from American children in our preschool studies.

Very few children, even among the fifth and sixth graders, explained the day/night cycle in terms of the axis rotation of the earth (Response No. 7). Some children knew that the day/night cycle has to do with the movement of the earth but could not explain how (Response No. 8). Other responses

TABLE 7.5

Percentage of Responses to the Question "How does this happen?" in Relation to the Day/Night Cycle

Responses	American sample			Greek sample		
	Grade			Grade		
	1	3	5	K	3	6
1. Do not know/No response	15	0	0	23.3	10	20
2. Intuitive explanations (clouds or night cover the sun, sun moves behind mountains)	55	35	20	33.3	30	6.7
3. God made it that way	5	5	0	3.3	0	0
4. Animistic and artificialistic (night comes so that people can sleep, the sun goes to sleep, hides, etc.)	0	0	0	20	0	0
5. Nonexplanatory	0	0	0	13.3	6.7	0
6. Assimilatory (e.g., the sun revolves around the earth, the earth rotates and the sun moves up/down)	5	5	0	3.3	10	6.7
7. Correct (the earth rotates around its axis)	10	25	35	0	13.3	16.7
8. The earth moves unspecified	0	15	10	0	10	26.7
9. The earth revolves around the sun	0	10	10	3.3	16.7	13.3
10. Mentions both movements of the earth	10	0	15	0	3.3	10
11. Other	0	5	5	0	0	0
12. Missing	0	0	5	0	0	0

revealed interesting misconceptions. For instance, some children believed that the day/night cycle is caused by the earth's revolution around the sun or thought that it is the sun that revolves around the earth; others knew that the earth rotates around its axis but nevertheless attributed the change from day to night to the up/down or east/west movement of the sun and the moon. Finally, some children thought that the moon is stationed in some part of the sky where it is always night and that the earth's axis rotation causes the day/night cycle because it makes our side of the earth face the moon! (Response No. 6)

Examples from children's explanations of the day/night cycle are described below.

Heather (Grade 5)

Experimenter: Where is the sun during the day?

Child: Out in the sky.

Experimenter: Where is the sun during the night?

Child: Behind the clouds.

Experimenter: How does this happen?

Child: When the sky changes the clouds go in front of the sun and it stays there until the moon goes behind and the sun comes back out.

Patrick (Grade 1)

Experimenter: Where is the sun during the day?

Child: Up in the sky.

Experimenter: Where is the sun during the night?

Child: Down under the earth.

Experimenter: How does this happen?

Child: The sun goes down and the moon glows.

Experimenter: Where is the moon during the night?

Child: Up in the sky.

Experimenter: Where is the moon during the day?

Child: I don't know.

Experimenter: How does this happen?

Child: Maybe clouds cover it up.

Andrea (Grade 5)

Experimenter: Where is the sun during the day?

Child: It stays in the same place but we move around.

Experimenter: Where is the sun at night?

Child: We move around and we can't see the sun because it's facing the opposite side.

Experimenter: How does this happen?

Child: The earth turns around in its place.

Experimenter: Where is the moon during the night?

Child: Well we can see it. I don't really know whether it goes anywhere or not.

Experimenter: Where is the moon during the day?

Child: Well, probably it still is in orbit but it goes to a different part of the earth so we can't see it.

Experimenter: How does this happen?

Child: Because it's up and we can see it and then it goes to another part of the earth.

Experimenter: So tell me how does it change from day to night?

Child: The earth moves around on itself (shows earth rotating) and we face the sun during the day and away from it at night.

Randy (Grade 3)

Experimenter: Where is the sun during the day?

Child: In space.

Experimenter: Where is the sun during the night?

Child: In space.

Experimenter: How does this happen?

Child: The sun has no orbit. It can't move.

Experimenter: Where is the moon during the night?

Child: In space.

Experimenter: Where is the moon during the day?

Child: In space.

Experimenter: How does this happen?

Child: It stays in space.

Experimenter: So tell me how does it change from day to night?

Child: The earth rotates. At night it faces the moon and then during the day it faces the sun.

TABLE 7.6
Percentage of Responses to the Question "Point to the Earth" in a
Picture of the Solar System

Responses	American sample			Greek sample		
	Grade			Grade		
	1	3	5	K	3	6
1. Do not know/No response	6	0	0	10	0	3.3
2. Points to sun	69	20	12	33.3	46.7	10
3. Points to earth	13	46	75	0	3.3	20
4. Points to another planet	0	34	13	10	43.3	56.7
5. Shows area between two planets or other uninterpretable response	12	0	0	3.3	6.7	10
6. The question was not asked because the child did not recognize the picture of the solar system	0	0	0	40	0	0
7. Missing	0	0	0	3.3	0	0

The Location of the Earth, Sun, and Moon in the Solar System

In these questions the children were shown a picture of the solar system and were asked if they knew what this picture represented. If they did, they were asked to point first to the earth, then to the sun, and last to the moon. The responses to the question "Point to the earth" showed the expected shift from a geocentric to a heliocentric view of the solar system. As can be seen in Table 7.6, most of the younger children pointed to the sun when asked to point to the Earth (Response No. 2). The older children gave fewer geocentric responses but many of them could not distinguish the earth from other planets (Response No. 4).

TABLE 7.7
Percentage of Responses to the Question "Point to the Sun" in a
Picture of the Solar System

Responses	American sample			Greek sample		
	Grade			Grade		
	1	3	5	K	3	6
1. Do not know/No response	13	0	6	6.7	6.7	0
2. Center (correct)	25	73	88	6.7	53.3	86.7
3. A planet	50	20	6	23.33	23.3	13.3
4. Shows area between two planets, or nonsensical response, or not here	12	7	0	16.7	16.7	0
5. Not applicable	0	0	0	43.3	0	0
6. Missing	0	0	0	3.3	0	0

TABLE 7.8
Percentage of Responses to the Question "Point to the Moon" in a
Picture of the Solar System

	American sample			Greek sample		
	Grade			Grade		
Responses	1	3	5	K	3	6
1. Do not know/No response	31	33	31	13.33	13.33	3.3
2. Correct	0	27	50	3.3	26.7	43.3
3. A planet	63	40	19	10	43.3	36.7
4. Other	6	0	0	30	16.7	16.7
5. Not applicable	0	0	0	40	0	0
6. Missing	0	0	0	3.4	0	0

Responses to the question "Point to the sun" showed again the expected developmental shift from a geocentric to a heliocentric view of the solar system (see Table 7.7). Most of the younger children pointed to one of the various planets when asked to point to the sun (Table 7.7, Response No. 3), and there were even some fifth-grade children who did not know that the sun is in the center of the solar system (Response No. 2). Finally, responses to the question "Point to the moon" (Table 7.8) showed that many children thought that the moon was a planet (Response No. 3), and that the number of children who could identify the moon correctly increased with age (Response No. 2).

Relative Size of the Earth, Sun, Moon, and Stars

As predicted, the majority of the younger children in our studies thought that the earth is bigger than the sun, the moon, and the stars. Table 7.9 shows children's responses to this question from the first study we conducted (Vosniadou, 1987). As can be seen, 75% of the first-grade children and quite

TABLE 7.9
Percentage of Responses to the Question "Think about the Earth, the
Sun, the Moon, and the Stars. Which is the Biggest: the Earth, the
Sun, the Moon, or the Stars?"

	Grade		
Responses	1	3	5
1. Earth	75.00	26.67	12.50
2. Sun	18.75	53.33	50.00
3. Moon	0.00	13.33	37.50
4. Stars	6.25	6.67	0.00

a few of the third- and fifth-grade children (26% and 12.5% respectively) thought that the earth is bigger than the sun, moon or stars (Response No. 1) The percentage of the children who were willing to say that the sun is larger than the earth increased with age (Response No. 2), but still, many fifth-grade children considered the earth or the moon to be bigger than the sun.

Gravity

The gravity concept was investigated by asking two key questions. In both questions the children were shown the drawing depicted in Fig. 7.1 in which a little girl is supposed to be standing upside down at the bottom of the earth. In the first question the children were asked "Suppose there were a little girl here at the bottom of the earth; would she fall off?" The second question was asked with respect to a ball that the little girl at the bottom of the earth supposingly held in her hands: "Now suppose this little girl on the bottom of the earth had a ball in her hand. If she dropped the ball where would the ball go?"

As can be seen in Table 7.10, many first-grade children (30%) thought that the girl pictured at the bottom of the earth would fall, supporting the intuitive model hypothesis according to which things fall in a downward direction (Question 1, Response No. 2). It is interesting to note that many children who responded correctly to this question apparently changed their mind when asked where the ball that the girl supposingly drops from her hands would fall (Table 7.10, Question 2, Response No. 1). Seventy-five percent of the first-grade children and 35% and 30% of the third- and fifth-grade children in our

(A)
"Suppose there were a little girl here at the bottom of the earth; would she fall off?"

(B)
"Now suppose this little girl on the bottom of the earth had a ball in her hand. If she dropped the ball where would the ball go?"

FIG. 7.1. Questions posed to children in order to investigate their understanding of gravity.

TABLE 7.10
Percentage of Responses to the Gravity Questions

Question 1: "Suppose there was a little girl here at the bottom of the earth. Would she fall off?"

	Grade		
	First	Third	Fifth
1. She would fall down, away from the earth (up/down gravity)	30	5	0
2. She would fall, but we wouldn't because we are inside the earth	25	25	20
3. She would not fall (correct gravity)	25	70	75
4. Do not know	20	0	5

Question 2: "Now suppose this little girl on the bottom of the earth had a ball in her hand. If she dropped the ball, where would the ball go?"

	Grade		
	First	Third	Fifth
1. The ball would fall down, away from earth (up/down gravity)	75	35	30
2. Toward center of earth (correct gravity)	20	60	55
3. It would float around in space	5	5	15

sample said that the ball would fall away from the earth, revealing in this way an intuitive concept of gravity. Quite a few children expressed the belief that the people do not fall off the earth because we live deep inside of it (Question 1, Response No. 2).

The following are some examples from the protocols of Robert, Selena, and Sarah.

Robert (Grade 5)

Experimenter: Can people live at the bottom of the earth?

Child: No. They'd fall.

Experimenter: Now, remember this is the earth (shows styrofoam sphere). Suppose there were a little girl here at the bottom of the earth. Would she fall off?

Child: Yes.

Experimenter: Why?

Child: Because the bottom is flat plus you'd be upside down.

Experimenter: Now suppose this little girl on the bottom of the earth had a ball in her hand. If she dropped the ball where would it go?

Child: Down (away from the earth)

Experimenter: Why?

Child: Because it's upside down. It can't go up (meaning back up, toward the earth).

Selena (Grade 1)

Experimenter: Can people live at the bottom of the earth?

Child: No. We all live inside the earth. We can't live on the bottom. If we lived on the bottom we would fall off.

Experimenter: Now remember this is the earth. Suppose there were a little girl here on the bottom of the earth. Would she fall off?

Child: No.

Experimenter: Why not?

Child: Because she's on the ground. We only live here (the child shows the inside of the sphere). We don't live on the outside.

Experimenter: What is below the earth?

Child: I don't know.

Experimenter: Is there something that holds the earth?

Child: Gravity.

In the first example, Robert believes that people cannot live at the bottom of the earth because they would fall. In the second example, Selena believes that people will not fall because they are inside the earth. They cannot live on the outside of the sphere because they would fall. Although Selena knows something about gravity, she believes that gravity holds the earth rather than the people on the earth.

Sarah (Grade 3)

Experimenter: Can people live at the bottom of the earth?

Child: No, because at the bottom, they'd maybe not have a good life. I am not sure.

Experimenter: Why don't they fall off?

Child: They don't fall off because of gravity.

Experimenter: Now remember this is the earth. Suppose there were a little girl here at the bottom of the earth. Would she fall off?

Child: No.

Experimenter: Why not?

Child: Because of gravity.

Experimenter: Now suppose this little girl at the bottom of the earth had a ball in her hand. If she dropped the ball where would it go?

Child: It would roll some place near a house.

Experimenter: Why?

Child: It can't fall.

Experimenter: What is below the earth?

Child: Nothing.

Experimenter: Is there something that holds the earth?

Child: No.

Sarah knows about gravity and says that people would not fall off at the bottom of the earth. Yet she seems to be uncomfortable with the idea that people actually live there because they "may not have a good life."

Earth Shape

American children's responses to the factual question "What is the shape of the earth?" and, to the question "Draw a picture of the earth so that its real shape shows," did not appear to support the intuitive model hypothesis. Most of the children in our sample said that the earth is either a "circle" or "round" and drew a circle to depict its shape. However, children's difficulties with the notion that the earth is a sphere became apparent in their responses to the generative questions "If you were to walk for many days where would you end up?" "Would you ever reach the edge of the earth?", "Does the earth have an edge?" Sixty percent of the first-grade children and 20% of the third-grade children in the first elementary-school study we conducted answered these questions by saying that the earth has an edge. Thus, while most children had been exposed to the information that the earth is a sphere, they could not use this information generatively. They answered the factual questions correctly but converted to an intuitive model of a flat earth when asked the question about the earth's edge.

In a different question, the children were shown the picture of a farm house on what appeared to be flat land and were asked: "Why does the earth look flat in this picture, but the one you drew is round?" Several interesting misconceptions about the shape of the earth were revealed in this way. Some children said that the earth is round but also flat like a disk or like a truncated sphere. Others thought that there are two earths: a flat one on which we live and a round one that is up in the sky. Finally, some children tried to solve the conflict between the apparent flatness of the earth and its assumed roundness by saying that the earth is like a hollow sphere and that people live on flat ground inside the sphere!

The following is an extract from the protocol of a child with a hollow earth sphere from a study conducted in India, in which children demonstrated their beliefs regarding the earth's shape by selecting among styrofoam models of the earth.

Indrilla (age 6)

Experimenter: What is the shape of the earth?

Child: Spherical.

Experimenter: Where do people live on the earth?

Child: They live inside the earth on the land

Experimenter: Can people live on the bottom of the earth?

Child: Yes.

Experimenter: Why don't they fall?

Child: Because they are on flat land.

Experimenter: Is there an end or an edge to the earth?

Child: No.

Experimenter: If you dug a hole through the earth what would you see on the other side?

Child: A planet.

Experimenter: From these models pick up the one that is the same shape as the earth.

Child: (picks up the hollow earth model and tells the experimenter) This is part of it; the other half is air.

Experimenter: Where do people live on earth? Show me on your model.

Child: (points to the inside bottom) We live all over inside on the bottom on the flat parts.

Experimenter: Could a person reach the end or the edge of the earth?

Child: No; you would go round and come back to where you started (child traces the circle on the inside bottom of her hollow earth model with her finger).

Table 7.11 shows the earth shape models of Indian and American elementary schoolchildren (from our second study of elementary-school children in the US) as a function of age.

As can be seen, the predominant model of the earth's shape among 6-year-

TABLE 7.11
Earth Shape Models of Indian and American Children as a function of Age

Age:	6 yrs.		8 yrs.	
Sample:	India %	USA %	India %	USA %
Model:				
Sphere	16	13	58	80
Questionable sphere	5	25	11	7
Truncated sphere	5	0	5	7
Hollow sphere	11	30	11	0
Pancake	47	6	5	6
Flat earth	16	13	5	0
Two earths	0	13	0	0
Mixed	0	0	5	0

old children is the hollow sphere in the U.S. data and the disk in the Indian data.

The following is an example of the disk earth model from the protocol of an Indian child.

Rakesh (age 6)

Experimenter: What is the shape of the earth?

Child: Round like a circle.

Experimenter: Where do people live on earth?

Child: In the middle, on top.

Experimenter: Can people live on the bottom of the earth?

Child: No.

Experimenter: Why not?

Child: Because they would drown around.

Experimenter: Is there an end or edge to the earth?

Child: Yes.

Experimenter: Can a person fall off there?

Child: Yes.

Experimenter: Where would they fall?

Child: Into the ocean.

Experimenter: If you dug a hole through the earth to the other side, what would you see?

Child: I don't know.

Experimenter: From among the models, pick the one that is the same shape as the earth.

Child: (picks up the disk)

Experimenter: Show me where the people live.

Child: (indicates the middle of the top surface of the disk)

Experimenter: Does the earth have an end or edge? Show me on your model.

Child: (indicates the rim of the disk model is the edge)

Experimenter: Could a person fall off there?

Child: Yes.

Experimenter: What is below the earth?

Child: Ocean.

The belief that the earth is shaped like a disk and that it floats upon a sea or ocean of water was very strong in the Indian sample, whereas only one child in our American sample gave this response. In a similar study conducted in Samoa (Brewer, et al., 1987) a model unique to the Samoan children was discovered. This model was based on the notion that the earth is shaped like a ring with people living along its perimeter. These models have been interpreted as demonstrating culture-specific influences on children's conceptual development. Apparently, the view that the earth floats on water is a dominant one in Indian cosmology while there is evidence suggesting that in Samoa physical and social space is organized in the form of a ring (e.g., in the villages huts are arranged in a cyclical fashion and so is furniture arranged within each hut).

THE PROCESS OF CONCEPTUAL CHANGE

I have argued that children start their knowledge acquisition in astronomy by constructing an intuitive cosmological model of a flat, stationary earth in a geocentric solar system in which the sun and the moon move in an up/down direction and cause the day/night cycle. Eventually this intuitive model changes to that of a spherical earth, which rotates around its axis and revolves around the sun in a heliocentric solar system in which the day/night cycle is caused by the axis rotation of the earth and not by the movement of the sun and the moon. In this section I will focus on three aspects of the process of conceptual change that I think deserve particular attention: The sequence of acquisition of the various concepts that comprise the domain of astronomy, the different levels of understanding a counterintuitive concept, and the misconceptions that children construct. I will argue that the presence of misconceptions shows that intuitive knowledge consists of certain fundamental experiential beliefs and that conceptual change is achieved when these beliefs are replaced with different explanations.

Sequence of Acquisition

The individual concepts that comprise the domain of astronomy seem to have a relational structure that influences their acquisition. One example is the interrelationship that exists between the earth shape and gravity concepts. Children cannot have an understanding of gravity if they do not know that the earth is spherical. At the same time, they cannot have a spherical earth concept without some knowledge about gravity, for otherwise they cannot understand how it is possible for people to live at the bottom of the earth without falling. Some misconceptions regarding the shape of the earth can be traced to lack of knowledge about gravity. For example, the idea that people live *inside* a hollow sphere appears to be an attempt to reconcile the information that the earth is a sphere with the belief that people cannot live at the bottom of a sphere without falling.

Understanding that the earth is spherical is a prerequisite to understanding many other astronomy concepts. One of these is the explanation of the day/night cycle. For instance, one child in our sample knew that the earth rotated around its axis but thought that the earth is round like a disk, not like a sphere. This child interpreted the earth's axis rotation to mean that the pancake-like earth turns around. This movement cannot, however, explain the day/night cycle and the child was understandably confused. At least 80% of the children in our sample who explained the phenomenon of the day/night cycle on the basis of the axis rotation of the earth, knew that the earth is spherical, that the moon revolves around the earth, that the moon does not have its own light but takes its light from the sun, and believed in a heliocentric rather than a geocentric model of the solar system.

Levels of Understanding

Children seem to go through different levels of understanding a concept when this concept contradicts an intuitive model. At a first, superficial level, children simply seem to memorize the adult/scientific model to which they are exposed without connecting it to the intuitive model. Thus, they can answer factual questions correctly but rely predominantly on their intuitive model to answer generative questions. At this level, the scientific and intuitive models coexist, unconnected from each other, and are used independently to answer different kinds of questions about phenomena that belong to the same fundamental class.

Something like this happens, for example, in the case of children who hold the inconsistent belief that gravity operates for people but not for balls; or those who say that the earth is round but that it also has an end from which people can fall; or in the case of children who say that the earth rotates around its axis but explain the day/night circle on the basis of the movement of the sun.

A second level of understanding emerges when children become aware of the fact that there are two contradictory explanations for the same phenomenon and attempt to resolve them by assimilating the scientific model to their intuitive model. This assimilation gives rise to various misconceptions. One such misconception is that the earth is a hollow sphere; another is that the sun revolves around the earth rather than that the earth revolves around the sun; also, that the earth's axis rotation causes the day/night cycle because it makes our side of the earth face the stationary moon. Similar misconceptions have been documented in many other knowledge domains and are found in children as well as in adults (see Clement, 1983; Driver & Easley, 1978; diSessa, 1962; White, 1983; McCloskey, 1983).

Finally, a third level of understanding of the scientific model is achieved when this model starts being used in a generative way. The generative use of the scientific model does not imply that the intuitive model is extinguished. The two models may still coexist but, unlike the first level of understanding, the person is aware of their simultaneous existence and can make consistent use of them as the situation and/or need dictates.

Misconceptions

I have paid particular attention to students' misconceptions because I believe that understanding how misconceptions are formed is fundamental to understanding how the change from an intuitive to a scientific model occurs. Before proceeding, I must clarify that the term misconception does not refer to children's intuitive knowledge, i.e., the knowledge children construct on the basis of everyday experience. Words such as "alternative frameworks" or "preconceptions" have been used to refer to what is here called intuitive knowledge. Rather, the term misconception is used to refer to children's misunderstandings of scientific explanations, misunderstandings that seem to occur from their attempts to assimilate the scientific information into their intuitive models. Misconceptions provide interesting information about the nature of children's intuitive knowledge and about the process of conceptual change.

Evidence for the presence of misconceptions in children's ideas regarding the shape of the earth was first provided by Piaget (1929), Nussbaum and Novak (1976), Nussbaum (1979), and Sneider and Poulos (1983). My colleagues and I wanted to confirm further the presence of such misconceptions and, most important, to investigate whether they represented transitory and inconsistent problem-solving attempts or were used by the children in a consistent fashion (Vosniadou & Brewer, submitted).

In order to determine whether children made consistent use of a given misconception of the earth, we first created a list of possible misconceptions. Then we derived the expected responses to all questions investigating the earth-shape concept if we assumed that the children made consistent use of one of these misconceptions. For example, we reasoned that if children believed that the earth is a hollow sphere, they should say that the earth is "round," that "there is no end/edge to the earth" or that "there is an end/edge but people cannot fall off it because they live inside the earth", that "the earth is flat on the inside where people live and round on the outside", and so on.

Once the expected pattern of responses to the various earth-shape questions was determined for each misconception, we compared the expected responses with the obtained ones. The criteria used were fairly stringent. For example, a child who said that there is no end/edge to the earth could not be assumed to be making consistent use of a disk misconception, even in those cases where this response was the child's only deviation from the response pattern expected for this misconception.

Using this procedure, we were able to determine that about 85% of the children in the sample used in a consistent fashion either a misconception or a spherical earth model. Some children gave internally inconsistent responses. On the whole, the results suggested that there was a relatively high degree of consistency in children's ideas about the shape of the earth.

Having determined that misconceptions are used in a consistent fashion, the next question was to explain why these misconceptions are formed in the first place. Adults do not go about telling children that the earth is a disk or a hollow sphere. Why do children come up with these strange ideas about the shape of the earth? In order to explain the construction of alternative models of the shape of the earth, one is forced to make certain assumptions about the nature of children's intuitive knowledge and about the process of restructuring this knowledge.

First, the presence of misconceptions suggests that intuitive knowledge is constructed out of a set of fundamental beliefs based on everyday experience. Some of these experiential beliefs are the following: the ground is flat, the earth has an end/edge, the edges of the earth are flat, the sky is located above the earth, and there is ground or water all the way down underneath the earth (see Vosniadou & Brewer, submitted, for a more extensive discussion of this issue). Second, it appears that children do not like to question their experiential beliefs. When they become aware of the conflict that exists between the culturally accepted information and their experience of a flat earth, they do not want to believe that their experiential beliefs are wrong. What they try to do is solve the conflict by creating a misconception that succeeds in reconciling the culturally accepted information with their beliefs.

These two assumptions can explain how the various misconceptions regarding the shape of the earth are formed. For example, the misconception of a dual earth (i.e., that there are two earths: a flat one on which people live and a round one which is up in the sky), allows children to solve the sphere/flat conflict without changing any of their experiential beliefs. The children who have constructed this misconception answer our questions in a way that shows that they still believe that the earth is flat, it has an end, there is ground all the way down, and the sky is above the earth. The only thing that has changed is that they have now added to their knowledge base the information that there is another earth which is up in the sky.

A detailed examination of children's responses has revealed that there is a progression of more and more advanced misconceptions, depending on how many of their experiential beliefs children have replaced with a new explanatory framework. For example, the hollow-earth view is a more advanced misconception than the dual-earth and the disk earth. The children who hold the view that the earth is a hollow sphere have given up their experiential belief that the earth is flat, that something supports the earth, and the sky is located on top of the earth. These children conceptualize the earth as a sphere suspended in space. However, they still hold the experiential belief that the ground is flat and that people cannot live on the periphery of a sphere because they would fall.

IMPLICATIONS FOR INSTRUCTION

I have argued that students' intuitive concepts are based on a synthesis of certain fundamental experiential beliefs and that misconceptions are caused when students try to reconcile the scientific concepts with their experiential beliefs. Within such a framework, conceptual change can happen only when students understand the limitations of their experiential beliefs and the need to replace them with different explanations.

This analysis implies that for instruction to be effective teachers must be aware of students' experiential beliefs. Second, they must be capable of providing students with reasons which make them question their beliefs and third, with a different explanatory framework to replace the one they already have. Finally, the sequence of instruction must not violate the order of acquisition of the various concepts that comprise a given domain.

A limited look at some astronomy instruction in local schools and a detailed examination of the astronomy units in four leading science series I have recently undertaken have revealed severe problems both in the sequence and contents of instruction. For example, in one series examined, the authors organized the material to be acquired around scientific information about the moon, the sun, and the earth. Therefore, they included a unit on the moon at grade one that takes the children from a description of the size and shape of the moon to an explanation of its phases. However, the explanation of the phases of the moon is a difficult concept, which presupposes rather sophisticated knowledge about the location of the earth, sun and moon in the solar system, the relative size and movements of the solar objects, and how light is reflected. In fact, this concept is so difficult that most adolescents and adults do not know how to explain it adequately.

With respect to the content of instruction it is important to notice that usually no explanations are provided of concepts such as the shape, movement, size, and location of the earth, sun, moon, and stars. The children are simply told facts such as "the earth is round like a ball," "the earth rotates around its axis," "the stars are like the sun," "the sun is bigger than the earth," and "the sun is located in the middle of the solar system." As we have seen, these "facts" are inconsistent with children's experiential beliefs and children find it difficult to believe them. For instruction to be effective, we must explain to students why the earth is round when it appears to be flat; how it is possible for the earth to move around its axis when we do not feel any movement; how it is possible for the sun to be bigger than the earth but for the moon to be smaller than the earth when their apparent size is about the same; why stars have their own light but the moon does not, and so on.

Explanations are usually provided in the case of phenomena such as the day/night cycle, the phases of the moon, or the seasons. Unfortunately these explanations are for the most part incomplete and inaccurate either because they do not take into consideration the order of acquisition of the relevant concepts or because they do not address all of students' underlying experiential beliefs.

In one experiment I have recently conducted I tested third graders' understanding of the day/night cycle before and immediately after they read a two-page text from a leading science series on the day/night cycle written for their grade level (Vosniadou, 1989b). The results were rather revealing. Out of the 23 children investigated, 6 provided adequate explanations of the day/ night cycle (e.g., in terms of the axis rotation of the earth) before they read the text and only 8 after they read it. Two children became confused after reading the text and thought that the day/night cycle is caused by the earth's revolution around the sun, and not by its axis rotation.

There were two main reasons for children's failures to understand the text. First, many of the children did not have an adequate earth shape model in the first place and as a result they could not understand the information about the earth's movement or could not see how this movement could explain the day/

night cycle. Second, many children who understood how the earth moves formed the misconception previously mentioned according to which the earth's axis rotation causes the earth to face the moon and thus to cause the night. These children said that the moon does not move, and answered our generative question, "What changes do we need to make to have day time all the time?", by saying that "We must get rid of the moon!" Needless to say, an adequate explanation of the day/night cycle must include not only information about the shape and movement of the earth, but also about the movement, shape, size, location, and light of the sun, moon, and stars.

Some researchers have focused their attention on students' misconceptions and have argued that it is important to make students confront these misconceptions and replace them with scientific concepts. While I believe that this approach is in the right direction, I think that focusing on students' misconceptions alone may not always provide a solution to the problem of restructuring. If misconceptions are formed because of students' inadequate attempts to replace their experiential beliefs with a different explanatory framework, then what is needed for misconceptions to be abandoned is for students to replace their experiential beliefs with a new explanatory framework. For an illustration, let us take once more the example of the concept of the earth's shape. Telling a child who believes that people live on flat ground inside the earth that the earth is not hollow will not immediately solve the child's problem with the notion of a spherical earth. Children believe that the earth is a hollow sphere because they do not understand how people can live at the bottom of the sphere without falling and because they cannot reconcile their perception of a flat earth with the idea that the earth is round. What children need in order to get rid of this misconception is a lesson on gravity and a lesson on how round things can sometimes appear to be flat. Otherwise one misconception will be replaced with another and children will remain confused.

Finally, science instruction must also be aimed toward increasing children's metaconceptual awareness. Children often find scientific explanations incredible and see no reason for questioning their beliefs, which are much more consistent with their phenomenal experience. When we teach science we must provide children with situations that will make them understand that their beliefs are not true facts about the world but theoretical constructions which can be subject to falsification. This can be done by showing children that there are certain empirical observations that their beliefs cannot explain and that there are other explanations that should be preferred because of their greater empirical adequacy. Instructional programs that aim at enriching students' experiential knowledge without making them aware of their naïve theory-building attempts fail to create this necessary metaconceptual awareness. For while science-naïve individuals are not bad at synthesizing their everyday experience into meaningful explanations (to the extent that this is possible without controlled experiments) they are not really aware of the theoretical nature of this activity.

CONCLUSIONS

I have argued that conceptual development in astronomy proceeds through the gradual restructuring of students' intuitive model of a flat and stationary earth located in a geocentric solar system to the currently accepted scientific view. In order for this radical restructuring of knowledge to occur, students must learn to question their intuitive beliefs and to replace them with a new explanatory framework. For instruction to be effective, we must create the circumstances for students to become aware of the theoretical nature of their intuitive constructions and of the need to replace them with explanations which account for the relevant empirical observations more adequately.

ACKNOWLEDGMENTS

The research reported in this chapter was supported in part by a grant from the U. S. National Science Foundation, NSF BNS 85-10254, and in part by the U. S. Office of Educational Research and Improvement. The publication does not necessarily reflect the views of the agencies supporting this research. I thank Marlo Schommer, Ann Jolly, Marcy Dorfman, Ala Samarapungavan, Maria Zafrana, and Christos Ioannides for help in collecting and scoring the data.

REFERENCES

Brewer, W. F., Hendrich, D. J., & Vosniadou, S. (1987, January). *Alternate knowledge systems: A cross-cultural study of cosmological schemata.* Paper presented at the second meeting of the International Society on Cross-Cultural Cognition, Honolulu.

Clement, J. (1982). Students' preconceptions in introductory mechanics. *American Journal of Physics, 52,* 66–71.

Clement, J. J. (1983). A conceptual model discussed by Galileo and used intuitively by physics students. In D. Gentner & A. L. Stevens (Eds.), *Mental models* (pp. 325–339). Hillsdale, NJ: Lawrence Erlbaum Associates.

diSessa, A. (1982). Unlearning Aristotelian physics: A study of knowledge based learning. *Cognitive Science, 6,* 37–75.

Driver, R., & Easley, J. (1978). Pupils and paradigms: A review of literature related to concept development in adolescent science students. *Studies in Science Education, 67,* 3–12.

Kuhn, T. S. (1957). *The Copernican revolution.* Cambridge, MA: Harvard University Press.

Mali, G. B., & Howe, A. (1979). Development of earth and gravity concepts among Nepali children. *Science Education, 63,* 685–691.

McCloskey, M. (1983). Naive theories of motion. In D. Gentner & A. L. Stevens (Eds.), *Mental models* (pp. 199–324). Hillsdale, NJ: Lawrence Erlbaum Associates.

Novak, J. D. (1977). An alternative to Piagetian psychology for science and mathematics education. *Science Education, 63*, 83–93.

Nussbaum, J. (1979). Children's conceptions of the earth as a cosmic body: A cross-age study. *Science Education, 63*, 83–93.

Nussbaum, J., & Novak, J. D. (1976). An assessment of children's concepts of the earth utilizing structural interviews. *Science Education, 60*, 535–550.

Osborne, R., & Wittrock, M. C. (1983). Learning science: A generative process. *Science Education, 67*, 489–508.

Piaget, J. (1929). *The child's conception of the world.* London: Routledge & Kegan Paul.

Sneider, C., & Poulos, S. (1983). Children's cosmographies: Understanding the earth's shape and gravity. *Science Education, 67*, 205–221.

Viennot, L. (1979). Spontaneous reasoning in elementary dynamics. *European Journal of Science Education, 1*, 205–221.

Vosniadou, S. (1987, April). Children's acquistion and restructuring of science knowledge. In N. Fredericksen (Chair), *Children's procedural knowledge in science.* Symposium conducted at the annual meeting of the American Educational Research Association, Washington, DC.

Vosniadou, S. (1988, April). Knowledge restructuring and science instruction. In J. Greeno (Chair), *Conceptual models of science learning and science instruction.* Symposium conducted at the annual meeting of the American Educational Research Association, New Orleans.

Vosniadou, S. (1989a, August). On the nature of children's naive knowledge. In the *Proceedings of the 11th annual conference of the Cognitive Science Society*, Ann Arbor, MI.

Vosniadou, S. (1989b, September). *Children's naive models and the comprehension of expository text.* Paper presented at the second biennial conference of the European Association for Research on Learning and Instruction, Madrid.

Vosniadou, S., & Brewer, W. F. (1987). Theories of knowledge restructuring in development. *Review of Educational Research, 57*(1), 51–67.

Vosniadou, S., & Brewer, W. F. (1990). A cross-cultural investigation of knowledge acquisition in astronomy: Greek and American data. In H. Mandl, E. DeCorte, N. Bennett, & H. C. Friedrich (Eds.), *Learning and instruction: European research in an international context* (Vol. 3). Oxford, England: Pergamon.

Vosniadou, S., & Brewer, W. (submitted). *Mental models of the earth. A study of conceptual change in childhood.*

White, B. Y. (1983). Sources of difficulty in understanding Newtonian dynamics. *Cognitive Science, 7*, 41–65.

8 Children's Biology: Studies on Conceptual Development in the Life Sciences

Joel J. Mintzes
John E. Trowbridge
Mary W. Arnaudin
University of North Carolina at Wilmington

James H. Wandersee
Louisiana State University, Baton Rouge

> *Learners look for meaning and will try to find regularity and order in the events of the world even in the absence of complete information. This means that naive theories will always be constructed as part of the learning process.*
>
> *Resnick (1983)*

For the past decade we have focused our research efforts on two fundamental, yet fascinating questions: How do children view the world of living things? and How do these viewpoints change as children mature into adolescents and young adults? In attempting to answer these questions, we have spoken with hundreds of young people in many schools located in several states. The viewpoints these youngsters shared have delighted and often surprised us. Above all, they have given us a deep and abiding respect for the ability of the human mind to construct meaning out of experience.

In this chapter we wish to share some of our findings, in the hope that the reader might begin to recognize and explore, and possibly accommodate his or her teaching to the "naïve theories" and "alternative conceptions" that students bring with them to the study of biology. We believe that children's biological concepts are worth studying not simply as objects of curiosity but as potential impediments to learning; impediments which, in some cases, are remarkably tenacious and resistant to change (Ausubel, Novak, & Hanesian, 1978).

> [A]ll students the weak as well as the strong learners come to their first science classes with surprisingly extensive theories about how the natural world works.

They use these "naive" theories to explain real world events . . . . Then, even after instruction . . . they still resort to their prior theories . . .

Resnick (1983)

To bring you up to date, we begin with a brief overview of some 60 years of previous research on children's biology. We then describe three of our own recent studies and finally we offer some suggestions to those who are committed to meaningful learning in the biology classroom.

SIX DECADES OF CHILDREN'S BIOLOGY

In 1929, Piaget published his now classic study, *The Child's Conception of the World*. Though he later regarded his early efforts as merely preliminary (*un peu adolescent*), Piaget's research on the child's concept of *life* undoubtedly served as the single most influential work of its kind for many years.

In short, Piaget proposed a four-stage theory that chronicles the emergence of the life concept. The youngest of Piaget's children (ages 3–7) ascribed life to any object exhibiting *activity* (e.g., a falling rock; a noisy toy) or *usefulness*. Somewhat older children (7–8) look upon *movement* of any kind as the defining feature of life (e.g., an automobile; a rocking chair). This stage is followed by a third one (9–11), in which living things are characterized by *spontaneous movement* (e.g., a river; the sun). Finally at about 11 to 12, children limit life to *plants* and *animals*.

An avalanche of research followed on the heels of Piaget's work, some of which produced findings in general agreement with his stage theory (Russell & Dennis, 1941) but soon a series of anomalous results began to accumulate. Studies in non-Western cultures failed to replicate Piaget's results (Jahoda, 1958). Other studies found that more than 50% of the general adult population attributes life to one or more inanimate objects. More recent work suggests that the development of the life concept progresses independently of Piaget's stages of "operational thought" (Williamson, 1981) and that even well-educated college students who have taken previous biology courses have poorly differentiated life concepts (Brumby, 1982).

Perhaps more damaging to Piaget's work on the life concept and his underlying stage theory is the recent emergence of a *conceptual change* view of cognitive development (Carey, 1987). This view suggests that the acquisition of biological concepts in childhood reflects a fundamental reorganization of the knowledge structure between the ages of 7 and 10. This restructuring, which closely parallels major intellectual revolutions in the history of science, involves the forging of new relationships among existing concepts and the construction of new, abstract, defined concepts.

In a series of elegant studies, Carey compared the understandings of 4-, 6-, and 10-year-old children in several biological domains. Her youngest children embedded their explanations of life processes within an intuitive theory of human behavior. They ascribed activities such as eating, breathing, and sleeping to social and psychological needs. By age 10, children develop an autonomous domain of "intuitive biology" wherein explanations approximate those held by naïve adults. Carey suggests that this transition probably depends on the kind of "strong restructuring" that characterizes major conceptual shifts in the evolution of scientific disciplines (Mintzes, 1989).

While Piaget and his adherents gradually moved away from the study of children's biological concepts, a cadre of other researchers, working concurrently and independently, began to investigate such issues as children's understandings of the human body, reproduction, heredity, and evolution.

Until recently it was assumed that children's knowledge of the *human body* is quite limited. Indeed, in an early study some workers found that youngsters believe the inner body consists of nothing but recently eaten food (Schilder & Wechsler, 1935). In contrast, more recent studies have demonstrated that even young children have well-developed concepts of body parts (Catherall, 1981; Gellert, 1962; Johnson & Wellman, 1982; Porter, 1974). In a study by Porter, when 10-year-old children were asked to draw their internal body parts, the majority of youngsters depicted the heart, brain, skeletal elements, veins, kidneys, lungs, muscles, ribs, and stomach.

The size, shape, and location of internal organs drawn by children show considerable consistency from one study to another. The heart is shown in the chest cavity, correctly proportioned but in the shape of a valentine; the stomach is lower and larger, and the lungs are higher and smaller than they should be.

Children's physiological concepts are also well documented (Gellert, 1962). For example, most young children recognize the stomach as a repository of food but the concepts of digestion, distribution, and egestion generally don't emerge until early adolescence. Similarly, the nose, mouth, and throat are associated with breathing in children under 10 but the concept of gas exchange develops much later (Nagy, 1953). Additionally, in a study on mind/brain concepts (Johnson & Wellman, 1982), it was found that youngsters (ages 5–8) ascribe to the brain only a limited set of intellective functions (e.g., thinking, dreaming) while older children (age 10) exhibit a more comprehensive understanding of the brain's role in motor tasks and sensation. Only adults judged the brain necessary for involuntary bodily functions.

A number of studies have examined children's concepts of *reproduction* (Kreitler & Kreitler, 1966; Moore & Kendall, 1971; Piaget, 1929) and *heredity* (Clough & Wood-Robinson, 1985; Deadman & Kelly, 1978; Kargbo, Hobbs, & Erickson, 1980). Piaget proposed that reproduction concepts emerge in a series of stages: a *pre-artificialistic* stage in which children lack a true concept of origins; an *artificialistic* stage in which beginnings are acknowledged but the parent's role is denied, and a *naturalistic* stage in which the role of the mother is recognized and, much later, that of the father. In subsequent work, however, neither Kreitler and Kreitler nor Moore and Kendall found evidence of an artificialistic stage. The most frequent explanation given by the Kreitler's Israeli children (ages 4–5) is that babies are created in the mother's belly from the food she eats, while Moore and Kendall's middle-class American children attributed babies to divine sources (e.g., God, Jesus).

When asked to explain how physical traits are passed from parents to offspring, many children as young as 7 have firmly established ideas. Kargbo et al. found some who believe that mothers contribute more than fathers to the genetic makeup of their children. Many youngsters claim that certain traits, such as height, are inherited from the father while others, like hair and eye color, are derived from the mother. Apparently many children (and adults) subscribe to a kind of pre-Mendelian belief in the blending of parental traits in offspring.

Finally, several studies have examined concepts of *evolution* among preadolescent youngsters and teen-agers. Apparently even 10- and 11-year-olds understand that change is a universal phenomenon and variation is common to all living things (Neuberger, 1966). However, concepts of adaptation and natural selection are consistently misconstrued (Brumby, 1979, 1984; Clough & Wood-Robinson, 1985; Deadman & Kelly, 1978; Jungwirth, 1975). Adaptation is often seen as a response to environmental change; a notion that Jungwirth has called "preconceived adaptation" and "inverted evolution." The concept of selection is commonly associated with individual organisms rather than populations and is seen as an explanation of why some individuals survive and others die. Explanations of the mechanism of evolution commonly enlist Lamarckian views on the inheritance of acquired characteristics; this is a belief common among adolescents and even among college students with prior coursework in biology.

RECENT STUDIES IN CHILDREN'S BIOLOGY

Reviewing published research in the domain of children's biology we soon discovered, despite a hundred or so previous studies, that the area remains a wide-open and fertile field (Mintzes & Arnaudin, 1984; Wandersee, Mintzes, & Arnaudin, 1987, 1989). Accordingly we undertook a series of cross-age studies, initially focusing our attention on children's concepts of *animal classification* (Mintzes & Trowbridge, 1987; Trowbridge & Mintzes, 1985, 1988), the *human circulatory system* (Arnaudin & Mintzes, 1985, 1986; Mintzes, 1984), and *photosynthesis* (Wandersee, 1983, 1986). In this way we hoped to tap a wide range of alternative conceptions in animal, plant, and human biology.

Though each is unique, the studies we describe have several common features. Each sampled the viewpoints of learners at several stages of conceptual development, including the upper elementary (fifth) grades, the middle school (eighth) grades, the high school (tenth/eleventh) grades, and the early college (freshman/sophomore) years.

Sample sizes were relatively large and participants represented a reasonably diverse cross-section of the school-age population. Subjects in each of the first two studies were approximately 500 students enrolled in the public schools of North Carolina; those in the third study were 1,400 students attending parochial schools in nine western and midwestern states.

Each of the studies employed instruments composed of forced-choice and free-response items. In the first two, clinical interviews, concept maps (Novak & Gowin, 1984), and sorting tasks served as additional sources of data.

Finally, each of the studies sought to explore and analyze student viewpoints on their own terms without comparison with any external standard. We were interested primarily in *describing* how learners view the living world rather than evaluating the "correctness" of student responses or categorizing them into any a priori set of hypothetical "stages."

Children's Concepts of Animal Classification

Studies in New Zealand (Bell, 1981), Great Britain (Ryman, 1974), and the Soviet Union (Natadze, 1963) suggested that learners of virtually every age group subscribe to a host of alternative conceptions about animals. We wondered whether American students might adhere to the same notions and to what extent these ideas change as a function of age or grade level. The questions we posed to our subjects probed the following issues: What is an animal? Which animals have a backbone? Which animals are considered fish? Amphibians? Reptiles? Birds? Mammals?

What is an Animal?   We began to probe this issue by asking our subjects to identify instances of animals in a set of line drawings depicting a cow, a seagull, a fish, a butterfly, a pine tree, and a mushroom. In response, we found virtually all of the subjects agreeing that a cow is an animal and the overwhelming majority also including a seagull in that category. However, except for college biology majors, about a quarter of our subjects failed to include the fish and a third to a half omitted the butterfly. None of the participants included the pine or mushroom.

These findings gave us our first insight into the problems students have in learning concepts of animal classification. It appeared that many learners undergeneralize the concept; that is, they seem to subscribe to a limited or highly restricted view of the animal kingdom.

To probe this question further, we asked our subjects simply to list the names of 10 animals. To our amazement about two-thirds of them listed only vertebrates. Furthermore, the large majority of subjects included 6 or more mammals and at least 1 bird on their list. Interestingly these responses did not vary as a function of age or grade level. The most common animals listed at all grade levels were cat, dog, bird, cow, and horse—typical pets and farm animals.

We then asked our participants to define the term *animal*, and again the responses seemed to confirm our hypothesis that learners have a restricted understanding of its meaning. However, in this task we did discover some age-related differences. For example, the elementary and middle school students were more likely to include *appendages* in their definitions than high school and college students (i.e., "Animals have legs"). On the other hand, older students mentioned *respiration* and *reproduction* more frequently (i.e., "Animals breathe;" "Animals have babies"). Other frequently mentioned traits did not vary by grade level ("Animals move"; "Animals have hair or fur"; "Animals live outside or in the woods").

On the basis of these findings we concluded that for many learners of every age group the concept *animal* has a much narrower meaning than that assigned to it by biologists. The label "animal" is used almost exclusively in reference to common *vertebrates*, especially to mammals and birds. But what do these students actually know about vertebrates? For example, how well do they differentiate between vertebrates and invertebrates? These questions became the focus of our remaining inquiries.

Which Animals Have a Backbone?   To address this question we presented our subjects with a set of line drawings depicting common vertebrates (penguin, whale, bat, snake) and invertebrates (crayfish, spider). The task was simply to identify those animals that have a backbone. Two follow-up items posed similar problems but in verbal rather than pictorial form.

In response to the pictorial task, the overwhelming majority (80% or better) at every grade level recognized the penguin and whale as *vertebrates*. A somewhat smaller proportion included the bat in that group. However, the snake was included by fewer than one in five of the elementary-school children, by about half of the secondary students and fewer than two-thirds of the college biology majors. Similarly the crayfish was judged to be a vertebrate by some 40% of the elementary and middle school students, dropping to 5% among college majors. Only a small number (10% or less) of students suggested that a spider has a backbone.

The verbal tasks revealed comparable results. For example, the turtle was judged to be an *invertebrate* by more than a quarter of the subjects, the snake by more than a third and the eel by more than a half. By contrast, the vast majority recognized the mammals (human, mouse, seal) and the bird (owl) as vertebrates and the earthworm and snail as invertebrates.

Taken as a whole, these findings seemed to suggest that learners of all ages differentiate between vertebrates and invertebrates largely on the basis of conspicuous external morphological attributes, such as segmentation, body covering, appendages, and overall body shape and perceived texture. Furthermore, it appears that students consider and weigh ambiguous and conflicting pieces of information, ultimately arriving at a decision based on the relative size or perceived importance of body parts. Accordingly, the eel and the snake are classified as invertebrates by virtue of their long, slender, limbless bodies and absence of obvious external segmentation, while the turtle is also an invertebrate because of its prominent shell. Likewise certain invertebrates, such as the crayfish, are misclassified as a result of pronounced segmentation and oversized appendages.

In a final series of questions we provided our subjects with lists of examples and nonexamples of five major vertebrate classes. Their task was to identify the *fish*, *amphibians*, *reptiles*, *birds*, and *mammals*. The student responses suggested a wide range of alternative conceptions, which seemed to stem from linguistic, perceptual, and associative properties of the organisms. Cross-age comparisons suggested that many of these conceptual difficulties are overcome as students progress through the school years; others are considerably more tenacious.

Among the difficulties that students seem to overcome is the tendency to categorize all aquatic organisms as *fish*, including the whale and the seal, but especially those commonly labeled "fish" such as the starfish and jellyfish. On the other hand, the tenacious problems include labeling the turtle an *amphibian* and the penguin a *mammal*. Presumably the former is a product of familiarity with terrestrial and aquatic species. The latter may result from the penguin's short, squat stature, its inability to fly, the abundance of down feathers (which resemble fur) and the ecogeographical association with the antarctic seal.

Children's Cardiovascular Concepts

This study grew out of a previous investigation by Catherall (1981), who interviewed 32 Canadian schoolchildren about concepts of the human cardiovascular system. Building on Catherall's work, we asked fourth-grade children and college first-year students to develop concept maps displaying their knowledge of the cardiovascular system. Using the maps as a point of departure, we subsequently interviewed each of them.

Based on the interview responses, a paper-and-pencil instrument was developed and administered to subjects in the 5th, 8th, and 10th grades and the freshman/sophomore college years. The following questions and answers summarize our findings.

What Does Blood Look Like?   The interviews revealed four alternative conceptions of the structure of blood. These alternatives were presented to our subjects in the form of an illustrated multiple-choice question. The students were asked to select the picture that most closely resembles their own idea of the structure of blood as seen through a microscope.

Almost two-thirds of the elementary–school children chose the picture depicting blood as simply a *red liquid.* This did not surprise us, since most children of this age have neither observed blood with the aid of a microscope nor received formal instruction on it. Accordingly, the children had only their "perceptual knowledge" upon which to base their responses.

The popularity of this response dropped sharply, however, at higher grade levels, and in its place emerged two additional ideas; that blood is made of *cells suspended in a red liquid,* and that it consists of *red cells lacking an intercellular liquid.* Each of these notions implies the assimilation of the concept "cells," but neither includes an understanding of "plasma," the straw-colored liquid in which the cells are suspended.

It appeared that older students were attempting to reconcile their perceptual knowledge (that blood is a red liquid) with their school-based knowledge (that blood contains cells). As a result, these students *constructed* idiosyncratic hybrids, which, based on cross-age comparisons, seem to be remarkably intransigent, accounting for more than half of the college-age responses.

At this point it began to look as though our subjects subscribed to a set of well-defined ideas about the structural characteristics of blood. Accordingly, we then directed their attention to the functions of blood.

What Does Blood Do?   In order to probe this issue, we asked our subjects to explain why blood is important to the body. In response, the vast majority of the elementary-school children provided general, vitalistic explanations; "it keeps you alive " "it keeps you going." Interestingly, this type of response also characterized almost half of the middle school and high school students, dropping to a fourth of our college-age subjects.

As the vitalistic responses declined several functional responses emerged. The most common functions assigned to the blood were *oxygen transport,* followed by *transport of nutrients.* These responses increased steadily across grade levels, suggesting an incremental shift toward the scientifically acceptable view.

Turning their attention away from blood, we then queried our subjects about the structure and function of the heart.

What Does the Heart Look Like Inside? We presented the students with several illustrations and then asked them to select the one that looked most like their own understanding of the inner structure of the heart. At the elementary-school level a *three-chambered,* amphibian-like heart was the most frequently chosen (40%). This heart, which bears the closest resemblance to a "valentine," was also picked by no fewer than a quarter of all subjects at successive grade levels.

Among middle and high school students the *three and four-chambered* hearts were chosen in equal numbers, while college students preferred the four-chambered over the three-chambered heart in a ratio of 2:1. Interestingly 10% of all our participants opted for a *solid* heart traversed by tubes.

These findings seemed to imply that students progress toward a scientifically acceptable view of heart structure as they move through the school years. However, our interviews had revealed an interesting phenomenon. While many college students apparently subscribe to a four-chambered heart, few can explain the significance of the right and left sides of the heart. Apparently many students have little understanding of how the heart's structure relates to its function.

What Does the Heart Do? In response to a multiple-choice question, the majority (65–80%) of students at every grade level seemed to understand that the heart pumps blood. Strikingly, however, as many as one-third of them ascribed additional functions to the heart, including cleaning, filtering, making and storing blood. Furthermore, these students were remarkably confident of their responses, with 85% or more suggesting that they were "sure" or "very sure."

Probing further into this issue we discovered that, with the exception of college biology majors, fewer than one-third understood that the right heart pumps deoxygenated blood, while the left pumps oxygenated blood. More than 20% of the middle and high school students suggested that dirty blood is pumped by one side and clean blood by the other. Many students simply dismissed the concept of a double pump altogether.

We now think that some of these notions have their origins in oversimplified explanations offered by teachers, television commentators, and journalists. For example, in a syndicated article by Hochman (1982), appearing in a Sunday supplement, the author informs us that the heart, "pumps blood, which is rich in oxygen and other nutrients, to all parts of the body." No mention is made of the right heart or its role in the pulmonary circulation. To investigate this further, we asked our subjects about the path taken by a drop of blood in its journey through the body.

Where Does Blood Go After It Leaves the Heart? Students were asked to

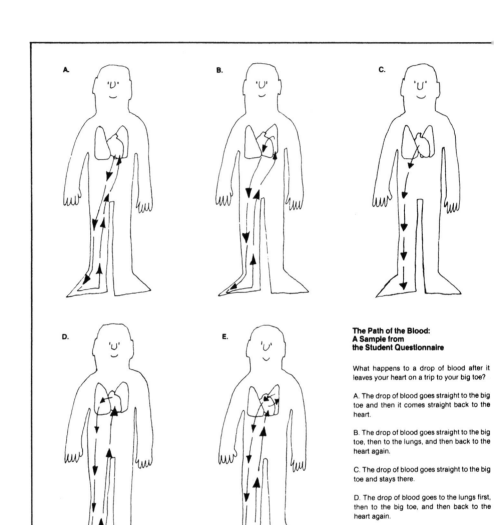

The Path of the Blood:
A Sample from
the Student Questionnaire

What happens to a drop of blood after it leaves your heart on a trip to your big toe?

A. The drop of blood goes straight to the big toe and then it comes straight back to the heart.

B. The drop of blood goes straight to the big toe, then to the lungs, and then back to the heart again.

C. The drop of blood goes straight to the big toe and stays there.

D. The drop of blood goes to the lungs first, then to the big toe, and then back to the heart again.

E. The drop of blood goes straight to the big toe, then back to the heart, then to the lungs, and then back to the heart again.

FIG. 8.1.   Where does blood go after it leaves the heart? A sample item from the inventory of cardiovascular concepts. From: Arnaudin, M. W., & Mintzes, J. The cardiovascular system: Children's conceptions and misconceptions. *Science and Children,* 1986, *23*(5). Copyright 1986 by Katy Kelly. Reprinted with permission.

select from several illustrations the one which looks most like their own understanding of the route taken by a drop of blood to a body part (Fig. 8.1). The most frequently chosen pattern at the elementary, middle and high school levels (heart–toe–heart) suggested adherence to a *systemic circulatory pattern* only. Interestingly, a significant proportion of elementary students chose a one-way (heart–toe) pattern, while college students tended to include the lungs enroute to or from a body part other than the heart. Only a small number of students (15% or less) subscribed to a double (systemic and pulmonary) pattern of blood flow.

Probing the issue of the pulmonary circulation further, we asked the students to select from several illustrations showing "where air goes after you breathe it in." In response, some 30%–45% of them suggested that air tubes carry it either to the heart or to other body parts. Others claimed that air taken into the lungs is simply expelled without distribution to body parts. Responses such as these imply that many students see no vital, blood-borne connection between the circulatory and respiratory systems and therefore have no need to postulate a pulmonary circulation.

The final issue we wished to explore was the notion of an open versus a closed circulation. *What happens to blood when it gets to a body part?* Our interviews had revealed four alternative conceptions in this area. Accordingly, students were asked to select from four illustrations depicting: a completely open system, a completely closed system, a partly open system (some blood remains in the vessels and some leaves to bathe the cells), and a quasiclosed system (blood leaves vessels but is confined to the interior of cells).

The most popular responses at all levels were the partly open and the quasiclosed models, together accounting for half to two-thirds of the answers. The scientifically acceptable (closed) model was chosen by fewer than 20% of the students. No differences were found in the pattern of these responses across grade levels, suggesting a set of tenacious misconceptions underlying students' understanding of the circulatory system.

Children's Concepts of Photosynthesis

The tapestry of life is woven out of thin air by sunlight. Botanist Daniel Arnon (1982) says that photosynthesis "eminently merits its distinction as the most important biochemical process on earth." Yet, until recently, photosynthesis was a mystery even to scientists. Today, virtually all elementary-school children learn how plants manufacture their own food by fixing carbon dioxide in the presence of sunlight and generating oxygen as a waste product.

This study built on previous work by Martin (1979) and by Lavender and Anderson (1982), who documented a number of misconceptions held by fifth graders and college students about photosynthesis. Accordingly, we decided to probe the following issues: What are the functions of soil, water, and carbon dioxide in plant growth and nutrition? What is the role of plants in the carbon cycle? What is the role of the leaf in photosynthesis?

Following a number of exploratory interviews, a paper-and-pencil instrument was developed and then administered to some 1,400 pupils in grades 5, 8, 11, and 14 (college sophomores). The instrument itself was composed of 12 tasks that were designed to reveal alternative conceptions through the use of illustrations in combination with forced-choice and free-response questions.

What Are the Functions of Soil, Water and Carbon Dioxide in Plant Growth and Nutrition?   We began to probe these issues by presenting our subjects with a variation on Van Helmont's classic 17th-century willow tree experiment. Van Helmont planted a 5-pound willow tree in 200 pounds of soil and permitted the tree to grow for 5 years. He then extracted a 164-pound tree and found that the soil had *not* lost weight. Van Helmont concluded that plants *do not* derive their food from the soil. Unfortunately his conclusion, that water is the source of plant growth, is equally inaccurate.

Presenting our subjects with a comparable problem, we first asked them whether the soil would lose weight, gain weight, or remain the same. In response, we found one fourth of the elementary-school children and about a third of the middle and high school students suggesting that the soil would *lose* weight. About one in six college students agreed.

When asked to explain their answers the students provided a set of revealing justifications. Scott, a fifth grader, put it simply, "Because the soil is the plant's food and without it a plant couldn't live." Vance, an eighth grader, said, "Because the plant ate minerals (food) from the soil. That's why the plant got big." A college sophomore, John, suggested that, "The plant sucked out all the proteins and minerals of the soil. This loss was not replaced."

The number of students who selected the scientifically acceptable (same weight) response increased substantially at successive grade levels, accounting for a fourth of the elementary school children, two-thirds of the high school pupils and 80% of the college sophomores. Interestingly however, the rationale provided by our subjects suggested that many of them experienced the same difficulty as Van Helmont. Said Donn, an eighth grader, "the soil had nothing to do with the plant. The water made the plant grow." Equally revealing was 11-grader Kevin's explanation: "The soil is moist from the water and the plant feeds on the water."

Curiously almost half of the elementary-school children and about one-fifth of the middle school students suggested that the soil would *gain* weight. The explanations indicated several problems. Some assumed that the soil was still wet when reweighed; others assumed the roots were still in the soil; still others thought the plant put food into the soil as it grew. A number of children indicated that they had misread the question.

We further probed the issue of plant nutrition in a subsequent item, asking our subjects "where most of the food of plants comes from." To our amazement more than 60% of the elementary and secondary students and about half of the college students said the *soil*.

Brenda, a fifth grader, told us that "the soil has bits of food in it and the roots find it and eat it." An eleventh grader, Wendy, explained that, "the food has got to come from the soil or people wouldn't spend so much money on fertilizer." Marti, a college sophomore, asserted that, "the roots are what sends food to the rest of the plant. The roots get food from the soil."

Fewer than 10% of all subjects suggested that plants manufacture food from carbon dioxide. One thoughtful college student, Matthew, suggested that, "the plants use CO_2 to produce sugars in photosynthesis. But wouldn't a better answer have been sunlight?"

Turning their attention away from nutrition, we then queried our subjects about the interdependence of plants and animals in the carbon cycle. *What is the role of plants in the carbon cycle?*

In a variation on Priestley's well-known "mouse in a jar" experiment, subjects were presented with an illustrated sequence suggesting that a mouse placed in a closed container would soon die. They were then asked to predict what would happen if a plant were placed in the container along with a mouse.

Except for the college students, about one-third of our subjects claimed that *both* the mouse and the plant would die. Many of our youngest participants suggested that food is the limiting factor at work. For example, David reminded us that, "you did not say you would refill his container of food or water the plant." Older students such as Craig, an eleventh grader, focused on oxygen; "The plant would not be able to produce enough oxygen to supply the mouse's quick metabolism. The mouse would die and the plant would die somewhat later."

A small proportion of students suggested that the plant would live but the mouse would die. A fifth grader, Casey, seemed to suggest that oxygen is a limiting factor for the mouse and sunlight for the plant: "because mice don't live underwater, and the plant has sunlight."

Again, the frequency of scientifically acceptable responses (*both live*) increased at successive grade levels, accounting for about one-third of the elementary, half of the secondary, and two-thirds of the college students. One fifth grader, Brent, explained it this way: "Well see if there is a plant the mouse will [live] because what the mouse breaths is the plant's food. And what the plant gives off the mouse can live on." Dan, an eleventh grader, provided a similar explanation, "The mouse gives off something so the plant can grow and the plant gives off something for the mouse to live."

Our final inquiry addressed the relationship of structure and function in plant nutrition. *What is the role of the leaf in photosynthesis?* We probed this issue with a forced-choice question, telling our subjects that most plants have leaves and then posing the question, "What is the main job of a leaf?"

The majority of students at every grade level accurately responded that leaves *make food.* This response characterized about half of the elementary-school children, some two-thirds of the secondary pupils, and 80% of the college students. Two additional responses that received substantial support were: leaves *catch the rain,* and leaves *capture the warmth of the sun.* Least support was given to the notion that leaves *shade the tender young shoots* of plants from the hot sun.

Responses to this question underscore a common finding in studies of children's biology; namely, that children often subscribe to contradictory beliefs (*leaves make food/food comes from the soil*), experiencing little in the way of cognitive dissonance. Fig. 8.2 summarizes a dozen of the most common misconceptions about photosynthesis. The original study uncovered 31 such problem areas (Wandersee, 1983).

Reflecting briefly on the *source* of these alternative views, we have come to believe that many have their origins in common language usage demonstrating a tendency among children and adults to attribute human traits to plants. A young mother might tell her child to "give the houseplants a drink." A garden shop sells fertilizers labeled "plant food."

Additionally, youngsters often dismiss things they cannot see as nonexistent. Since gases (carbon dioxide and oxygen) play a critical role in photosynthesis, the "commonsense explanations" children *construct* tend to build on the clearly observable: fertilizer, soil, and water.

CHILDREN'S BIOLOGY IN TEACHING

Our view of the educative process is constrained by two basic assumptions that define the working roles of students and teachers. The first of these assumptions is that *learners actively construct meanings* as they seek to make sense of their physical and biological surroundings. In so doing they generate links between sensory information and relevant aspects of prior knowledge. As we have seen, the meanings that learners construct are frequently at variance with those held by the scientific community and furthermore they are often stubbornly intractable, at least when confronted by conventional instruction.

The second assumption is that successful science teachers are *agents of conceptual change.* Their role is to assist students as they actively restructure meanings into forms that more closely approximate the scientifically acceptable view. This type of conceptual change teaching is intellectually demanding,

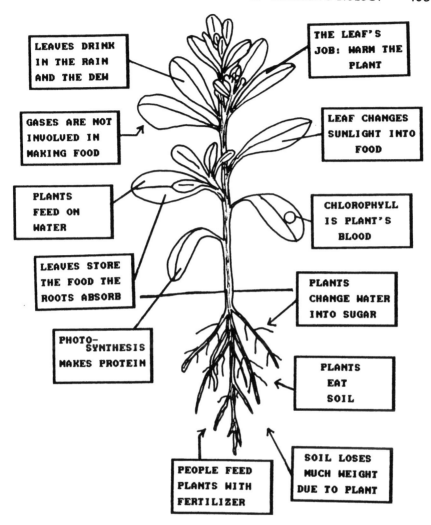

FIG. 8.2.   Children's concepts of photosynthesis. A dozen of the most common misconceptions.

requiring in-depth knowledge of the discipline and a broad understanding of children's thinking patterns. Rosalind Driver (1987) summarized the issue well:

> The teacher's role . . . becomes much more complex than a manager of a "delivery system." As a mediator between scientists' knowledge and children's understanding the teacher is required to act as a diagnostician of children's thinking and at the same time to carry a map in his/her head of the conceptual

domain which enables appropriate activities to be suggested and meanings negotiated.

When students and teachers perform their roles successfully the product is a state of *shared meaning* (Novak, 1981), a kind of congruence of mind. But how to effect such a state?

Over the past decade several workers, notably Driver and Oldham (1986), Erickson (1979), Hewson (1981), and Nussbaum and Novick (1982), have elucidated elements of an intervention strategy aimed at facilitating the transition from children's science to scientists' science. We present these elements now, in modified form, along with examples from our own work on children's biology.

Formulating and Sharing Conceptual Objectives

The notion that teachers should explicitly identify the desired outcomes of instruction is certainly an important contribution of the behaviorist school (Mager, 1962). At the time it was felt that understanding could not be measured directly, but only *inferred* by observing changes in student behavior. We believe, however, that recently developed techniques such as *concept mapping* (Novak & Gowin, 1984) can provide a direct and reasonably accurate picture of understandings held by students and teachers. Accordingly, we plan our lessons and begin our instruction by developing and presenting concept maps which display our own view of the biological domain in question and exemplify the outcomes we hope to encourage (Arnaudin, Mintzes, Dunn, & Shafer, 1984).

The concept map (Fig. 8.3) is a two-dimensional representation that depicts the most important concepts of a domain and the relationships among those concepts. As such it provides a kind of road map that guides instruction and, when presented to students, serves as an "advance organizer" of further learning.

Engaging Students in Multisensory Experiences

Students of all ages benefit from direct, "hands-on" experiences with living things. And so, at the outset of our lesson sequences we provide opportunities for students to "mess around" with the objects and events that are central to the concepts we wish them to learn. The purpose of this "experiential maneuver" (Erickson, 1979) is twofold. It provides a rich, varied and intensely personal matrix of prior knowledge; the "raw material" for constructing meanings. It also focuses students' attention and arouses curiosity in the domain we have targeted.

In our lessons on animal classification we try to provide opportunities for

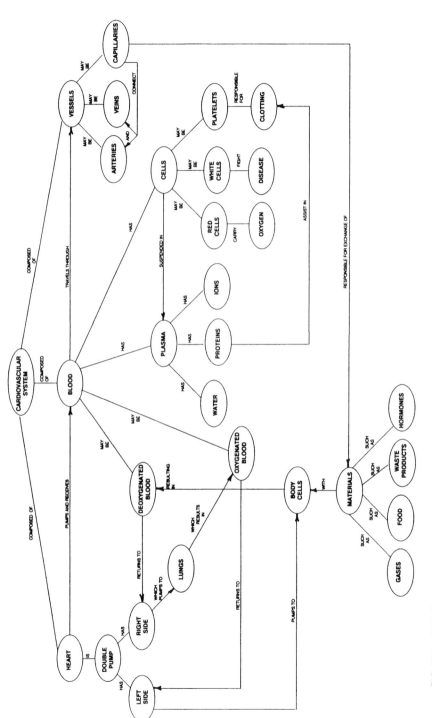

FIG. 8.3. Defining conceptual objectives. Part of a concept map depicting desired outcomes of a lesson sequence on the human cardiovascular system.

students to observe animals in their natural habitats; to collect specimens; handle, inspect, and care for several organisms, and compare and contrast animals using simplified criteria.

Lessons on the cardiovascular system begin with a slide/tape presentation of frog anatomy. This exercise is followed by a frog dissection with particular attention to comparing three- and four-chambered hearts and the pulmonary and systemic circulation.

We introduce our lessons on photosynthesis with a trip to a local greenhouse and a classroom activity in which students plant their own gallon-jar terraria, seal the mouths with plastic wrap, and observe plants growing in such a closed system

Eliciting and Clarifying Student Ideas

Perhaps the most novel component of conceptual change teaching is the provision for eliciting and clarifying student ideas. The consensus of opinion is that students' alternative conceptions, especially those that are well entrenched, must be externalized before they can be addressed. In this sense, science learning as science itself, is best promoted in the light of public scrutiny, amid the clash of opposing viewpoints. In order to accomplish this "externalizing" function we have enlisted a combination of clinical interviews and small group activities that focus on key concepts in the target domain.

For the beginning teacher who may be less familiar with students' ideas, the interview provides a flexible tool for probing cognitive structure. In a typical class of some 30 students, interviews with three or four individuals of varying ability levels can provide a wealth of insight into students' thinking patterns. The interviews need not be lengthy (15–20 minutes) and should contain open-ended questions that encourage divergent responses. Questioning is most revealing when it progresses from most inclusive concepts to least inclusive concepts and when it asks students to explain or justify their responses.

In our interviews on animal classification, we begin by asking our students to name five animals and to explain why each is an animal. These probes are followed by progressively more demanding ones: What do you mean by the word "animal"? How is an animal different from a plant? Can you name five animals with a backbone? Does a _____ have a backbone? How do you know? Can you name five animals without a backbone? Does a _____ lack a backbone? How do you know?

Experienced teachers who are more familiar with students' alternative viewpoints may devise forced-choice inventories (Fig. 8.1), which can be administered individually or, better yet, to small groups working cooperatively. We have found that groups of three to four students provide an optimal environment for the exchange of ideas.

Once the alternative views have been identified they are summarized on a posterboard and displayed prominently in the classroom. The teacher then calls on individuals to explain their ideas and provide a brief justification for them. Subsequently, class members are invited to comment on and argue for the strengths and weaknesses of each interpretation. During these class discussions the teacher serves as moderator and facilitator.

Activities such as these, which expose students' ideas to open criticism, can be extraordinary threatening. To avoid undermining students' confidence teachers must be unusually sensitive to the diversity of viewpoints that students express. They must also foster a similar attitude in class members by cultivating an atmosphere in which all ideas are deemed worthy of consideration.

Knowing something of the history of science can be helpful in this regard. We have found that students are reassured to discover that some of their ideas, though not currently acceptable to modern science, have a long and honored tradition in the development of present-day understandings (Wandersee, 1986).

Restructuring Student Ideas

The centerpiece and most critical phase of conceptual change teaching is the restructuring component. It is here that new meanings are built as learners make and break linkages among existing concepts and invent or import new concepts.

In her excellent review of the Children's Learning in Science Project at the University of Leeds, England, Rosalind Driver (1987) discussed teaching maneuvers that have been used to promote conceptual change. Focusing on selected problems in children's biology, we briefly illustrate how several of these techniques may be used in restructuring student ideas.

Animal Classification.   Students display several kinds of conceptual difficulties in classifying animals. Among these difficulties is the tendency to undergeneralize certain concepts (*Animals* are furry creatures). In instances such as these restructuring is aimed, as Driver has suggested, at "broadening the range of application of a concept." In other instances, students apparently overgeneralize or fail to discriminate between closely related concepts. (Turtles are *amphibians*). In these instances the aim of instruction is "differentiation of a conception."

We have found that both kinds of problems may be addressed by providing opportunities for students to classify living or preserved specimens while offering immediate feedback. In our work with young children we set up a large table with vertebrate and invertebrate specimens and ask children to sort them into two boxes labeled "Animals" and "Not Animals." After several children have sorted the specimens and recorded their responses, we intervene by suggesting that all of the specimens belong in the "Animals" box. At this point a lively interaction ensues as children seek to justify their responses and we focus attention on the critical attributes of the concept *animal*.

In subsequent lessons we ask children to sort specimens into boxes labeled "Animals with Backbones"/"Animals without Backbones"; "Amphibians"/ "Reptiles," and "Birds"/"Mammals." The goal is to help children develop a "mental model" of each concept as they practice skills of discrimination and generalization.

Cardiovascular System.   Students of virtually every age group have difficulty understanding the concept of a *closed system* of circulation. Our interviews revealed that the difficulty is traceable to a deeper, more fundamental set of problems.   Driver has suggested that it is necessary sometimes to "unpack a conceptual problem" before it can be addressed directly.

When we "unpack" the concept of a *closed system* we see that it depends on an understanding of the metabolic requirements of the cell, the nature of the extracellular compartment, the processes of diffusion and osmosis, the structure of capillaries and the composition of blood.   Accordingly, in our lesson sequence we "progressively shape a conception" of a closed system by focusing initially on the diffusion of metabolites in the simple *Amoeba*. From there we move to the "special problems" confronting higher, multicellular organisms (i.e., the cells are not in direct contact with the environment, so a transport system is required).   This leads ultimately to a consideration of capillaries and the movement of substances into and out of these vessels.

The lesson sequence is punctuated at the beginning with an opportunity to observe phagocytosis (i.e., "cell-eating") in *Amoeba,* and again at the end with a chance to observe capillary blood flow in the web of a frog's foot.

Photosynthesis.   The notion that plants obtain their food from exogenous sources (soil, water, or light) appears to be one of the most persistent in children's biology.   Our approach, similar to that of Driver, has been to acknowledge students' ideas, to suggest that scientists have a different one, and then to present the "alternative model."

We think that the notion of autotrophic nutrition is best understood when it is introduced as a conceptual bridge between lessons on energy flow in ecosystems and animal digestion.   In this way the plant is viewed in its ecological context as a natural energy transducer; the ultimate provider of all food and energy, and the primary source of oxygen in natural systems.

A simple experiment our students perform dramatically reveals the leaf as the food manufacturing organ of the plant and demonstrates the requirement of sunlight for photosynthesis. The students are told that plants make food and store it in the form of starch. They then take one plant (a geranium is good) and place it in a sunny window for 3 days. A second plant is placed in a dark closet for 3 days, where its store of starch is quickly depleted. A leaf from each plant is then placed in a boiling alcohol bath for 10 minutes to remove the plant pigments. To test for the presence of starch, a drop of iodine is placed on each leaf. A positive test (leaf turns dark purple or black) is seen in the "light" plant but not in the "dark" plant. (We recommend that a hotplate be used to heat the alcohol, and that the procedure be carried out in a well-ventilated area to avoid inhalation of potentially hazardous fumes.)

We wish to close with the words of Charles Darwin, who reminds us of the difficulties encountered by those who seek to foster conceptual change in biology. Having spent the better part of his life mustering evidence in support of evolution, he tells us, in *The Origin of Species* (1859), of his frustrating attempts to convince his peers:

> I by no means expect to convince experienced naturalists whose minds are stocked with a multitude of facts all viewed during a long course of years, from a point of view directly opposite to mine . . . . A few naturalists endowed with much flexibility of mind . . . may be influenced by this volume; but I look with confidence to the future—to young and rising naturalists who will be able to view both sides of the question with impartiality.

Perhaps impartiality is too much to ask for in our students as it is in our colleagues. However, if conceptual change teaching fails to move students toward scientifically acceptable views, at least we have planted the seeds of change that are likely to germinate, in subsequent encounters with biology.

ACKNOWLEDGMENTS

This research was supported, in part, by a grant from the Faculty Research and Development Fund of the University of North Carolina at Wilmington.

We gratefully acknowledge the encouragement of Dr. Joseph D. Novak, who stimulated our interest in children's biology.

REFERENCES

Arnaudin, M. W., & Mintzes, J. J. (1985). Students' alternative conceptions of the human circulatory system: A cross-age study. *Science Education, 69* (5), 721–733.

Arnaudin, M. W., & Mintzes, J. J. (1986). The cardiovascular system: Children's conceptions and misconceptions. *Science and Children, 23* (5), 48–51.

Arnaudin, M. W., Mintzes, J. J., Dunn, C. S., & Shafer, T. H. (1984). Concept mapping in college science teaching. *Journal of College Science Teaching, 14* (2), 117–121.

Arnon, D. I. (1982). Sunlight, earth life. *Sciences, 22* (7), 22–27.

Ausubel, D. P., Novak, J. D., & Hanesian, H. (1978). *Educational psychology: A cognitive view.* New York: Holt, Rinehart, & Winston.

Bell, B. F. (1981). When is an animal not an animal? *Journal of Biological Education, 15*(3), 213–218.

Brumby, M. (1979). Problems in learning the concept of natural selection. *Journal of Biological Education, 13* (2),119–122.

Brumby, M. (1982). Students' perceptions of the concept of life. *Science Education, 66*(4), 613–622.

Brumby, M. (1984). Misconceptions about the concept of natural selection by medical biology students. *Science Education, 68* (4), 493–503.

Carey, S. (1987). *Conceptual change in childhood.* Cambridge, MA: MIT Press.

Catherall, R. W. (1981). *Children's beliefs about the human circulatory system.* Master's thesis, University of British Columbia, Vancouver.

Clough, E. E., & Wood-Robinson, C. (1985). Children's understanding of inheritance. *Journal of Biological Education, 19* (4), 304–310.

Darwin, C. (1859). *On the origin of species.* London: John Murray.

Deadman, J. A., & Kelly, P. J. (1978). What do secondary school boys understand about evolution and heredity before they are taught the topics? *Journal of Biological Education, 12* (1), 7–15.

Driver, R. (1987). Promoting conceptual change in classroom settings: The experience of the children's learning in science project. In J. D. Novak (Ed.), *Proceedings of the second international seminar on misconceptions and educational strategies in science and mathematics.* Ithaca, NY: Cornell University.

Driver, R., & Oldham, V. (1986). A constructivist approach to curriculum development in science. *Studies in Science Education, 13,* 105–122.

Erickson, G. L. (1979). Children's conceptions of heat and temperature. *Science Education, 63*(2), 221–230.

Gellert, E. (1962). Children's conceptions of the content and structure of the human body. *Genetic Psychology Monographs, 65,* 293–405.

Hewson, P. W. (1981). A conceptual change approach to learning science. *European Journal of Science Education, 3*(4), 383–396.

Hochman, G. (1982). Bypass surgery: The heart of the matter. *Family Weekly,* May 30. Wilmington, NC: Wilmington Star News.

Jahoda, G. (1958). Child animism I: A critical survey of cross–cultural research. *Journal of Social Psychology, 47,* 197–212.

Johnson, C. N., & Wellman, H. M. (1982). Children's developing conceptions of the mind and brain. *Child Development, 53,* 222–234.

Jungwirth, E. (1975). Preconceived adaptation and inverted evolution (a case of distorted concept formation in high school biology). *Australian Science Teachers Journal, 21*(2), 95–100.

Kargbo, D. B., Hobbs, E. D., & Erickson, G. L. (1980). Children's beliefs about inherited characteristics. *Journal of Biological Education, 14* (2), 137–146.

Kreitler, H., & Kreitler, S. (1966). Children's concepts of sexuality and birth. *Child Development, 37,* 363–378.

Lavender, J., & Anderson, A. (1982). *Student responses to respiration, photosynthesis and nutrition* (BS 202 Working Paper No. 3). Unpublished manuscript, Michigan State University, East Lansing, MI.

Mager, R. F. (1962). *Preparing instructional objectives.* Belmont, CA: Lear Siegler, Inc./Fearon Publishers.

Martin, F. L. (1979). *The development of an instrument for determining botanically related misconceptions of beginning college botany students.* Unpublished PhD dissertation, University of Southern Mississippi, Hattiesburg.

Mintzes, J. J. (1984). Naive theories in biology: Children's concepts of the human body. *School Science and Mathematics, 84* (7), 548–555.

Mintzes, J. J. (1989). The acquisition of biological knowledge during childhood: An alternative conception. *Journal of Research in Science Teaching, 26*(9), 823–824.

Mintzes, J. J., & Arnaudin, M. W. (1984). *Children's biology: A review of research on conceptual development in the life sciences.* ERIC Document Reproduction Service No. ED 249 044.

Mintzes, J. J., & Trowbridge, J. E. (1987). Alternative frameworks in animal classification. In J. D. Novak (Ed.), *Proceedings of the second international seminar on misconceptions and educational strategies in science and mathematics.* Ithaca, NY: Cornell University.

Moore, J. E., & Kendall, D. C. (1971). Children's concepts of reproduction. *Journal of Sex Research, 7*, 42–61.

Nagy, M. H. (1953). Children's conceptions of some bodily functions. *Journal of Genetic Psychology, 83*, 199–216.

Natadze, R. G. (1963). The mastery of scientific concepts in school. In B. Simon & J. Simon (Eds.), *Educational Psychology in the USSR.* London: Routledge & Kegan Paul.

Neuberger, H. T. (1966). Conceptualizations of change held by ten and eleven year old children. *Journal of Research in Science Teaching, 4*(3), 180–181.

Novak, J. D. (1981). Applying learning psychology and philosophy of science to biology teaching. *American Biology Teacher, 43*(1), 12–20.

Novak, J. D., & Gowin, D. B. (1984). *Learning how to learn.* Cambridge, England: Cambridge University Press.

Nussbaum, J., & Novick, S. (1982). Alternative frameworks, conceptual conflict and accommodation: Toward a principled teaching strategy. *Instructional Science, 11*, 183–200.

Piaget, J. (1929). *The child's conception of the world.* New York: Harcourt Brace.

Porter, C. S. (1974). Grade school children's perceptions of their internal body parts. *Nursing Research, 23*(5), 384–391.

Resnick, L. B. (1983). Mathematics and science learning: A new conception. *Science, 220*, 477–478.

Russell, R. W., & Dennis, W. (1941). Note concerning the procedure employed in investigating child animism. *Journal of Genetic Psychology, 58*, 423–424.

Ryman, D. (1974). Children's understanding of the classification of living organisms. *Journal of Biological Education, 8*, 219–223.

Schilder, P., & Wechsler, D. (1935). What do children know about the interior of the body? *International Journal of Psychoanalysis, 16*, 355–360.

Trowbridge, J. E., & Mintzes, J. J. (1985). Students' alternative conceptions of animals and animal classification. *School Science and Mathematics, 85*(4), 304–316.

Trowbridge, J. E., & Mintzes, J. J. (1988). Alternative conceptions in animal classification: A cross-age study. *Journal of Research in Science Teaching, 25*(7), 547–571.

Wandersee, J. H. (1983). Students' misconceptions about photosynthesis: A cross-age study. In H. Helms & J. D. Novak (Eds.), *Proceedings of the international seminar on misconceptions in science and mathematics.* Ithaca, NY: Cornell University.

Wandersee, J. H. (1986). Can the history of science help science educators anticipate students' misconceptions? *Journal of Research in Science Teaching, 23*(7), 581–597.

Wandersee, J. H., Mintzes, J. J., & Arnaudin, M. W. (1987). Children's biology: A content analysis of conceptual development in the life sciences. In J. D. Novak (Ed.), *Proceedings of the second international seminar on misconceptions and educational strategies in science and mathematics.* Ithaca, NY: Cornell University.

Wandersee, J. H., Mintzes, J. J., & Arnaudin, M. W. (1989). Biology from the learners viewpoint: A content analysis of the research literature. *School Science and Mathematics, 89*(8), 654–668.

Williamson, P. A. (1981). The effects of methodology and level of development on children's animistic thought. *Journal of Genetic Psychology, 138,* 159–174.

III METHODS AND MEDIA FOR LEARNING SCIENCE

9 Science Activities, Process Skills, and Thinking

Michael J. Padilla
University of Georgia

The word activity, over the years, has become synonymous with those things that are good in science education. New science teachers leave teacher education programs ready to change the system, to call on the mystical powers involved in activity-oriented science. Publishers promote their textbooks and programs as "activity-centered," often with little regard to actual content. Professional journals support activities through first-person success stories and how-to-do-it articles. What is the rationale behind this "hands-on" approach? Why are activities considered more appropriate than other methods for achieving science objectives? Do certain kinds of activities contribute more to understanding of science than others? How does one change the curricular approach to stress process skills and thinking in science? These questions are a major focus of this chapter. After elaborating on several ways in which activities might positively affect learning, different kinds of activities will be defined and analyzed. Then one type—process skill activities—will be analyzed and illustrated in further detail.

ARGUMENTS FOR AN ACTIVITY APPROACH

Development of Logical Thought

Science educators have long employed arguments related to logical thinking for promoting science activities. Piagetian developmental theory became popular in science education circles during the 1960s and 70s, largely due to the close connection between the logic required to solve Piagetian tasks and the logic needed to be successful in science. In fact many of Piaget's original tasks were taken from science activities related to phenomena such as pendulums, buoyancy, and the behavior of light.

Research results regarding the onset and development of formal operational abilities reinforced the need for an activity-oriented curriculum. It was found that most students had not begun to develop formal abilities at age 11–12 as Piaget originally hypothesized (Chiapetta, 1976; Lovell, 1961). Renner, Grant, and Sutherland (1978) discovered that just 17% of the seventh graders and 23% of the eighth graders in their sample were operating at a formal level. More worrisome was the fact that only 34% of 12th graders had mastered the logic of formal thinking. Piaget himself (1972), reassessed his earlier work and hypothesized that his original subjects may have been a privileged group that displayed accelerated abilities.

These findings tended to explain the difficulties that many students had in learning the logic of science and caused educators to redouble efforts to promote logical thinking. The early, simplistic outgrowth of this work was an emphasis on acceleration of students from one stage to the next. "Our job was to teach students to use formal reasoning patterns, to move them into Piaget's formal operational period as quickly as possible" (Staver, 1986). What followed was failure. While many students were successfully trained to use a particular logical operation, what was learned was quickly forgotten and did not transfer to new problems or situations.

Constructivism

This early research into logical thinking began to focus more in the 1980s on the essential theme of Piaget's work, that knowledge is constructed by humans from previous knowledge and experience through interactions with the environment. Called constructivism, this view that children learn through activity that allows them to discover, internalize, and build their own understandings and meanings has emerged as a strong central treatise in science education today. It places the direct responsibility for learning on the learner's active construction of ideas. The role of the teacher in this kind of atmosphere is different from that in the traditional teacher-centered classroom. The teacher who believes in a constructivist approach realizes that knowledge cannot simply be transmitted to others, no matter how good that transmission is. For true learning to occur, the constructivist teacher believes, "It is absolutely necessary that learners have at their disposal concrete material experiences, and that they form their own active manipulations" (Piaget, in Schwebel & Raph, 1973, pp. ix–x.) Thus the teacher in this kind of classroom is more a facilitator and director than one who directly imparts information.

Physical and Emotional Nature of the Learner

The physical nature of the learner, especially during adolescent and early adolescent years, argues for an activity approach. Physical growth during this time is highly irregular. Muscular and body framework development often take place disproportionately, resulting in awkwardness and self consciousness. Increased physical activity is often a product of the typical high energy level of children this age. Thus, the physical aspects of moving and manipulation during an activity fit their developmental needs. Similar changes in early and midadolescence occur in the emotional nature of students. These students often manifest both adult and child-like behaviors in a short span of time. Self-assertion and independence are regularly mixed with insecurity and instability (Georgiady & Romano, 1977). Likewise, both young and old students continually learn how to interact with others by interacting with fellow students. Younger children learn new skills and older ones practice these skills in new situations. Activities can provide an important outlet for these energies and feelings. In addition, the group interaction can allow individuals to explore different roles among their peers, especially those involving leadership and cooperation.

Doing and Understanding

One of the most common justifications for promoting science activities in classrooms is embodied in the axiom:

> I hear ... and I forget
> I see ... and I remember
> I do ... and I understand
>
> —Ancient Chinese proverb quoted from *The ESS Reader* (Elementary Science Study, 1970).

The implied wisdom is that the learner will better understand and retain knowledge when firsthand, manipulative experience is possible. Students tend to remember what they do, especially if what they do is interesting to them. This seems reasonable, especially when an activity is performed in the proper context, with appropriate reinforcement. That is, activities appropriately connected to previous and future work can enhance knowledge acquisition.

Affective Goals—Success in Science

Certain affective goals also are better accomplished through an activity centered classroom. Activities can and should focus upon problems pertinent to the students' interests and needs. If designed in this fashion, then the boredom often seen in a teacher-centered, lecture-discussion classroom can be much less a problem. Also, activity science offers everyone a chance at being successful, even if only in a manipulative way. Young Johnny, not exactly the class scholar, can often share understandings gleaned from a more practical world that other more scholarly students find helpful in an activity. This success can help to form future positive feelings and attitudes toward science and even school in general. As Simpson (1979) states, "Success breeds success."

Promotion of Creative Thinking

Creativity has long been a goal of education. Yet the process of schooling great numbers of students in an organized fashion often precludes its promotion. Certain kinds of science activities can encourage this kind of thinking. Traditional science is often taught as a systematic acquisition of scientific knowledge. Creativity can be promoted by asking students to pose creative problems and propose their own methods for solving them. This approach requires a greater focus on individual students' ideas. It calls for a change in the atmosphere of the typical classroom to one in which student ideas are valued and pursued.

KINDS OF ACTIVITIES

Not all activities equally engage students intellectually. However, one major distinction is the instructional approach implied by the activity. Some simply direct students to follow directions, which, if heeded, result in the expected outcome. Others are more open-ended and demand student analysis of both the problem and the procedures used to solve the problem. A description of these extremes follows.

Recipe Labs

A recipe lab approach is one in which students perform a specified sequence of steps, much like those of a recipe for bread or a cake, to obtain a desired result. Often recipe labs are done in order to "prove" the truth involved in a statement made by a teacher or textbook. That is, after the text describes a phenomenon, lab work showing that phenomenon to be true follows.

Recipe lab work of this type is often criticized as promoting rote learning. It is likely that this type of activity does little to stimulate thinking and probably only serves to break up the boredom of listening to the teacher or reading the textbook. Thus recipe lab work meets the criteria of providing physical activity that matches students' energy needs, enhancing the potential for students remembering, and developing the potential for success. However, it promotes neither the development of logic nor creativity.

Open-ended Activities

On the other extreme are activities that begin with a question or problem and ask the students to participate in the solution. The procedures for solving the problem are not necessarily set and the answer is not known in advance. Posing potential solutions is one of the prime goals of these activities. Thus both the development of thinking and creativity are major outcomes of such activity. The active attempt to resolve the question is often more important than getting a correct answer.

There are various degrees of activities of this kind. Some activities stress the solution over the methods of attaining the solution, and these are generally content activities meant to develop content understandings. Others stress the "process" of getting answers and are process-skill oriented, meant to focus on creative and logical thinking processes of designing and carrying out an experiment or making a series of systematic observations to prove or disprove a hypothesis. It is this latter type, activities focused on the science process skills, that are the focus of the remainder of this chapter. These activities are the means by which scientific knowledge is expanded and extended. Specific skills involved in this process include observing, quantifying, identifying, and controlling variables; designing experiments; hypothesizing; defining operationally; organizing and collecting data; graphing, and generalizing.

THE SCIENCE PROCESS SKILLS

Several names have been used to describe science process skills. The scientific method, scientific thinking, and critical thinking skills are terms that have been used at various times. Today, however, "science process skills" is a broad expression commonly used. Popularized by the elementary curriculum project Science—A Process Approach (S–APA), these skills are defined as a set of broadly transferrable abilities, appropriate to many science disciplines and reflective of the true behavior of scientists. S–APA divided process skills into two types: basic and integrated. The basic or simpler process skills provide a foundation for learning the more complex integrated

TABLE 9.1
Basic Science Process Skills

Observing: Using the senses to gather information about an object or event.
Example: Describing a pencil as yellow or 20 cm long.

Inferring: Making an educated guess about an object or event based on previously gathered data or information.
Example: Saying that the person who used a pencil made a lot of mistakes because the eraser was well worn.

Measuring: Using both standard and nonstandard measures or estimates to describe the dimensions of an object or event.
Example: Using a meter stick to measure the length of a table or simply estimating its length.

Communicating: Using words or graphic symbols to describe an action, object, or event.
Example: Describing the change in height of a plant over time in writing or through a graph.

Classifying: Grouping or ordering objects or events into categories based on properties or criteria.
Example: Placing all rocks having a certain grain size or hardness into one group.

Predicting: Stating the outcome of a future event based on a pattern of evidence.
Example: Predicting the height of a plant in 2 weeks' time, based on a graph of its growth during the last 4 weeks.

---

skills. Each of the basic and integrated skills is listed and described in Tables 9.1 and 9.2, respectively.

Problem Solving and Process Skills

Before discussing science process skills, it is important to understand problem solving in a general way, since the end result of a process skill inquiry is the solution of a problem. A quick review of one writer's synthesis of the process will be helpful in this aim.

In the *Ideal Problem Solver* (1984), John Bransford states that a problem exists whenever the present situation is not the desired situation. Problem solving to him, then, is the act of trying to solve these problem situations so that answers can be found and progress made. Bransford describes a model for solving many types of problems and calls it his IDEAL problem-solving method with each letter of the word IDEAL standing for a distinct step in problem solution. The first component in his model is to *identify* the problem, which he calls "the most significant part of problem solving" (p. 12). Next comes *defining* and representing the problem, important because "different

TABLE 9.2
Integrated Science Process Skills

Controlling variables: Identifying variables that can affect an experimental outcome, keeping most variables constant while manipulating only the independent variable.
  Example: Realizing through past experience that amount of fertilizer and water need to be controlled when testing to see how the addition of organic matter affects the growth of beans.

Defining operationally: Stating how to measure a variable in an experiment.
  Example: Stating that bean growth will be measured in centimeters per week.

Formulating hypotheses: Stating the expected outcome of an experiment.
  Example: The greater the amount of organic matter added to the soil, the greater the bean growth.

Interpreting data: Organizing data and drawing conclusions from it.
  Example: Recording data from the experiment on bean growth in a data table and drawing a conclusion corresponding to the data.

Experimenting: Conducting an entire experiment, including asking an appropriate question, stating an hypothesis, identifying and controlling variables, operationally defining those variables, designing a "fair" experiment, conducting the experiment, and interpreting the results of the experiment.
  Example: The entire process of conducting the experiment on the affect of organic matter on the growth of bean plants, from question through interpreting data.

Formulating models: Creating a mental or physical model of a process or event.
  Example: The model of how atomic particles interact in the atom or how the processes of evaporation and condensation interrelate in the water cycle.

---

definitions of the problem will often lead to different treatments" (p. 15). The third element is *exploring* alternate approaches. "This involves an analysis of how you are currently reacting to a problem plus a consideration of options or strategies that might be employed" (p. 18); that is, a plan is developed for problem solution that considers differing alternatives. The last two components follow logically. They are *acting* on a plan and *looking* at the effects. These two steps imply carrying out at least one of the potential solutions generated in step three and logically drawing conclusions from the results of this action.

Skills as defined and used in science education mirror Bransford's model in a couple of ways. First, they are used to solve problems in science. Second, they typically, although not always, follow a logical order, starting with problem identification and usually finishing with a set of conclusions. Many times another cycle through particular components of the problem solving model is required because improvement on method is needed or the first attempt gave poor results. In science, this process is broadly termed experimenting and it is one of several skills grouped under the rubric of science process skills.

The Importance of Using a Process Approach

Besides the reasons given for the importance of activities in general, there are several strong arguments for inclusion of process skill activities. One is the generalizability of these skills to life, since many of life's problems can be analyzed and solutions proposed by applying process skills. Which brand of soap or corn flakes provides the best value? Are frozen, canned, or fresh green beans more economical? Should a hydroelectric, coal-burning, or nuclear plant be built in the local community? Which candidate better reflects an individual's viewpoint? All these questions can be addressed by collecting and organizing data and drawing conclusions from it. The skills of identifying and controlling appropriate variables, designing experiments, and defining operationally are all important parts in this process.

Process skill activities more accurately reflect the nature of science and the typical activity of scientists. Science is a dynamic enterprise; it is a search for answers, not just a collection of facts and conclusions. At any one time the information contained in a "textbook represents only our present conclusions about a body of scientific knowledge" (Hurd, 1970). Most students do not understand the true nature of science as an ongoing and tentative search, unless it is approached as a search and not a solution. Activities that focus on process skill acquisition provide the perspective necessary for students to begin to view science in this light. Each student acts as a scientist. The student actively observes, hypothesizes, collects data, and experiments.

The relationship between science process skills and formal operational abilities is another reason for stressing a process-oriented curriculum. Piaget operationally defined several abstract thinking abilities that together comprise formal operations (Inhelder & Piaget, 1958). Prominent among these abilities is what Piaget called "identification and control of variables."

> The formal operational thinker inspects his problem data, hypothesizes that such and such a theory or explanation might be the correct one, deduces from it that so and so empirical phenomena ought logically to occur or not occur in reality, and then tests his theory by seeing if these predicted phenomena do in fact occur. (Flavell, 1977)

In simpler language, a formal thinker can set up and conduct an experiment, *precisely the same activity involved in performing a process skill experimenting activity.* Not surprisingly, Padilla, Okey, and Dillashaw (1983) found a correlation of .73 between the two sets of abilities. However in a follow-up study, Padilla, Okey, and Garrard (1984) found that students formal operational abilities did not improve when given a 4-month process skill treatment. In spite of this result, there appears to be potential for developing formal reasoning abilities in students through the use of process skill activities, but over a much longer period of time.

IMPLEMENTING A PROCESS APPROACH

One of the major skills to be developed in middle and secondary school science is that of conducting an experiment. Many, if not most, of the other process skills can be thought of as components of this superordinate ability. Observing and quantifying are often used for data collection. Hypothesizing, identifying, and controlling variables; designing experiments, and defining operationally, are all parts of setting up an experiment. Graphing and generalizing are skills used in interpreting results.

The first step necessary for implementing process skill activities is choosing an appropriate unit topic. Some topics can more naturally involve students in collecting and analyzing data. Others, while they might be of great scientific interest or of interest to a particular science teacher, do not provide appropriate opportunities for manipulating materials and variables. Units involving measurements of certain aspects of the five senses or those stressing pollution assessment in the local school area or measurement of local weather conditions with home-made devices can work exceedingly well. Others, such as theoretical electricity, atoms and molecules, and black holes are extremely difficult.

After unit topics are selected, the students must be given opportunities to practice the process skills. If process skill activities are new to students, then individual skills, such as observing, graphing, collecting data, using tables, forming appropriate hypotheses, and operationally defining variables, should probably be practiced before being combined in a true experiment. Initial training should also stress appropriate strategies for task completion. For example, brainstorming techniques can work well for identifying variables and defining operationally. A check of the brainstormed variable lists would also indicate whether all variables have been controlled except the manipulated and responding variables. Soon students should be grouping these separate skills for the purpose of solving problems by conducting an experiment. This method helps them understand the role of each skill in the meaningful scientific context of experimenting.

Initially, experimenting activities should involve relatively simple or familiar problems. Situations involving a small number of variables or dealing with commonplace problems within the students' environment are important starting points. After a reasonable facility with skills and simpler problems is attained, then the teacher can proceed slowly to more complex situations.

CONDUCTING AN EXPERIMENT—SOME EXAMPLES

The following are examples of experiments that students might perform. Suggestions of appropriate answers and decisions are given to teachers reading this article so that they can see the direction that the activity might take. When using these or similar activities in a classroom, *it is important that students not be given answers.* Instead it is of greater consequence that they try their own ideas and through success and failure begin to formulate their notions of experimenting. This will not only stimulate greater development of logical thinking and better concept acquisition, but will also spur more creative approaches to problems.

Electromagnetism

The first step in setting up an experiment is asking an appropriate question. Many such questions can be posed concerning a topic such as electromagnetism.

- How does the number of winds of wire affect electromagnet strength?
- How does the mass of the iron core affect electromagnet strength?
- How does the amount of electric current affect electromagnet strength?

One of these questions must then be chosen and an appropriate hypothesis formed, for example, "electromagnet strength will increase with increased winds of wire."

Variables must then be identified, perhaps by brainstorming a list of those that might affect the hypothesis. The manipulated or independent variable (e.g., number of winds of wire) and the responding or dependent variable (e.g., electromagnet strength) must be chosen. Both of these variables must then be operationally defined so that they can be measured. This can be accomplished by again using brainstorming techniques. To continue the example, one appropriate operational definition for electromagnet strength might be the number of paper clips that the magnet can pick up. Number of winds of wire does not need to be operationally defined since it is already measurable as stated. All other appropriate variables should be controlled, if possible. In our example, the type of nail and wire used, the strength of the batteries, and the conditions under which the paper clips are picked up all have to be standardized.

Once variables have been identified and operationally defined, an experimental design must be chosen. How many trials should be performed? In what order should the tests occur? What specific data should be recorded? Questions such as these must be answered before data can be collected and organized. Five trials might be appropriate for our example. These choices allow for experimental error and a fair comparison of different conditions. Once the design is chosen, the data collection can begin.

Data organization can be expedited with students by discussing a suitable table before data collection begins. With younger students, the teacher might start by recommending an appropriate table; however, more experienced students should soon be suggesting their own. Data might be further organized by using a class chart upon which all results are placed. This allows for a smooth transition from data organizing to the important step of generalizing. One significant aspect of this step is that generalizations can take many forms. Some investigations provide relatively clean results, which allow for a simple statement of the relationship between the manipulated and responding variables; for example, electromagnet strength increases with an increased number of winds of wire. Other types of generalizations simply pose further questions to be answered through future experiments; for example, would the electromagnet results be the same if precautions were taken to demagnetize the paper clips after every trial? This second type of generalization is very important if students are to begin to understand the true nature of science. Teachers must not only allow further questions, but encourage them.

Dandelions

A simple weed such as the dandelion can provide another example for generating an experiment. Several appropriate questions are possible.

- What proportion of dandelion seeds will germinate in a wet paper towel?
- How does temperature affect the germination rate of the seeds?
- Will presoaking or refrigeration of dandelion seeds affect their germination rate?

Once a question is chosen, a hypothesis is formulated; for example, a temperature above 25°C will adversely affect germination rate. Appropriate variables must then be identified:

- Manipulated variable (e.g., temperature)
- Responding variable (e.g., germination rate)
- Controlled variable (e.g., amount of water, age of seeds, etc.)

Each variable must then be operationally defined.

The experiment must then be designed. How many and which temperatures will be tested? How long should the seeds be subjected to a particular temperature? What length of time will be allowed for germination? After these questions are answered and the design is set, the data can be collected and organized, using charts or graphs. Generalizations from the organized data in the form of conclusions or questions can then be made.

A Note on Difficulty

The example questions given may be too simple for advanced high school students; however, they can serve as good starting points for most students through the 10th grade. Once the described process is somewhat internalized, designing experiments becomes a matter of generating appropriate questions through which the process skills can be further practiced. Examples of appropriate questions for consumer include: (It is important to note that many researchable questions can be generated from other concrete topics.)

Does one fast food chain provide more meat in a hamburger than others?
Is one brand of paper towel stronger than the others? Or more absorbent?
Will one brand of dishwasher liquid wash more dishes per unit cost?
Is it more economical to buy boneless meat or a piece with the bone in?
Does one brand of antacid neutralize more acid than the others?

A FINAL CONSIDERATION

Teachers wishing to implement a productive, activity-centered classroom need to spend an adequate amount of time not only doing the right kinds of activities, but also discussing and integrating activity results. Activities, by themselves, do not promote understanding in children. Teachers should enrich the activities by spending the necessary class time getting students to make sense of their experiences and by helping them connect activities to past and future science knowledge.

REFERENCES

Bransford, J. (1984). *The ideal problem solver*. New York: W. H. Freeman.

Chiapetta, E. (1976). A review of Piagetian studies relevant to science instruction at the secondary and college level. *Science Education, 60,* 253–261.

Elementary Science Study (1970). *The ESS reader,* Newton, MA: Education Development Center.

Flavell, J. (1977). *Cognitive development,* Englewood Cliffs, NJ: Prentice-Hall.

Georgiady, N. P., & Romano, L. G. (1977). Growth characteristics of middle school children: Curriculum implications. *Middle School Journal*, pp. 12–23.

Hurd, P.D. (1970). *New curriculum perspectives for junior high school science.* Belmont, CA: Wadsworth.

Inhelder, B., & Piaget, J. (1968). *The growth of logical thinking from childhood to adolescence,* New York: Basic Books.

Lovell, K. (1961). A follow-up study of Inhelder and Piaget's the growth of logical thinking. *British Journal of Psychology, 52,*143–153.

Padilla, M., Okey, J., & Dillashaw, F. (1983). The relationship between science process skills and formal thinking abilities. *Journal of Research in Science Teaching, 20,* 239–246.

Padilla, M., Okey, J., & Garrard, K. (1984). The effects of instruction on integrated science process skill achievement. *Journal of Research in Science Teaching, 21,* 277–287.

Piaget, J. (1972). Intellectual evolution from adolescence to adult. *Human Development, 15,* 1–12

Renner, J., Grant, R., & Sutherland, J. (1978). Content and concrete thought. *Science Education, 62,* 215–221.

Schwebel, M., & Raph, J. (1973). *Piaget in the classroom,* New York: Basic Books.

Simpson, R. D. (1979). Breeding success in science. *Science Teacher, 46,* 24–26.

Staver, J. (1986). *The constructivist epistomology of Jean Piaget: Its philosophical roots and relevance to science teaching and learning.* Paper presented at an American–Japanese seminar on science education sponsored by the National Science Foundation and the Japan Society for the Promotion of Science, Honolulu.

10 Explaining Science Concepts: A Teaching-with-Analogies Model

Shawn M. Glynn
University of Georgia

Analogical reasoning can play an important role in scientific discovery, insight, and explanation. For example, Johannes Kepler, the eminent 17th-century astronomer, wrote: "And I cherish more than anything else the Analogies, my most trustworthy masters. They know all the secrets of Nature . . ." (quoted in Polya, 1973, p. 12). Kepler attempted to explain astronomical phenomena, such as the motion of the planets, in terms of precise physical laws. In a letter in 1605, he drew an analogy between planetary motion and clockwork:

> I am much occupied with the investigation of the physical causes. My aim in this is to show that the celestial machine is to be likened not to a divine organism but rather to a clockwork . . . insofar as nearly all the manifold movements are carried out by means of a single, quite simple magnetic force, as in the case of a clockwork, all motions are caused by a simple weight. Moreover, I show how this physical conception is to be presented through calculation and geometry. (quoted in Rutherford, Holton, & Watson, 1975, Unit 2, p. 68)

Joseph Priestley (1773–1804), a distinguished physical scientist, also found analogical reasoning to be useful. On the basis of an analogy, Priestley proposed the "law of electrical force," which was later verified experimentally by the French physicist Charles Coulomb. Here are the events that led to Priestley's proposal:

> Priestley verified Franklin's results, and went on to reach a brilliant conclusion from them. He remembered from Newton's Principia that gravitational forces behave in a similar way. Inside a hollow planet, the net gravitational force on

an object (the sum of all the forces exerted by all parts of the planet) would be exactly zero. This result also follows mathematically from the law that the gravitational force between any two individual pieces of matter is inversely proportional to the square of the distance between them. Priestley therefore proposed that forces exerted by charges vary inversely as the square of the distance, just as do forces exerted by massive bodies . . . . We call the force exerted between bodies owing to the fact that they are charged "electric" force, just as we call the force between uncharged bodies "gravitational" force . . .

Priestley's proposal was based on reasoning by analogy, that is, by reasoning from a parallel, well demonstrated case. Such reasoning alone could not prove that electrical forces are inversely proportional to the square of the distance between charges. But it strongly encouraged other physicists to test Priestley's hypothesis by experiment. (Rutherford et al., 1975, Unit 4, p. 35)

One of the strongest statements in support of analogies as aids to discovery, insight, and explanation in science, is that of the English physicist N. R. Campbell who, in his 1920 book *Physics, the Elements,* pointed to the billiard ball model of the kinetic theory of gases and argued:

Analogies are not "aids" to the establishment of theories; they are an utterly essential part of theories, without which theories would be completely valueless and unworthy of the name. It is often suggested that the analogy leads to the formulation of the theory, but that once the theory is formulated the analogy has served its purpose and may be removed or forgotten. Such a suggestion is absolutely false and perniciously misleading. (Quoted in Hesse, 1966, p. 4)

Robert Oppenheimer, in an invited address to the American Psychological Association in 1955, made the following comments about the role of analogy in scientific understanding:

Analogy is indeed an indispensable and inevitable tool for scientific progress . . . . Whether or not we talk of discovery or of invention, analogy is inevitable in human thought, because we come to new things in science with what equipment we have, which is how we have learned to think, and above all how we have learned to think about the relatedness of things. We cannot, coming into something new, deal with it except on the basis of the familiar and the old-fashioned. The conservation of scientific enquiry is not an arbitrary thing; it is the freight with which we operate; it is the only equipment we have. We cannot learn to be surprised or astonished at something unless we have a view of how it ought to be; and that view is almost certainly an analogy. We cannot learn that we have made a mistake unless we make a mistake; and our mistake is almost always in the form of an analogy to some other piece of experience. (Oppenheimer, 1956, pp. 129–130)

Observations such as those made by Kepler, Priestley, Campbell, and

Oppenheimer are common in the science literature. Taken together, these observations suggest that analogies can be valuable aids to scientific understanding.

Given the importance of analogical reasoning to scientific understanding, it is not surprising that analogies are used often by authors of science textbooks to explain concepts to students. Science teachers often embellish the authors' analogies or, when the author has not provided an analogy, the science teacher often provides one.

Sometimes the analogies that text authors use to explain new concepts are clear and well developed, while other times they are vague and potentially confusing. What authors need is a model to guide their use of instructional analogies. Teachers who wish to extend or modify an author's analogy also need such a model. Teachers could use the model to develop their own analogies when none is offered in the text—analogies that are targeted to the specific background knowledge of the children they teach.

Later in this chapter, a Teaching-with-Analogies model will be presented and illustrated. Teachers and text authors can use this model to explain new concepts to students. To set the stage for this model, the processes of science text comprehension and analogical reasoning will be discussed.

UNDERSTANDING SCIENCE TEXT

A science text is one that explains science concepts and how they are related, or more simply, "how things work." Science text comes in many forms: textbooks, journals, magazines, manuals, newspapers, and software. These forms can be either paper- or computer-based. A current trend in instruction is to supplement conventional science textbooks with computer-based modules, which contain practice drills, diagnostic tests, remedial exercises, and interactive and noninteractive simulations.

In all its forms, science text plays a vital role in the instruction of science. In elementary school, high school, and college, students rely heavily on text for much of the science knowledge and skills they must learn.

Comprehending the concepts in a science text can be difficult for a student. To facilitate students' meaningful comprehension of science text, teachers and text authors must help students relate new concepts to concepts with which they are already familiar (Glynn, Britton, & Muth, 1990). If familiar concepts and new ones are related correctly, then the student will comprehend the text in a meaningful fashion. Otherwise, comprehension will break down and the student will not understand critical text concepts. Analogical reasoning is one of the most effective ways for students to integrate their existing knowledge with text knowledge (Vosniadou & Brewer, 1987).

ANALOGICAL REASONING AND SCIENCE LEARNING

Frequent use of analogies to explain everyday events underscores their potential value as instructional tools. The following expressions are commonplace in casual conversation: "Let me give you an analogy..." "It's just like..." "It's the same as..." "It's no different than..." The process of relating concepts by means of analogy is a basic part of human thinking, and authors, teachers, and students are certain to use it. One way to ensure that they use it effectively is to provide them with a model of analogical reasoning.

It is common for the teacher's edition of science textbooks to point out, in the introduction, all of the special features incorporated into the design of the text to facilitate students' comprehension of science concepts. These features include: advance organizers; structured overviews; highlighted concept names; margin notes; introductory, adjunct, and review questions; illustrations; cartoons; boxed examples; concept summaries; lists of important terms; conceptual activities; and glossaries. These features, along with supplementary materials such as workbooks, resource books, videotapes, films, and software are promoted in the teacher's edition as valuable aids to comprehension.

Features such as these can be valuable aids to comprehension, under certain conditions, as many research studies have shown (Britton & Glynn, 1987; Britton, Glynn, Meyer, & Penland, 1982; Glynn, 1978; Glynn, Andre, & Britton, 1986; Glynn & Britton, 1984; Glynn, Britton, & Muth, 1985; Glynn, Britton, & Tillman, 1985; Glynn & Di Vesta, 1977, 1979). Analogies rarely are mentioned in textbook introductions. This tends to be true even in textbooks in which authors make excellent use of analogies. In a number of research studies, analogical reasoning has been shown to facilitate comprehension and problem solving (Alexander, White, & Mangano, 1983; Bean, Singer, & Cowan, 1985; Clement, Brown, & Zietsman, in press; Gick & Holyoak, 1980, 1983; Halpern, 1987; Hayes, 1987; Vosniadou & Brewer, 1987). So, why not promote this valuable aid to comprehension in the introduction to the text?

One reason why analogies are not promoted, even in textbooks that make extensive use of them, is that the skill of writing good analogies is what psychologists call "procedural," rather than "declarative." Procedural knowledge is knowledge of "how to do something" rather than "how to explain it in words." Because teachers, authors, and publishers do not have guidelines or a model for what constitutes a good instructional analogy, the development and evaluation of analogies are fairly subjective, as they are more of an art than a science. Therefore, teachers, authors, and publishers may not feel comfortable about promoting them in textbooks as aids to comprehension until a model becomes available for designing and evaluating instructional analogies.

The following sections provide answers to the questions most commonly asked about instructional analogies by teachers and authors.

What Is an Analogy?

Strictly speaking, an *analogy* is a process: it is a process of identifying similarities between different concepts. While the terms analogy and metaphor are frequently substituted for one another, analogy tends to be used more often in scientific and technical contexts. Metaphor is used more often in literary contexts (e.g., "Her spectacular departure was the icing on the cake"). Since the examples presented in this chapter are from science textbooks, analogy will be used rather than metaphor.

How Do Analogies Help Students Learn?

Meaningful learning has been defined by Wittrock (1985, pp. 261–262) as a "student generative process that entails construction of relations, either assimilative or accommodative, among experience, concepts, and higher-order principles and frameworks. It is the construction of these relations between and within concepts that produces meaningful learning." When an analogy is drawn between concepts, a powerful relation is constructed that leads to the meaningful learning described by Wittrock. An analogical relationship is powerful because it comprises an entire set of associative relationships between features of the concepts being compared.

In science texts, analogies are used in a relatively precise fashion to transfer ideas from a familiar concept to an unfamiliar one. We will call the familiar concept the analog and the unfamiliar one the *target*. Both the analog and the

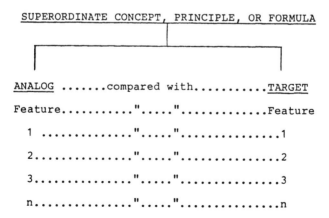

FIG. 10.1.   An abstract representation of an analogy, with its constituent parts.   Note that the analog and the target are subordinate to a superordinate concept, principle, or formula.

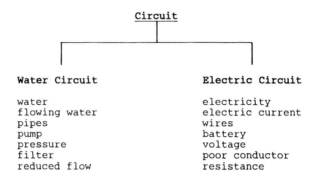

FIG. 10.2. An analogy can be drawn between a water circuit and an electric circuit because they share the similar mapped features; "Circuit" is the superordinate concept.

target have characteristics, or features. If the analog and the target share common or similar features, an analogy can be drawn between them. An abstract representation of an analogy, with its constituent parts, appears in Fig. 10.1 (note that the analog and the target are subordinate to a superordinate concept).

The target concept of an electric circuit will be used to illustrate the analogy representation. The water circuit will be the analog concept. Some corresponding electric and water circuit features appear in Fig. 10.2. An analogy can be drawn between the electric and water circuits because they share the similar features mapped out in Fig. 10.2. An analogy can also be represented visually, by using a diagram such as that in Fig. 10.3.

Note that the electric circuit and the water circuit are both circuits; that is,

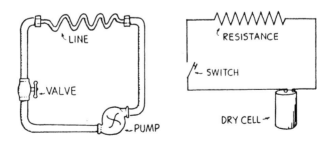

FIG. 10.3. Analogy between a simple hydraulic circuit and an electric circuit. (From *Conceptual Physics*, p. 513, by Paul G. Hewitt, 1987, Menlo Park, CA: Addison-Wesley Publishing Company, Inc. Copyright 1987 by Addison-Wesley. Reprinted by permission.)

they are subordinate to the superordinate concept of Circuit. There are other kinds of circuits that might be used to draw an analogy. For example, in a pinball machine, the pinballs (corresponding to electrons or water molecules) travel a circuit and are pushed by a plunger (corresponding to a battery or a pump). The pinballs even meet "resistance" in the form of bumpers and funnels. Other analogies could be drawn by teachers who keep the abstract representation of an analogy and its constituent parts in mind when thinking about circuits.

Sometimes, there is no conventional name for the superordinate concept that subsumes an analog and a target. For example, authors of biology tests frequently draw an analogy between the camera and the human eye. Here are some of the similar features:

Camera	Human Eye
lens	lens
inverted image	inverted image
film	retina
lens cap	eyelid
focus	lens accommodation
aperture	pupil dilation

What is the name of the superordinate concept that subsumes the analog camera and the target human eye? Visual Device is one possibility, but it is certainly not as familiar a name as Circuit was in the previous example. Superordinate concepts often do not have familiar labels. Nevertheless, the role of the superordinate concept in the representation of an analogy and its constituent parts is an important one. The identification and naming of the superordinate concept can suggest other analogies; it also can stimulate students to generalize what they have learned and apply their learning to other contexts. Therefore, although it might be difficult to identify and name the concept that subsumes an analog and its target, it is beneficial to do so for purposes of meaningful comprehension.

How Do Analogies and Examples Differ?

Sometime students confuse an example of a concept with an analogy. An example is an instance of a concept, not a comparison between similar features of two concepts. Consider a science textbook that describes the relationship between an electric spark and lightning. Lightning is not *like* a big spark, it *is* a big spark! So, lightning is an example of the concept of electric spark.

How Do You Tell a Good Analogy from a Bad One?

How good an analogy is depends upon how well it achieves its purpose. In general, if an analogy is serving an explanatory purpose, the following three criteria can be used to judge its appropriateness: (1) the number of features compared, (2) the similarity of the features compared, and (3) the conceptual significance of the features compared.

The explanatory power of an analogy generally increases as the number of similar features shared by the analog and target increases. However, it is possible to draw a "good" analogy on the basis of a few (or even one) similar features, if those features are directly relevant to the specific goals of the teacher or author. For example, the following analogy is drawn on the basis of only one similar feature, but it is a very important one in terms of the teacher's goals: The moon acts like a mirror reflecting the light of the sun.

An analogy is considered "bad" if it is difficult to identify and map the important features shared by the analog and the target. For example, in the sixth-grade Heath Science text (Barufaldi, Ladd, & Moses, 1981), three models of the atom appear in the drawing labeled "Billiard ball model; Plum pudding model; Rutherford's model: a nucleus surrounded by rapidly moving electrons" (p. 116). The titles of the first two models are historically accurate. Furthermore, they draw helpful analogies for readers who are familiar with billiard balls and plum pudding.

Unfortunately, few sixth graders are familiar with billiards and plum pudding. The titles should be maintained since they are historical; however, the text should explain billiards and plum pudding for the concepts and the associated analogies to be understood. Perhaps, an analogy could be used to explain plum pudding by comparing it with chocolate chip ice cream, a concept with which more sixth graders would be familiar.

A good analogy puts new ideas into terms with which students are already familiar. Analogies drawn by a teacher or author between concepts covered early in a text and those covered later (such as fractions and proportions in a math text) are particularly effective because there is assurance that the earlier concepts (which function here as analogs) are part of every student's knowledge base. Also, these analogies are particularly powerful because they prompt readers to connect related concepts and form conceptual systems.

Can Analogical Reasoning Hurt Comprehension?

The correspondence of features between two concepts is never identical; otherwise the corresponding concepts would be identical. When teachers, authors, or students intentionally or inadvertently compare features that do not correspond to one another, misunderstanding and misdirection result.

A careful examination of all aspects of an analogy is a prerequisite to using it effectively. An analogy easily can lead students down the wrong path. For example, students who believe that electricity in a wire is like water in a hose often conclude, erroneously, that if the wire is cut, the electricity will "leak out."

Teachers should explain to students that analogies are double-edged swords. An analog can be used to explain correctly and even predict some aspects of the target concept. At some point, however, every analogy breaks down. At that point, miscomprehension and misdirection can begin.

Occasionally, authors warn readers about the potential dangers of analogies. This is a good practice and it should be adopted by all authors who use analogies. More than 25 years ago, Eric Rogers (1960), in his classic text, *Physics for the Inquiring Mind,* introduced his chapter on electric circuits by praising analogies and then cautioning his readers about them:

> To this day in teaching elementary electricity we liken electric circuits to hydraulic circuits of water pipes full of water all the way around, with pumps, taps, flowmeters, pressure gauges . . . to correspond to generators, switches, ammeters, voltmeters. . . . Like many uses of analogy in teaching, this does make things easier for the beginner to understand. . . . Yet saying the electric circuit is "just like" the water circuit does not prove the electric circuit will have such behavior. "Current flow" is a hindsight description, put in after we have found that the electric circuit does have experimental properties which resemble those of a water circuit. As such, it is good teaching, but if misused as an attempted proof, would be bad science. (This seems a long complaint against a teacher's kindly illustration. Yet it was the great mistake of medieval science to argue "what must be" from some authoritarian statement; and present-day popularizers of science make the mistake of building hard-won knowledge into glib analogies from which the science is then apparently produced. Attempts to make physics clearer by analogies may mislead the reader unless he is warned.) (pp. 505–506)

A recent recommendation for the use of analogies, with caution, can be found in *Concepts in Physics,* an introductory physics textbook by Miller, Dillon, and Smith (1980):

> Models and analogies can be of great value in physics if they are used with care and discrimination. It is important, for example, to guard against the danger of believing that a model or analogy is an exact representation of some physical system. One should always regard a model critically and remember that an analogy means no more than: under certain special conditions, the physical system being studies behaves as if . . . (p. 253)

Authors should explain to readers, as Rogers (1960) and Miller et al. (1980) did, that eventually every analogy breaks down. Readers must understand this.

ANALOGIES IN SCIENCE TEXTBOOKS

A good analogy puts new ideas into terms with which readers are already familiar. Frequently, authors will use a concept that they covered in an earlier chapter to introduce—by way of analogy—a new concept. Consider the following example in which Paul Hewitt (1987), the author of the text *Conceptual Physics,* uses concepts related to the flow of heat (in his Chapter 21) to introduce concepts related to the flow of electric charge (in his Chapter 34):

> Recall in your study of heat and temperature that heat flows through a conductor when a difference in temperature exists across its ends. Heat flows from the end of higher temperature to the end of lower temperature. When both ends reach the same temperature, the flow of heat ceases.

> In a similar way, when the ends of an electrical conductor are at different electric potentials, charge flows from the higher potential to the lower potential. Charge flows when there is a potential difference, or difference in potential (voltage), across the ends of a conductor. The flow of charge will continue until both ends reach a common potential. When there is no potential difference, no flow of charge will occur. (pp. 509–510)

In the sections that follow, several more analogies and analogy-based problems developed by Paul Hewitt will be presented, as his work is exemplary. Analogies drawn by an author between concepts covered early in a text and concepts covered later are particularly effective because the author can be reasonably confident that the earlier concepts (which function here as analogs) are part of most readers' knowledge base. Also, these analogies are particularly powerful because they prompt readers to connect related concepts and form conceptual systems.

To better understand when and how an analogy should be used to explain a new concept, 43 elementary school, high school, and college science textbooks were examined for examples of elaborate analogies. In all the textbooks, there were many examples of simple, one-or-two sentence analogies, such as "Mitochondria are the powerhouse of the cell;" however, elaborate analogies, those that ran on for a paragraph, a page, or several pages, were relatively rare. Elaborate analogies compared and contrasted many features of two major concepts.

High school physics and physical science textbooks appeared to contain the greatest number of elaborate analogies. Why do high school textbooks have a greater number of elaborate analogies? Perhaps elementary school textbook authors use few elaborate analogies because the knowledge base of their readers is so limited and because it is not possible to cover concepts in the depth needed to support analogies. On the other hand, college textbook authors do use elaborate analogies, but not as often as high school textbook authors. College textbook authors may assume that the stronger comprehension capabilities of college students preclude the need for as many analogies. College textbook authors may also be under pressure to cover more material, forcing them to sacrifice some elaborate analogies.

Why do physics textbooks appear to have more elaborate analogies than textbooks in other sciences? Perhaps it is because physics concepts are about very basic phenomena that either do not lend themselves to unaided physical observation (e.g., electrons) or, if they are directly observable, they are often misperceived (e.g., trajectories), or confused with everyday uses of the concept (e.g., speed and velocity). Because of these characteristics, physics concepts need more "conceptual support" when introduced in textbooks. Analogies can provide some of this conceptual support by helping readers to perceive, understand, or reinterpret physics concepts in terms of concepts with which they are already familiar. Although elaborate analogies were most common in physics textbooks, it is important to keep in mind that

TABLE 10.1
Physics and Physical Science Textbooks

Beiser, A. (1964). *The science of physics.* Palo Alto, CA: Addison-Wesley.

Dull, C. E., Metcalfe, H. C., & Williams, J. E. (1963). *Modern physics.* New York: Holt, Rinehart, & Winston.

Genzer, I., & Younger, P. (1969). *Physics.* Morristown, NJ: Silver Burdett.

Haber-Schaim, U., Dodge, J. H., & Walter, J. A. (1986). *PSSC Physics.* Lexington, MA: D.C. Heath.

Harnwell, G. P., & Legge, G. J. F. (1967). *Physics: Matter, energy, and the universe.* New York: Reinhold.

Hewitt, P. G. (1987). *Conceptual physics.* Menlo Park, CA: Addison- Wesley.

Hirsch, A. J. (1981). *Physics: A practical approach.* Toronto: John Wiley.

Hirsch, A. J. (1986). *Physics for a modern world.* Toronto: John Wiley.

Johnson, G. P., Barr, B. B., & Leyden, M. B. (1988). *Physical science.* Menlo Park, CA: Addison-Wesley.

Karplus, R. (1969). *Introductory physics.* New York: W. A. Benjamin.

Krauskopf, K. B., & Beiser, A. (1986). *The physical universe.* New York: McGraw-Hill.

Leyden, M. B., Johnson, G. P., & Barr, B. B. (1988). *Introduction to physical science.* Menlo Park, CA: Addison-Wesley.

Miller, F., Dillon, T. J., & Smith, M. K. (1980). *Concepts in physics.* New York: Harcourt, Brace, Jovanovich.

Murphy, J. T., & Smoot, R. C. (1972). *Physics principles and problems.* Columbus, OH: Charles E. Merrill.

Pasachoff, J. M., Pasachoff, N., & Cooney, T. M. (1983). *Physical science.* Glenview, IL: Scott, Foresman.

Physical Science Study Committee. (1965). *Physics.* Lexington, MA: D. C. Heath.

Rutherford, F. J., Holton, G., & Watson, F. G. (1975). *Project physics.* New York: Holt, Rinehart, & Winston.

Taffel, A. (1986). *Physics: Its methods and meanings.* Newton, MA: Allyn & Bacon.

Wong, H. K., & Dolmatz, M. S. (1984). *Physical science: The key ideas.* Englewood Cliffs, NJ: Prentice-Hall.

textbooks in other sciences, particularly chemistry, included elaborate analogies.

The high school physics and physical science textbooks examined are listed in Table 10.1. (Physical science is the study of changes in matter and energy; in addition to physics, it includes areas of study such as chemistry and astronomy.)

THE TEACHING-WITH-ANALOGIES MODEL

The Teaching-with-Analogies (TWA) Model (Glynn; 1989; Glynn, Britton, Semrud-Clikeman, & Muth, 1989) is based on a survey of 43 science textbooks and an analysis of the analogies used in those textbooks. The most effective analogies from the standpoint of instructional design were identified. The authors of these analogies performed certain key operations that have been incorporated into a model which can serve as a guide for teachers and authors of science textbooks. The TWA model for using an analogy to explain a science concept contains the following six operations:

1. Introduce Target
2. Cue Retrieval of Analog
3. Identify Relevant Features of Target and Analog
4. Map Similarities
5. Draw Conclusions about Target
6. Indicate where Analogy Breaks Down

The author of a well-designed analogy performs each of these operations for the reader, although not necessarily in the order listed. To illustrate these operations, here are excerpts from Paul Hewitt's (1987) chapters on *Electric Currents* and *Electric Circuits,* in which he draws an extended analogy between currents of water (the analog) and currents of electricity (the target):

Electric Current

The last chapter discussed the concept of electric potential, or voltage. This chapter will show that voltage is an "electrical pressure" that can produce a flow of charge, or *current,* within a conductor. The flow is restrained by the *resistance* it encounters. (p. 509)

Flow of Charge

To attain a sustained flow of charge in a conductor, some arrangement must be provided to maintain a difference in potential while charge flows from one end to the other. The situation is analogous to the flow of water from a higher

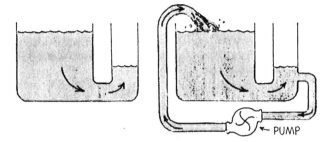

FIG. 10.4.   (left) Water flows from the reservoir of higher pressure to the reservoir of lower pressure. The flow will cease when the difference in pressure ceases. (right) Water continues to flow because a difference in pressure is maintained with the pump. (From *Conceptual Physics,* p. 510, by Paul G. Hewitt, 1987, Menlo Park, CA: Addison-Wesley Publishing Company, Inc.   Copyright 1987 by Addison-Wesley.   Reprinted by permission.)

reservoir to a lower one [see Fig. 10.4 left]. Water will flow in a pipe that connects the reservoirs only as long as a difference in water level exists. (This is implied in the saying, "Water seeks its own level.") The flow of water in the pipe, like the flow of charge in the wire that connects the Van de Graaff generator to the ground, will cease when the pressures at each end are equal. In order that the flow be sustained, there must be a suitable pump of some sort to maintain a difference in water levels [Figure 10.4 right]. Then there will be a continual difference in water pressures and a continual flow of water. The same is true of electric current. (pp. 509–510)

Voltage Sources

Charges do not flow unless there is a potential difference. A sustained current requires a suitable "electrical pump" to provide a sustained potential difference. Something that provides a potential difference is known as a *voltage source.* (p. 511)

There is often some confusion between charge flowing *through* a circuit and voltage being impressed *across* a circuit. To distinguish between these ideas, consider a long pipe filled with water. Water will flow *through* the pipe if there is a difference in pressure *across* or between its ends. Water flows from the high-pressure end to the low-pressure end. Only the water flows, not the pressure. Similarly, you say that charges flow *through* a circuit because of an applied voltage *across the circuit.* You don't say that voltage flows through a circuit. Voltage doesn't go anywhere, for it is the charges that move. Voltage causes current. (pp. 511–512)

Electrical Resistance

The amount of current that flows in a circuit depends on the voltage provided by the voltage source. It also depends on the resistance that the conductor offers to the flow of charge, or the *electrical resistance*. This is similar to the rate of water flow in a pipe, which depends not only on the pressure behind the water but on the resistance offered by the pipe itself. The resistance of a wire depends on the *conductivity* of the material (that is, how well it conducts) and also on the thickness and length of the wire. (p. 512)

A Battery and a Bulb

It is a bit misleading to say that electrons flow "out of" the battery, or "into" the bulb; a better description is to say they flow *through* these devices. The flow of charge in a circuit is analogous to a pump, the wires to the pipes, and the bulb to any device that operates when the water is flowing. The water flows through both the pump itself and the circuit it connects. It doesn't "squash up" and concentrate in certain regions, but flows continuously. Electric current behaves the same way. (pp. 525–526)

Electric Circuits

Any path along which electrons can flow is a circuit. For a continuous flow of electrons, there must be a complete circuit with no gaps. A gap is usually provided by an electric switch that can be opened or closed to either cut off or allow electron flow.

The water analogy is quite useful for gaining a conceptual understanding of electric circuits, but it does have some limitations. An important one is that a break in a water pipe results in water spilling from the circuit, whereas a break in an electric circuit results in a complete stop in the flow of electricity. Another difference has to do with turning current off and on. When you *close* an electrical switch that connects the circuit, you allow current to flow in much the same way as you allow water to flow by *opening* a faucet. Opening a switch stops the flow of electricity. An electric circuit must be closed for electricity to flow. Opening a water faucet, on the other hand, starts the flow of water. Except for these and some other differences, thinking of electric current in terms of water current is a useful way to study electric circuits. (pp. 526–527)

In the analogy Hewitt has drawn between currents of water and currents of electricity, he effectively has performed all of the operations specified in the TWA model. In the electric current excerpt, he introduces the target concepts of voltage, current, and resistance. Next, in the flow of charge excerpt, he cues the reader to retrieve from memory information about currents of water. Hewitt realizes that some readers will have only fragmentary knowledge of a water flow system, so he provides a good deal of information about a water flow system. In the flow of charge excerpt, Hewitt identifies and maps similar features: "The flow of water in the pipe, like the flow of charge in the wire ..." Plus, his use of water circuit and electric circuit diagrams (refer back to Fig. 10.3) helps readers to identify and map similar features.

In addition to explaining new concepts, analogies can be used to clear up old misconceptions! In the excerpts about "voltage sources" and "a battery and a bulb," Hewitt does exactly this. He uses his analogy to counter some popular misconceptions that readers either already have or are likely to develop. It is important to keep in mind that analogies can be used to straighten out readers' misconceptions, particularly since one of the most popular arguments against using analogies is that they can sometimes cause misconceptions.

Hewitt draws conclusions for readers about the target concepts. For example, in the electrical resistance excerpt, he compares electrical resistance with the resistance water encounters in a pipe and draws the following conclusion for the reader: "The resistance of a wire depends on the conductivity of the material . . . and also on the thickness and length of the wire."

Finally, in the electrical circuit excerpt, Hewitt indicates where the analogy breaks down. He explains how a break in an electric circuit differs from that in a water pipe and how an electrical switch differs from a faucet. By doing so, he reduces the likelihood that his readers will overgeneralize from the analog to the target concept, and form some misconceptions.

Paul Hewitt's use of analogies is excellent. He performed all of the six operations specified in the TWA model. If an author were to perform only some of the operations, leaving some to the reader, the technical quality of the analogy would be reduced because it is possible that the reader might fail to perform an operation or might perform it poorly.

In our survey of textbooks of physics and of physical science, we have found many instances in which authors suggested an analog to readers, but then left the readers to make sense (or nonsense) of it for themselves. Under these circumstances, the students could identify irrelevant features of the target and analog, map them, draw wrong conclusions about the target, and fail to realize where the analogy breaks down. In short, the students' understanding of the target concept could be both incomplete and incorrect.

The Science Teacher's Use of the TWA Model

Teachers who keep the TWA model in mind can interpret textbook analogies for their students. If the author fails to perform some of the operations specified in the model, the teacher can perform them. For example, suppose the author of a science text draws an analogy between electricity in a wire and water in a hose, but fails to point out where this analogy breaks down, namely, that electricity does not spill out if the wire is cut. The teacher can remedy this failure on the author's part by performing this essential operation for the students.

Teachers should familiarize students with this model so they will learn how to interpret, criticize, and extend an author's analogy on their own. When this model has been used in science education classes to dissect an author's analogy, the discussions that ensued between the teacher and students, and the students themselves, enabled the teacher to identify students' misconceptions and knowledge gaps that otherwise would have gone undetected. The discussion also prompted students to tie together concepts they previously viewed as unrelated.

Teachers and students also are encouraged to use the model as a guide when generating their own analogies. They may wish to do this when the textbook author has not provided an analogy. For example, "listen in" on the following conversation between a seventh grade science teacher. Miss Davis, and one of her students, John.

John: I'm worried about the next science test, Miss Davis.

Miss Davis: Oh, what's giving you trouble, John?

J: The stuff on electricity and electric circuits in our text.

MD: Electricity can be a tough unit all right. Have you read your textbook carefully?

J: I sure have, lots of times. The reading is really hard. All the new terms get me confused.

MD: What were some of those confusing terms?

J: Well, I sort of know what a "circuit" is, but I'm not sure what "voltage" and "resistance" mean.

MD: What were some of the other electricity terms or ideas that you read about?

J: Uh, I read about "wires" and "batteries" and "switches."

MD: Yes, these are important parts of an electric circuit. You seem to remember all the important ideas from your reading. Can you put these ideas together and explain to me how an electric circuit works?

J: Ah, no. That's the problem. I can't get a picture in my head of how this electricity stuff works.

MD: Well, don't be discouraged, John. You learned a lot of important bits and pieces from the text. Let me see if I can help you put these bits and pieces together, so you will understand how an electric circuit works. Perhaps an analogy might help. Do you recall when you and your classmates set up the aquarium in the classroom?

J: Sure!

MD: And do you remember me explaining how the water circulated in the aquarium?

J: That was easy, not like this electricity stuff. When you explained how the water circulates, I could actually see the pump and filter.

MD: Right! Well, now I'm going to help you "see" how the electric circuit works by comparing it to water circulation in the aquarium. Look at the classroom aquarium while I describe again how the water flows through it in a circuit, or a connected path. A current of water is drawn through a pipe from the aquarium by a pump which controls pressure. The water then flows through a filter, which slows the flow and catches impurities. Finally, the water returns to the aquarium through a pipe. Do you remember and understand that, John?

J: Sure, Miss Davis.

MD: Fine. Now think about this question. What might the water correspond to in an electric circuit? That is, what flows in the circuit?

J: Electricity?

MD: Exactly! Very good. Now, the water is carried from the aquarium into the filter and back into the aquarium by means of plastic pipes. What do these pipes correspond to in an electric circuit?

J: The metal wires?

MD: Right again. Now, in the aquarium, the pump provided the pressure to move the water through the tubes. In an electric circuit, what device provides the pressure to move the electricity through the circuit?

J: How about a battery?

MD: Yes, indeed, a battery, or a generator. Now, for a tougher question. Like a pump, the battery produces a sort of electrical pressure. What's the correct name for this electrical pressure?

J: I bet it's voltage.

MD: And I bet you're right! Now here's a really tough question. We stuffed cotton in the aquarium filter to clean the water. This also had the effect of reducing the amount of water that flowed through the pipes in a given period of time. Likewise, in an electric circuit, the use of some poorly conducting metals in wires can reduce the amount of electricity that flows in a given period of time. In an electric circuit, what do you call this reduction in flow?

J: Resistance!

MD: Correct, John, I think you've got it. To sum up, let's list here on the board the features of our aquarium water circuit which correspond to those in electric circuit. [See Figure 10.2] Now, John, keeping these features in mind, explain to me how an electric circuit works.

J: OK, I'll give it a try. An electric circuit is an unbroken wire path through which electricity can flow. In order for the electricity to flow, there must be a source of voltage, such as a battery. How much electricity will flow through a circuit in a given period of time depends on how much resistance there is in the material which makes up the wire. So how's that? I guess I've got this circuit business down pat.

MD: Very impressive, but we're not done yet. I still have a few tricky questions.

J: OK, Miss Davis, give me your best shot.

MD: Look at this diagram (Figure 10.5) of an electric circuit; it's similar to the one in your textbook. The circuit contains a charged battery and a lit light bulb. What would happen to the electricity flowing through the circuit if you cut the wire and pulled the ends apart? Would you get a different result if you cut the wire before or after the light bulb?

J: Those are tricky questions, for sure. Hmm, let me use the aquarium water circuit analogy. If I cut the pipe returning water to the tank, the water would continue to flow, but probably spill out on the floor. On the other hand, if I cut the pipe taking water from the tank just above the water line, then the water would stop flowing. Now, I'll apply this analogy to your circuit. If I cut the wire before the bulb, then electricity would flow but spill out of the wire. If I cut behind the bulb, then electricity would stop flowing. Am I right?

MD: No, you are not, although your reasoning is good. When you cut or break an electric circuit at any point in the circuit, the electricity stops flowing everywhere in the circuit. That's the function of an electrical switch, by the way; it interrupts the circuit, stopping the flow of electricity.

J: But why wasn't I right, Miss Davis? I used the analogy.

MD: Because, John, no analogy is perfect. Analogies help us to understand some aspects of a new concept, but at some point every analogy breaks down.

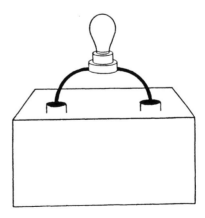

FIG. 10.5   Diagram of an electric circuit, with a charged battery and a lit bulb.

J: If analogies can lead us to wrong conclusions sometimes, then I think we shouldn't use them at all.

MD: That, John, would be like "throwing the baby out with the bath water" if you'll forgive me using another analogy. Analogies can be a big help to me when I explain new concepts and to you when you try to understand them. The trick is to use analogies carefully, keeping in mind their limitations and the wrong ideas which can arise when an analogy is carried too far. Used carefully, analogies can help you a lot, John, just as they've helped many of the famous scientists you've read about in your textbook.

J: Which scientists?

MD: Oh, astronomers such as Johannes Kepler, who drew an analogy between the movements of the planets and the workings of a clock. And physical scientists such as Joseph Priestley, who suggested the law of electrical force by drawing an analogy from the law of gravitational force.

J: Oh, yes, I remember their names. They used analogies, huh?

MD: Certainly. Analogies are important thinking tools. They can help us to make the jump between old ideas we already understand and new ideas we're trying to learn.

J: Is science the only area where I can use analogies?

MD: You can use analogies in all your subjects, John. They are powerful tools for understanding and problem solving. But do keep in mind their limitations.

J: I will, Miss Davis. And thanks a lot. I'm not worried about the test anymore.

Teaching a Science Concept with Several Analogies

In the preceding fictitious conversation, the teacher effectively used an analogy to explain a complicated concept a student encountered in a textbook.

Even if the text author has provided an analogy for a key concept, teachers and students may wish to generate another one so they can examine the concept from more than one perspective. For example, the author might use a "flowing water" analogy to explain the concept of electric current. The teacher and students, however, wishing to examine the concept from a different perspective, might generate a "moving crowd" analogy, in which electric current is compared with masses of people moving through tunnels.

The advantage of generating alternative analogies and viewing a concept from more than one perspective is that each perspective brings particular features of the concept into clearer focus. Thus, the teacher and the students who generate multiple analogies for a concept will have a more comprehensive understanding of that concept and its relationship to other concepts.

Although the focus in this fictitious conversation was on the elementary-school teacher's use of the TWA model, high school and college teachers can use the model in a similar way. Analogical reasoning can facilitate comprehension in students of all ages.

FUTURE RESEARCH

The TWA model was derived from an analysis of science texts, particularly physics and physical science texts. It is essential, however, that empirical studies be conducted to validate this model. A program of studies has been initiated to do just that. Hopefully, other researchers also will study and extend this model.

Science teachers should familiarize their students with this model. Systematic procedures for training students in the use of this model should be developed, and these procedures should be validated in classroom settings. Ethnographic studies of teacher–student–textbook interactions that involve analogies would be particularly appropriate.

Because the model proposed here was derived from an analysis of science texts, it is not clear to what extent this model generalizes across the curriculum to disciplines other than science. The model might generalize to other disciplines; however, textbook surveys and empirical studies must be conducted to verify this.

Finally, a great deal more research is needed on ways to facilitate analogical reasoning among science students. More information is needed on how individual differences in cognitive development and science knowledge influence the generation and use of analogies. More information is also needed concerning the circumstances under which analogies can be counterproductive, resulting in increased confusion instead of comprehension.

SUMMARY AND CONCLUSIONS

This chapter has shown that one of the most effective ways for students to integrate their existing knowledge with text content is by using analogical reasoning. Teachers and text authors can provide analogies for students, and students can be trained to generate their own analogies.

Analogies can put new concepts into familiar terms for students. Analogies can be used to transfer ideas from a familiar concept (the analog) to an unfamiliar one (the target).

In the representation of an analogy presented here, the analog and the target are subordinate to a superordinate concept. The identification and naming of the superordinate concept can suggest other analogies; it also can stimulate students to generalize what they have learned and apply their learning to other contexts.

An analogy should be used cautiously. An analog concept can be used to explain correctly and even predict some aspects of the target concept. At some point, however, every analogy breaks down. At that point, miscomprehension and misdirection can begin. Teachers and authors must make students aware of this.

Analogies drawn by a teacher or author between concepts covered early in a text and concepts covered later are particularly effective because there is some assurance that the earlier concepts (which function as analogs) are part of every student's knowledge base. These analogies prompt students to connect related text concepts and form conceptual systems.

Analogies that are effective from the standpoint of instructional design contain certain key features which have been incorporated into a model. The Teaching-with-Analogies model can serve as a guide for teachers and text-book authors. It can also serve as a guide for students who wish to interpret, criticize, and extend an instructional analogy or create one of their own.

The process of understanding new concepts by means of analogy is an inherent part of human cognition. The tendency to reason analogically is, in effect, "hard-wired" in human beings. It is important, therefore, that text-book authors, teachers, and students use analogies effectively as aids for understanding and insight in science. Toward this end, a model has been proposed for using analogies to explain concepts in science texts. Future research will focus on validating this model and developing procedures for helping authors, teachers, and students to use the model effectively.

REFERENCES

Alexander, P., White, C., & Mangano, N. (1983). Examining the effects of direct comprehension in analogical reasoning on reading comprehension. In J. Niles & L. Harris (Eds.), *Searches for meaning in reading/language processing and instruction.* Rochester, NY: National Reading Conference, pp. 36–41.

Anderson, J. R. (1980). *Cognitive psychology.* San Francisco: Freeman.

Barufaldi, J., Ladd, G., & Moses, A. (1981). *Health science.* Lexington, MA: Heath.

Bean, T., Singer, H., & Cowan, S. (1985). Analogical study guides: Improving comprehension in science. *Journal of Reading, 29,* 246–250.

Britton, B. K., & Glynn, S. M. (1987). *Executive control processes in reading.* Hillsdale, NJ: Lawrence Erlbaum Associates.

Britton, B. K., Glynn, S. M., Meyer, B. J. F., & Penland, M. J. (1982). Effects of text structure on use of cognitive capacity during reading. *Journal of Educational Psychology, 74,* 51–61.

Clement, J., Brown, D. E., & Zietsman, A. (in press). Not all preconceptions are misconceptions: Finding "anchoring conceptions" for grounding instruction on students' intuitions. *International Journal of Science Education.*

Gick, M. L., & Holyoak, K. J. (1980). Analogical problem solving. *Cognitive Psychology, 12,* 306–355.

Gick, M. L., & Holyoak, K. J. (1983). Schema induction and analogical transfer. *Cognitive Psychology, 15,* 1–38.

Glynn, S. M. (1978). Capturing readers' attention by means of typographical cuing strategies. *Educational Technology, 18*(11), 7–12.

Glynn, S. M. (1989). The Teaching-with-Analogy Model. In K. D. Muth (Ed.), *Children's comprehension of text* (pp. 185–204). Newark, DE: International Reading Association.

Glynn, S. M., Andre, T., & Britton, B. K. (1986). The design of instructional text: Introduction to the special issue. *Educational Psychologist, 21,* 245–251.

Glynn, S. M., & Britton, B. K. (1984). Supporting readers' comprehension through effective text design. *Educational Technology, 24*(10), 40–43.

Glynn, S. M., Britton, B. K., & Muth, K. D. (1985). Text-comprehension strategies based on outlines: Immediate and long-term effects. *Educational Technology, 53,* 129–135.

Glynn, S. M., Britton, B. K., Muth, K. D. (1990). Thinking out loud about concepts in science text: How instructional objectives work. In H. Mandl, E. De Corte, S. N. Bennett, & H. F. Friedrich (Eds.), *Learning and instruction: European research in an international context* (Vol. 2, pp. 215–223). Oxford: Pergamon.

Glynn, S. M., Britton, B. K., Semrud-Clikeman, M., & Muth, K. D. (1989). Analogical reasoning and problem solving in science textbooks. In J. Glover, R. Ronning, & C. Reynolds (Eds.), *Handbook of creativity: Assessment, research, and theory.* New York: Plenum Press.

Glynn, S. M., Britton, B. K., & Tillman, M. H. (1985). Typographical cues in text: Management of the reader's attention. In D. H. Jonassen (Ed.), *The technology of text* (Vol. 2). Englewood Cliffs, NJ: Educational Technology Publications.

Glynn, S. M., & Di Vesta, F. J. (1977). Outline and hierarchial organization as aids for study and retrieval. *Journal of Educational Psychology, 69,* 89–95.

Glynn, S. M., & Di Vesta, F. J. (1979). Control of prose processing via instructional cues. *Journal of Educational Psychology, 71,* 595–603.

Halpern, D. (1987). Analogies as a critical thinking skill. In D. Berger, K. Pezdek, & W. Banks (Eds.), *Applications of cognitive psychology.* Hillsdale, NJ: Lawrence Erlbaum Associates.

Hayes, D. (1987). *Directing prose learning with analogical study guides.* Paper presented at the American Educational Research Association meeting, Washington, DC, April.

Hesse, M. B. (1966). *Models and analogies in science.* Notre Dame, IN: University of Notre Dame Press.

Hewitt, P. G. (1987). *Conceptual physics,* Menlo Park, CA: Addison-Wesley.

Miller, F., Dillon, T. J., & Smith, M. K. (1980). *Concepts in physics.* New York: Harcourt, Brace, Jovanovich.

Oppenheimer, R. (1956). Analogy in science. *American Psychologist,* 127-135.

Polya, G. (1973). *Mathematics and plausible reasoning* (Vol. 1.) Princeton, NJ: Princeton University Press.

Rogers, E. M. (1960). *Physics for the inquiring mind.* Princeton, NJ: Princeton University Press.

Rutherford, F. J., Holton, G., & Watson, F. G. (1975). *Project physics.* New York: Holt, Rinehart & Winston.

Vosniadou, S., & Brewer, W. (1987). Theories of knowledge restructuring in development. *Review of Educational Research, 57,* 51–67.

Wittrock, M. C. (1985). Learning science by generating new conceptions from old ideas. In L. H. T. West & A. L. Pines (Eds.), *Cognitive structure and conceptual change.* Orlando, FL: Academic Press.

11 Learning Science in Software Microworlds

Patricia E. Simmons
The University of Georgia

By 1994, the Office of Technology Assessment predicts that more than 4,000,000 microcomputers will be in the schools. In each of the last 10 years, computing technologies and uses of these technologies have increased in the public school setting (Becker, 1986). Approximately one-fourth of high school science teachers use computers; however, the pattern of use is low at all grade levels and in all subject areas. Surveys conducted by Lehman (1985), Becker (1986), Weiss (1987), and National Science Teachers Association (1987) have shown that most science educational software in use is drill and practice, followed by tutorials, programming, and word processing. Information from these most recent surveys on current uses of microcomputers and software indicated that computer-using teachers perceived that student motivation, student–student cooperation, student independence, and opportunities for high-ability students all increased when using microcomputers (Becker, 1987). Clearly, the appropriate use of microcomputers and educational software can result in desirable cognitive and affective learning outcomes for our science students that are consistent with current goals in science education (National Science Teachers Association, 1989). The challenge for science teachers at all levels becomes one of synthesizing educational technologies and effective instructional strategies to provide optimal learning experiences for all students.

Advancements in computer technologies for educational settings have resulted in the development of two kinds of educational software: intelligent tutoring systems and "cognition enhancers" (Dede, 1987). The term cognition enhancer refers to empowering environments, hypermedia, and microworlds. The use of a cognition enhancer is predicated on the idea of building a "partnership" between the information technology available (e.g.,

241

computer microworlds) and the learner's cognitive strengths. Because of the current hardware and software limitations on available computer technologies, "cognition enhancers" are emerging as one of the most powerful learning tools available for science instruction.

WHAT IS A COMPUTER MICROWORLD?

A computer microworld is "a structured environment that allows the learner to explore and manipulate a rule-governed universe, subject to specific assumptions and constraints, that serves as an analogical representation of some aspects of the natural world" (Pea, 1984). Computer microworlds are idealized environments composed of objects, relationships among objects, and operations that transform the objects and their relationships (Thompson, 1985). Seymour Papert (1980) first described the idea of computer microworlds in relation to using Logo turtles (dynaturtles) to teach principles of Newtonian physics. For example, students learned about Newton's Law of action and reaction by using two Logo turtles, each of which behaved the opposite of the other.

The idea underlying the construction of computer microworlds is that these "artificial realities" will enable learners to manipulate the realities in ways which learners cannot manipulate the "real world" (diSessa, 1982, 1988). The computer microworld is constructed so that learners interact with an artificial reality that leads them beyond their initial levels of understanding, and moves them toward a "deeper structure" of understanding of the microworld reality.

WHY SHOULD WE USE COMPUTER MICROWORLDS?

The fundamental view of the learner, based on current cognitive research in science learning, is that the learner *constructs* understanding, *understands* by knowing relationships, and *links* new information to previous knowledge, which fits established schemata (Resnick, 1983). Teachers need to provide the kinds of learning environments that enable learners to be successful and engage in the cognitive tasks that have been described. This requires the learner to be active in the classroom, employ scientific reasoning, and interact with appropriate scientific models that stimulate and enhance cognitive growth (Larkin & Chabay, 1989).

Computer microworlds represent a medium between concrete models and abstract thinking models. DiSessa (1988) stated that the design of computer microworlds should be based on two kinds of heuristics: the concept of mega-microworlds and the idea of textured microworlds. A mega-microworld is predicated on the premise that scientific understanding is built around multiple perspectives that are well integrated and applicable to real-life situations. Thus, students would build clusters of perspectives with which to view and understand the world. The textured microworld is built around the idea that teachers have precise expectations about students' learning, in terms of the kinds of relationships and understanding which students are constructing through their microworld experiences. Rather than simply have students experience the computer microworld and then assess their success or failure in understanding the principles and ideas contained within the microworld, teachers can determine and tailor specific kinds of experiences into the microworld. Gaps in students' learning and understanding are dealt with by changing the system of understanding of the learner, not just presenting the learner with cognitive conflicts and forcing minor changes in learners' conceptual frameworks or "naïve" theories to occur.

The computer microworld used as a cognition enhancer enables learners to explore, experiment, and manipulate artificial systems and models of scientific realities (Dede, 1987). Students can spend time developing their understanding of scientific concepts and problem solving on a metacognitive level, rather than bogging down in logistical details of problem solving or rote learning of numerous facts. An artificial reality that enables learners to explore scientific principles and laws that are fundamental to an understanding of the real world but which cannot be demonstrated in the real world with all of the constraining and uncontrollable variables, lends itself to an ideal situation for learners to explore their ideas on how reality works.

The terms "computer simulation" and "computer microworld" are often used interchangeably in the literature. Although microworlds and simulations share many common features, a major distinction between the two is that the simulation may or may not have an educational application (Hale, personal communication, 1990). Simulations are representations of models with rules that specify certain interactions between the user and the simulation. The user (learner) constructs an understanding of the rules, the model, and the interactions. Microworlds contain a theme (realistic or abstract) in the learning environment which may or may not be based on a particular model (for example *The Factory*). Because many characteristics of simulations and microworlds overlap with each other, the examples cited in this chapter will include computer programs which may be considered as simulations and or as microworlds.

WHAT DO WE KNOW ABOUT THE COGNITIVE AND AFFECTIVE OUTCOMES FROM RESEARCH WITH EXISTING COMPUTER MICROWORLDS?

One principal obstacle to student understanding and comprehension is the failure of learners to separate mental actions (e.g., understanding principles, conceptual linkages, and scientific inquiry from the attributes (e.g., facts) of an object (Thompson, 1985). In a study with a geometry computer microworld (*Motions*) elementary teachers interacted with the microworld to understand transformation geometry. Although this study focused on math education, several interesting results were reported and should be noted by science teachers. When the teachers' understanding of rotation, motions in a coordinate system, and symmetries of plane figures were faulty, they received a different kind of response from their interactions with the microworld. In a more traditional teacher-centered setting (no microworld), the responses they received from the teacher provided no intrinsic value to them. That is, students had difficulty recognizing and understanding why a particular way of thinking was inconsistent with accepted ways of thinking. By experiencing and "playing around" with various problems with the *Motions* microworld (e.g., being asked to generate a set of motions that result in a specific movement of an object), the teachers were able to rethink their understanding about unexpected behaviors of objects. This caused them to modify their explanations and predictions about the principles underlying those behaviors.

The teachers who participated in the computer treatment also tended to play with a problem and explore their ideas about a problem before engaging in problem solution. Nontreatment teachers did not do this. Thompson (1985) noted that this tendency lo play with problems extended to noncomputer-based settings of problem solving.

In the physical sciences, one application of a computer microworld (an intelligent tutor system) was described by White and Frederickson (1987). In this software, a physics microworld was contained within an interactive simulation (*QUEST*). *QUEST* consisted of a series of interactive simulations about an electrical circuit. The principal feature of *QUEST* was the design of the microworld. A progression of learners' mental models about circuit behavior, which emphasized qualitative scientific models, formed the basis for the series of microworlds. Students selected, built, modified, and tested various circuits and their components. At the completion of each set of activities in a microworld, the learner developed a more refined mental model about circuit behavior.

In another set of microworld simulations, *ThinkerTools*, an understanding of Newtonian mechanics was emphasized (White, in press; White & Horwitz, 1987; 1989). The goal of this set of computer microworlds was to expose students, in this case, sixth graders, to more simplified microworlds. In these microworlds, students did not have to contend with the multiple forces affecting motion, but focused on an "idealized" world in which friction or gravity did not affect the behaviors of objects. The design of these computer microworlds was based on physical science phenomena and models that could be understood by 11- and 12-year-olds, but also provided flexibility to investigate various kinds of problems on Newtonian mechanics. Students had to develop an understanding of Newtonian mechanics (force, acceleration), an understanding of the relationships between factors that caused velocity to change, and a mental representation for the concept of velocity (e.g., objects launched from tabletops with differing horizontal velocities). To facilitate students' acquisition of this kind of model about Newtonian mechanics, the series of computer microworlds were constructed to build upon the increasing complexities of the Newtonian laws governing the behaviors of objects. Students first experimented with a microworld with no friction or gravity operating on the object. Impulses were applied to move the object to the right or left direction. Students were expected to discover that a given set of impulses administered to the object resulted in the object moving in a scalar fashion on the screen. A more complex microworld had students deal with gravity in a world where motion was based upon constant acceleration in a vertical dimension and constant speed in a horizontal dimension. Thus, the students had to develop a mental model of understanding about the first microworlds before progressing to the next microworld. At each level, learners had to refine their mental models on Newtonian mechanics.

One goal of *ThinkerTools* is to design instruction based on microworlds that would enable students to develop and acquire a desired mental model about Newtonian mechanics. The subject matter (force, acceleration) is embedded within the activity, so that learners are required to experience and experiment with the concepts while engaging in scientific inquiry. For example, students were given a set of laws and asked to indicate which laws were correct and which were incorrect by using the computer microworlds available to them.

Another goal of *ThinkerTools* is to have students understand and experience the process of change of scientific knowledge. The students engage in discussions about predictions on the behavior of the microworld, rule out laws that did not apply by formulating, predicting, and testing their ideas within the microworld, and discuss the applicability of their findings and conclusions. The kind of behaviors by students was determined to indicate success in understanding scientific processes and inquiry.

An interesting finding was that students attended only to solving the problem given to them, such as formulating a law about the behavior of the microworld (White & Horwitz, 1988). The students terminated their learning after discovering the desired relationships, and did not extend their scientific inquiry to implications for real-world applications of their findings.

Students received a physics misconceptions paper-and-pencil test to assess their understanding of Newtonian mechanics in real-world problem-solving situations. Forty-one sixth graders received the *ThinkerTools* curriculum daily over a 2-month span, compared with a control group of 37 sixth graders who received the standard curriculum. The treatment group exhibited statistically significant differences on the paper-and-pencil outcomes from the control. There were no significant differences noted due to gender or ability (based on the California Achievement Test).

One interesting finding of this study was a comparison between the paper-

and-pencil assessment performances of the sixth graders receiving the treatment with a second control group of high school physics students who received traditional text-based Newtonian physics instruction. On some problems, the sixth graders performed as well as the high school students. For example, on one problem examining the trajectory of a ball when it is kicked off the edge of a cliff, nearly all of the sixth graders responded correctly. Most of the high school students responded incorrectly on this item. This is not surprising, since the majority of high school and college students respond incorrectly to these kinds of items. The observation that the *ThinkerTools* students performed well may indicate that the use of an appropriate microworld may aid in students' understanding of the behavior of various physical phenomena. However, students were assessed with only a few items on the paper-and-pencil assessment. A paper-and-pencil format may not reveal as much rich information about learners' mental models as other kinds of assessments. On another problem dealing with spiral motion, the high school students and the sixth graders performed equally well.

When the *ThinkerTools* curriculum was evaluated for effectiveness of facilitating students' understanding of Newtonian mechanics, the evidence suggested that the use of computer microworlds may be able to help students develop, enhance, and refine their mental models about principles and relationships in science. Certainly, the preliminary results indicated that much more research is needed in this area of cognition.

In the life sciences, computer software, such as *Catlab* or *Birdbreed*, are based upon real-world models of cat and bird populations. Learning experiences that employ genetics simulation enable learners to manipulate and use their knowledge about genetics in a different problem solving context from typical textbook or verification laboratories. Kinnear (1983a) summarized comparisons between the characteristics of actual experimentation versus computer-simulated experimentation. The actual experiment is a situation in which only one trial is conducted, redesign of the experiment is rare, teacher-centered procedures are employed, convergent thinking is encouraged, unfamiliar organisms and large numbers of offspring are produced at one time, and strains used in the experiment are usually pure breeding stock. By contrast, the computer-simulated experiment via the microworld environment allows for multiple repetitions and redesigns of experiments and student design of experiments. Divergent thinking is encouraged, familiar organisms and small numbers of offspring are generated, and the organism can consist of any genetic composition.

Many secondary and tertiary students perceived genetics problem solving (textbook and verification laboratories) to be nonmeaningful and based on rote performance (Kinnear, 1983b; Longden, 1982; Stewart, 1982). What is required is a learning context that is more meaningful and results in more meaningful learning for students.

The learner must not only develop an understanding of the principles and concepts in genetics, but engage in and understand how to use scientific inquiry skills (Kinnear, 1983b). These simulations allow the user to generate individuals based on a random number generator of allelic frequencies in real-world populations. In *Catlab*, the learner selects various characteristics of cats, such as coat color, presence or absence of a tail, and so forth. The information the learner is given about the genetic composition of the cat is based only on the outward appearance of the cat.

Learners must construct cats and then determine how to use the cats in solving problems about inheritance. As an example, white coat color in cats is due to the presence of a masking gene, that is, the presence of white "covers up" the presence of orange or gray or stripes. In a study with high school students using *Catlab*, two white cats were crossed. The students expected to generate white kittens, which indicated to them that white was a "pure" color (Simmons, 1989); white kittens may be generated, but orange, gray, black, and various colored and striped cats may also be generated. A variety of colored and striped kittens appeared. The students expressed great surprise and had to reformulate their mental model of the inheritance pattern of white coat color in cats (Simmons, 1989).

An examination of 300 genetics textbook problems revealed that 48% of the problems dealt with probabilistic reasoning and understanding (Kinnear, 1983b). In a series of studies conducted by Kinnear, students interacted with genetics simulation of parakeets (*Birdbreed*). *Birdbreed* was employed to examine students' understanding of probability in a computer-based problem-solving context. Students decided what kind of data to generate (offspring of birds selected from specific breeding stocks) and then determined the relevancy of that data toward solving the problem. The results from this study involving 59 university-level students revealed that a majority rated the computer-based problem-solving tasks to be very valuable cognitively and affectively. These students had completed prerequisite introductory biology courses with textbook-based problems. When asked to indicate if the computer-based problems required them to use and learn different problem-solving skills from textbook problems, 75% responded yes. Additional comments made by students indicated that their understanding of genetics and probability (genetics ratios) had shifted to a view that was more congruent with real-world genetics. However, there were some students who did not reconcile their understanding in the computer-based problem-solving context to their prior experiences. They expressed great frustration when the data did not match their expectations. These students viewed their genetic data as deterministic and not probabilistic in nature.

In another study, a sample of 44 university level students enrolled in a biology course solved computer-based problems, in which the problem statement or goal was given to the student. The majority of students indicated that this microcomputer experience was challenging, cognitively valuable, interesting, and valuable as a learning experience.

WHAT ARE THE IMPLICATIONS OF USING COMPUTER MICROWORLDS FOR STUDENTS' LEARNING AND FOR TEACHERS' INSTRUCTION?

Piaget's writings (1973) on the developmental stages of psychological growth influenced the perspective from which learning is viewed. This perspective, now called constructivism, was defined as the view of psychological development (intelligence), which has as a central tenet, the interactions between the endogenous character of the child and the child's environment. These interactions are critical and lead the child to construct more advanced stages of knowledge. The child must discover and construct a meaning and understanding of the universe by oneself. The construction of more advanced states of knowledge cannot be done by the teacher for the child; the teacher can provide the opportunities and experiences which may lead to the development and construction of knowledge by the child.

An essential part of the application of constructivism in the learning environment is that students need to explore their ideas. Computer microworlds lend themselves to an instructional use of providing environments in which students can explore ideas by learning problem-solving skills and domain specific knowledge (Papert, 1980; Pea, 1984). Enhanced cognitive performances would be the result of learning environments containing appropriate models with which to engage students in enhanced conceptual understanding and problem solving (Pea, 1984).

Piaget (1973) stated that socialization was necessary for learners to develop intellectually. Cooperative learning contexts (Johnson & Johnson, 1979) help provide learners with opportunities to engage in socialization. Instructional approaches employing cooperative learning can utilize the potential of computer microworlds to engage students in cognitive growth. For instance, White (in press) employed an instructional approach that focused on group problem solving and experimentation with physical science computer microworlds. Students began by learning about principles and concepts governed by the rules in the computer microworld system and then shifted to transferring these principles and laws to another context, such as a laboratory.

What is the teacher's role?

The lack of use of computers and educational software, such as microworlds, has been ascribed principally to a lack of teacher knowledge about computers and their instructional applications (Woodrow, 1989). This barrier to the use of software can be overcome by appropriate preservice and in-service experiences for science teachers at all levels. The goals for these kinds of experiences should parallel the experiences that science students will undergo when they begin to use computer microworlds. First, computer literacy needs to be stressed. This can be accomplished through an approach that highlights the everyday applications of software (word-processing lesson plans or tests, planning lessons with interactive simulations such as *Molecular Velocities, Catlab, Geology Search, Oh Deer!* or *Voyage of the MiMi*). These kinds of experiences may help to demonstrate the educational applications and potential of using computer microworlds to enhance science learning and teaching.

Scientists employ and refine their mental models about the scientific phenomena they study while they study them. As scientists construct, employ, and modify qualitative and quantitative models to help them explain and predict the behaviors of various scientific phenomena, teachers need to plan instruction that parallels these processes with their students. This aspect of science (inquiry) is not very often discussed or modeled in science classrooms. Students need to have opportunities to use approaches that stress the development of qualitative mental models and reasoning patterns to understand scientific models. In particular, students can be made aware of and develop multiple mental models to explain how science functions, rather than learning or parroting only one "correct" model about science. Teachers need to be cognizant of and model the approaches and reasoning that scientists employ. When teachers are active role models of inquiry in their classrooms, students will be more likely to demonstrate similar kinds of behaviors and develop inquiring attitudes (Costa, 1985).

The teacher's role becomes critical during learning situations such as the ones described in this chapter. The teacher can engage students in meaningful dialogue to cause students to initiate further inquiry of their discoveries. By asking divergent questions of students or having students generate their own questions, teachers can help stimulate the development and enhancement of their students' conceptual understanding, problem-solving abilities, and the nature of scientific inquiry.

For example, the computer simulation, *Catlab*, can be embedded within a learning-cycle context (Simmons & Lunetta, 1987). The learning-cycle approach described by Renner, Abraham, & Birnie (1986) consists of three phases: exploration, conceptual invention, conceptual expansion. During exploration with *Catlab*, students interact with the simulation by experiencing information and concepts prior to the more formal discussion of major conceptual organizers. In the conceptual invention phase, the teacher leads discussions during which more precise scientific language and concepts are introduced. During the conceptual expansion phase, students extend their understanding by applying concepts, relating concepts to new information, redefining questions, and further investigating their ideas.

A computer simulation or microworld, such as *Catlab,* provides students with opportunities lo learn about scientific models by interacting with an artificial reality that is a good approximation of real world genetics. Learners can engage in problem-solving tasks in which they enhance their mental models about genetics principles by: (1) generating their own questions, (2) determining which variables to control or investigate, (3) interpreting and analyzing data, and (4) drawing conclusions about their data, which support or reject their hypotheses. Evidence from studies using *Catlab* in this context suggested that teaching strategies incorporating computer microworlds can enable teachers to provide successful learning experiences for their students, which result in cognitive growth and positive attitudes toward science and technology (Simmons, 1989; Simmons & Lunetta, 1987).

What is the student's role?

Previous research studies in problem solving have reported that both "novices" and "experts" approached problem solving using qualitative reasoning (Chi, Feltovich, & Glaser, 1981; Larkin, McDermott, Simon, & Simon, 1980). The "experts" typically employed qualitative reasoning extensively in problem solving before using quantitative reasoning skills. For instance, deKleer (1985) noted that engineers worked at understanding a circuit at a qualitative level before attempting to engage in quantitative problem solving. Thus the approach toward learning science should emphasize a qualitative reasoning approach (White & Frederickson, 1987). Instruction should employ quantitative reasoning as an extension of the qualitative reasoning that precedes it. This sequencing will enable students to confront and reconcile their mental models with "scientists' models" of the world and change the mental systems through which they view science (diSessa, 1988).

For example, if the principles underlying the basic steady-state circuit are taught in the context of traditional approaches, a quantitative model is introduced as soon as possible to students. By contrast, students can be taught through the use of qualitative physical models (as is common in most introductory texts) (White & Frederickson, 1987). Breakdowns in understanding and model evolution occur when the link between behaviors of charged electrical panicles and Newton's laws to circuit theory are not made by students. These linkages could be forged by examining circuit theory in terms of the more elemental components and developing models that help to explain the behaviors of components in a qualitative sense. White and Frederickson (1987) developed a computer microworld that focused on the distributions of positive and negative charge carriers in a circuit as would be found in a battery. Such physical models enabled students to focus from the macroscopic level to the microscopic level of circuit behavior.

In a previous study by White and Frederickson (1987) using this computer microworld, seven high school students with no formal instruction in circuit theory used the software. Students browsed through the topics available on the software, selected problems to try, and altered the circuitry. A trouble-shooting algorithm was also available for consultation by the students. Pretest results revealed that students exhibited misconceptions about circuit behavior and lacked an understanding of principal electricity concepts. The students worked approximately 1 week, 1 hour per day, with the software. All students were able to predict circuit behavior accurately and scored correctly on the posttest items. White and Frederickson (1987) noted that some students also modified the trouble-shooting algorithm to make the system more efficient.

Another interactive simulation by Lunetta, Lane, and Peters (1986) entitled *Models of Electric Current: Ohm's Law,* contains a simple circuit that can be enlarged to reveal a model of animated particulate motion. When current is applied to the circuit, the particles become animated. Students can vary certain parameters, such as voltage, in the circuit and note the effects on the behavior of the microscopic particles. These kinds of computer microworlds enable students to explain physical phenomena on a microscopic level, refining and redefining their mental models about electricity, and generalize to the contexts of macroscopic levels.

What are expected cognitive outcomes?

Conceptual understanding and reflection on problem-solving strategies and solutions, and successful outcomes are appropriate instructional outcomes. The literature on conceptual change research (Hewson, 1981; Osborne, 1982; Osborne, Freyberg, Tasker, & Stead, 1981; Zietsman & Hewson, 1986) indicates that children's ideas and theories about how the scientific world works are very resistant to change. Children employ theories derived from their previous experience with the world from which to reason and make sense of new experiences and concepts (Zietsman & Hewson, 1986). Such conceptions have been referred to as "alternative conceptions" or "alternative frameworks", since "it is not a matter of 'not understanding' but of 'understanding differently'" (Nussbaum & Novick, 1982) According to Hewson (1981), certain conditions must occur for children to consider changing or abandoning their current conception or view of how the world works. For them to change this view, children must recognize and be willing to integrate new conceptions into their existing conceptual frameworks. The new conception must appear to be plausible, intelligible, and coherent, and more useful than the previous conception. One problem in science learning and teaching is that scientists' view of the world may not be intelligible plausible, or useful to children's current view of the world. Thus, helping students learn how to change their view of the world (conceptual framework) is an important goal of science teaching. Teachers need to understand their students' view of science and the scientists' view of science to provide appropriate learning experiences and meet educational goals (National Science Teachers Association, 1989).

One way of helping teachers deal with changing students' conception of the world is through a conceptual change teaching strategy (Zietsman & Hewson, 1986). A conceptual change teaching strategy consists of learners being confronted by new conceptions, in which the outcomes of this confrontation depend on the interactions between the new conceptions and the "old" conceptions. If the new conceptions cannot be integrated within the overall conceptual framework of understanding, the learner rejects the new conception. If, however, the learner recognizes the need for integrating the new conception into the existing framework, then the framework will undergo change and learning can proceed with less difficulty. Thus, teachers must first diagnose learners' existing conceptions to determine if a conceptual change teaching strategy is needed for instruction.

The use of microcomputer simulations with conceptual change teaching strategies were reported by Zietsman and Hewson (1986) in a study with 34 10th-grade students in South Africa. Students received a remedial microcomputer treatment on physical science concepts of motion and velocity. One finding from this study indicated that more than 90% of the students responded to the microcomputer treatment (simulated tasks) the same way they responded to the real tasks. In addition, the pretest and posttest scores showed a significant difference in the conceptions of velocity held by students (working individually) who received the computer treatment and those did not receive the computer treatment. It should be noted, however, that fairly small sample sizes of students were compared in this study. Certainly, the finding that the treatment group outscored the nontreatment group would have been an expected outcome. The most interesting and significant aspect of this study was the context of the conceptual change strategy in which the computer treatment was embedded. Students demonstrated changes in their conceptions of velocity as a result of the treatment.

It should be noted that there are criticisms of the conceptual change approach of learning and teaching. DiSessa (1988) proposed another perspective, using as an example students' intuitive knowledge of physics. He viewed intuitive knowledge as consisting of large numbers of fragments, as opposed to the integrated naïve theories upon which the conceptual change view is based. It may be that students deal with real-world physics on a short-term basis, attending only to the immediate problem at hand, and do not conceptualize a larger integrated theory of physics (diSessa, 1988). Thus, the focus for conceptual change is moved to the level of students' systematic view of the physical world, rather than the replacement of students' naïve theories with the more accepted scientific theory of the physical world.

In a study, diSessa (1988) described an optics microworld dealing with ray tracing and other optics concepts. He found that although students would explore with the microworld for a period of time, they lost interest and did not view the microworld as connecting to their real-world experiences. The system lacked a critical component tying it to students' real world experiences. By modifying the microworld, the environment shifted from students playing with it to students connecting abstract questions to experiential and more meaningful learning.

An earlier chapter by Krajcik (this volume), stated the importance of using computer microworlds to allow students to experience firsthand models of science that are not easily observed or studied in nature. He presented a well-articulated discussion of the uses of chemistry computer microworlds to aid in students' understanding of scientific concepts.

In the life sciences, it may not be possible to study mammalian genetics and gene interactions with the organisms available for science laboratories. Microbial genetics can be fairly easily accomplished, but specialized nutrient media and sterilization apparatuses are usually required. At times, students find it difficult to understand the relevance of smearing E. coli, watching for color changes on a dish of gelatin, and relating that experience to the real-world genetics that affects them.

At this point, the use of interactive simulations, such as *Catlab* (mammalian genetics) or *Birdbreed* (avian genetics) were perceived by many students to be more familiar, and thus more relevant to their real-world experiences (Kinnear, 1983a; Simmons, 1989). It obviously is not possible to breed organisms such as cats, dogs, and parakeets in the two seconds during which the computer simulation can generate the offspring. The students' problem-solving tasks then become one of employing the computer simulation to investigate their understanding of concepts, such as probability, Mendelian inheritance, and gene interactions.

HOW CAN COMPUTER MICROWORLDS HELP LEARNERS' CONCEPTUAL UNDERSTANDING?

The previous studies described in this chapter strongly suggested that learners using computer microworlds reflect on their thinking processes, which result in more intrinsic learning values. Computer microworlds not only result in changes in quantitative learning experiences, but also in qualitative learning experiences (White, in press). These can enhance and enrich the quality of learning experiences available in science classrooms.

The potential applications of computers in the science classroom have expanded greatly from the range of number crunching and data-processing functions to powerful learning environments (Dede, 1987). Learning environments, like microworlds, enable students and teachers to transcend the routine mechanics of various kinds of problem-solving tasks and to concentrate on higher-order thinking skills. The evolution of learners' mental models about scientific phenomena and principles becomes the instructional focus.

Students need to rethink their understanding when cognitive conflicts arise (Costa, 1985). By helping students acquire and develop various mental models, they will have a more coherent set of mental models with which to explain, predict, and understand scientific phenomena from various domains (White & Frederickson, 1989). With computer microworlds, learners exhibited tendencies to explore with the microworld before jumping into a solution attempt (Thompson, 1985). Some studies indicated that these kinds of behaviors and approaches of learners toward problem solving may be transferred to noncomputer-based problem-solving contexts.

It is well known that most children and teen-agers find interacting with the microworlds in video games quite interesting (Lepper & Malone, 1987). Learners have found interacting with computer microworlds to be quite stimulating and motivating (Dede, 1987). Our task as science teachers then becomes one of channeling this motivation into educational situations that result in greater cognitive outcomes and more positive attitudes toward science and technology.

REFERENCES

Becker, H. J. (1986). *Instructional uses of school computers: Reports from the 1985 national survey.* Issues 1–4. Johns Hopkins University Center for Social Organization of Schools, Baltimore.

Becker, H. J. (1987). *The impact of computer use on children's learning: What research has shown and what it has not.* Center for Research on Elementary and Middle Schools, Johns Hopkins University, Baltimore.

Chi, M. Feltovich, P., & Glaser, R. (1981). Categorization and representation of physics problems by experts and novices. *Cognitive Science, 5,* 121–152.

Costa, A. L. (1985). (Ed.). *Developing minds: A resource book for teaching thinking.* Alexandria: Association for Supervision and Curriculum Development.

Dede, C. J. (1987). Empowering environments, hypermedia and microworlds. *Computing Teacher,* November, pp. 20–24.

deKleer, J. (1985). How circuits work. In D. G. Bobrow (Ed.), *Qualitative reasoning about physical systems.* Cambridge, MA: MIT Press.

diSessa, A. A. (1982). Unlearning Aristotelian physics: A study of knowledge-based learning. *Cognitive Science, 6,* 37–75.

diSessa, A. A. (1988). Knowledge in pieces. In G. Forman & P. B. Pufall (Eds.), *Constructivism in the computer age.* Hillsdale, NJ: Lawrence Erlbaum Associates.

Hewson, P. W. (1981). A conceptual change approach to learning science. *European Journal of Science Education, 3,* 383–396.

Johnson, D. & Johnson, R. (1979). *Learning together and alone: cooperation, competition, and individualization.* Englewood Cliffs, NJ: Prentice-Hall.

Kinnear, J. (1983a). *Using computer simulations to enhance problem-solving skills and concept development in biology students.* Computer ALITE Conference, Brisbane, Australia.

Kinnear, J. (1983b). Identification of misconceptions in genetics and the use of computer simulations in their correction. *Proceedings of the First International Conference on Misconceptions.* Cornell University, Ithaca, NY.

Larkin, J. H., & Chabay, R. W. (1989). Research on teaching scientific thinking: implications for computer-based instruction. In L. B. Resnick & L. E. Klopfer (Eds.), *Toward the thinking curriculum: Current cognitive research.* 1989 Yearbook of the Association for Supervision and Curriculum Development. Alexandria.

Larkin, J. H., McDermott, J. Simon, D. P., & Simon, H. A. (1980). Expert and novice performance in solving physics problems, *Science, 208,* 1335–1342.

Lehman, J. R. (1985). Survey of microcomputer use in the science classroom. *School Science and Mathematics, 85,* 578–583.

Lepper, M. R., & Malone, T. W. (1987). Intrinsic motivation and instructional effectiveness in computer based education. In R. E. Snow & M. S. Farr (Eds.), *Aptitude, learning, and instruction, vol 3: Conative and Affective Process Analysis.* Lawrence Erlbaum Associates: Hillsdale, NJ.

Longden, B. (1982). Genetics-are there inherent learning difficulties. *Journal of Biological Education, 16,* 135–140.

Lunetta, V. N., Lane, E. & Peters, H. (1986). *Models of electric current: Ohm's Law.* Conduit: Iowa City, IA.

National Science Teachers Association, (1987). *The 1985 microcomputer survey of secondary science teachers.* Author: Washington, DC.

National Science Teachers Association, (1989). *A task force report on the scope and sequence of science instruction in K–12 classrooms.* Author: Washington, DC.

Nussbaum, J., & Novick, S. (1982). Alternative frameworks, conceptual conflict, and accommodation: Toward a principled teaching strategy. *Instructional Science, 11,* 183–200.

Office of Technology Assessment. (1982). *Information technology and its impact on American education.* United States Government Printing Office: Washington, DC.

Osborne, R. J. (1982). Conceptual change for pupils and teachers. *Research in Science Education, 12,* 25–31.

Osborne, R. J., Freyberg, P., Tasker, R., & Stead, K. (1981). Description, analysis, and action: Three phases of a research project. *Research in Science Education, 11,* 52–58.

Papert, S. (1980). *Mindstorms: Children, computers, and powerful ideas.* New York: Basic Books.

Pea, R. (1984). *Integrating human and computer intelligence.* Technical Report No. 32. Bank Street College of Education: New York, New York.

Piaget, J. (1973). *The child and reality: Problems of genetic psychology.* New York: Grossman.

Renner, J. W., Abraham, M. R., & Birnie, H. H. (1986). The importance of the form of student acquisition of data in physics learning cycles. *Journal of Research in Science Teaching, 22,* 303–325.

Resnick, L. B. (1983). Mathematics and science learning: A new conception. *Science, 220,* 477–478.

Simmons, P. E., & Lunetta, V. N. (1987). Catlab: A learning cycle approach. *American Biology Teacher, 49,* 107–109.

Simmons, P. E. (1989). *Problem solving strategies and approaches of successful and unsuccessful subjects interacting with a genetics computer simulation.* National Association of Research in Science Teaching, San Francisco.

Stewart, J. (1982). Difficulties experienced by high school students when learning basic Mendelian genetics. *American Biology Teacher, 44,* 80–89.

Thompson, P. W. (1985). A Piagetian approach to transformation geometry via microworlds. *Mathematics Teacher,* September, pp. 465–471.

Weiss, I. R. (1987). *Report of the 1985–86 national survey of science and mathematics education.* Research Triangle Institute: North Carolina.

White, B. Y. (in press). A microworld-based approach to science education. In E. Scanlon & T. O'Shea (Eds.), *New Directions in Educational Technology.* New York: Springer Verlag.

White, B. Y., & Frederickson, J. R. (1987). *Causal model progressions as a foundation for intelligent learning environments.* Report No. 6686. BBN Laboratories: Cambridge, MA.

White, B. Y., & Frederickson, J. R. (1989). *Designing articulate microworlds that facilitate learning, understanding, and problem solving in science education.* American Educational Research Association: San Francisco.

White, B. Y., & Horwitz, P. (1987). ThinkerTools: Enabling Children to Understand Physical Laws. Report No. 6470. BBN Laboratories: Cambridge, MA.

White, B. Y., & Horwitz, P. (1988). Computer microworlds and conceptual change: A new approach to science education. In P. Ransden (Ed.), *Improving Learning: New Perspectives.* London: Kegan Paul, pp. 69–80.

Woodrow, J. E. J. (1989). Teachers' knowledge of educational applications of computers. *Journal of Computers in Mathematics and Science Teaching,* Summer, 31–38.

Zietsman, A. I., & Hewson, P. W. (1986). Effect of instruction using microcomputer simulations and conceptual change strategies on science learning. *Journal of Research in Science Teaching, 23,* 27–39.

APPENDIX
COMPUTER SOFTWARE

Birdbreed, Edutech, 1927 Culver Rd., Rochester, NY.

Catlab, Conduit, University of Iowa, Iowa City.

The Factory, Sunburst Communications, 39 Washington Ave., Pleasantville, NY.

Models of Electric Current: Ohm's Law, Conduit, University of Iowa, Iowa City.

Geology Search, McGraw-Hill, 8171 Redwood Highway, Novato, CA.

Molecular Velocities, Conduit, University of Iowa, Iowa City.

Oh Deer!, MECC, 3490 Lexington Ave. North, St. Paul, MN.

QUEST, BBN Laboratories, Cambridge, MA.

ThinkerTools, BBN Laboratories, Cambridge, MA.

Voyage of the MiMi, Holt, Rinehart, & Winston, 839 Mitten Rd., Burlingame, CA.

For more information on science software, the following readings and sources are recommended:

The 1988–1989 Educational Software Preview Guide (contact the editor, California Software Clearinghouse, Instructional Technology Center, San Mateo County Office of Education, 333 Main St., Redwood City, CA 94063) or the fall, 1988, issue of the *Journal of Computers in Mathematics and Science Teaching*, pp. 65–86

Journals from professional organizations, such as the National Science Teachers Association and the National Association of Biology Teachers, feature software reviews and how-to articles on using science software.

Author Index

Note: Italicized page numbers refer to bibliography pages.

A

Abimbola, I. O., 66, *83*
Abraham, M. R., 249, *255*
Adey, P., 67, 78, *83*
Aldridge, B. G., 4, *18*
Alexander, P., 222, *239*
Anderson, A., 189, *200*
Anderson, C. W., 12, *18*, 49, 50, 52, 54, 56, 60, *62*, *63*, 69, *83*, 110, 112, *114*, 117, 120, 129, 142, *145*, *146*
Anderson, J. H., 28, *35*
Anderson, J. R., 35, 239
Anderson, R. C., *35*
Andersson, B., 117–120, 123, 125, *145*
Andre, T., 222, *240*
Arnaudin, M. W., 182, 188, 194, *199*, *201*, *202*
Arnon, D. I., 189, *200*
Arons, A., 105, *114*
Atkin, M., 61, *62*
Ausubel, D. P., 28, *35*, 47, *62*, 68, *83*, 179, *200*

B

Baddeley, A., 9, *18*
Baird, J. R., 73, 78, 80, 82, *83*
Barufaldi, J., 226, *239*

Bean, T., 222, *239*
Becker, H. J., 241, *254*
Beiswenger, R. E., 12, 13, *19*, 91, 93, 105–107, 109–111, *115*
Bell, B. F., 183, *200*
Belt, B. L., 54, *62*
Ben-Zvi, R., 117–123, 125, 126, 132, 140, 143, *145*
Bereiter, C., 56, *63*
Berkheimer, G. D., 52, *62*
Birnie, H. H., 249, *255*
Blakeslee, T. D., 52, *62*
Bliss, J., 81, *83*
Bongaarts, J., *35*, 40
BouJaoude, S., 129, 132, *145*
Bradwein, P., 93, *114*
Bransford, J., 210, *216*
Brewer, W. F., 16, *19*, 129, 134, 136, 140, *147*, 150, 152, 154, 169, 172, *177*, 221, 222, *240*
Britton, B. K., 4, 9, 10, *18*, *19*, 221, 222, 230, *239*, *240*
Brown, D. E., 15, *18*, 239
Brown, H. J., 69, *83*
Brown, J. S., 53, 55, 56, *63*
Bruffee, K. A., 54, *63*
Brumby, M., 180, 182, *200*
Bruner, J. S., 47, *62*
Butzow, J., 103, *114*

C

Cahn, A. D., 28, *35*
Caravita, S., 30, *35*
Carey, S., 14, 16, *18, 19,* 49, *63,* 69, *83,* 180, 200
Carpenter, E. T., 91, *114*
Catherall, R. W., 181, 185, *200*
Chabay, R. W., 242, *255*
Champagne, A. B., 28, 30, *35*
Chi, M. T. H., 6, *18,* 250, *254*
Chiapetta, E., 206, *216*
Claxton, G. L., 67, 79, *83*
Clement, J. J., 15, *18,* 49, *63,* 113, *114,* 150, 169, *176,* 222, *239*
Clough, E. E., 181, 182, *200*
Cohen, M., 112, *114*
Collins, A., 53, 55, 56, *63*
Cosgrove, M. M., 117–119, *147*
Costa, A. L., 249, *254*
Cowan, S., 222, *239*

D

Darwin, C., 199, *200*
Dawson, C. J., 111, *114*
Day, J. D., 30, *35*
Deadman, J. A., 181, 182, *200*
Dede, C. J., 241, 243, 253, *254*
deKleer, J., 250, *254*
Dennis, W., 180, *201*
DeSena, A., 35
Di Vesta, F. J., 220, *240*
Dillon, T. J., 227, *240*
Dillashaw, F., 212, *216*
diSessa, A. A., 51, *63,* 150, 169, *176,* 242, 250, 252, 253, *254*
Driver, R., 60, 66, 80, 81, 82, *83, 84,* 129, 130, *145,* 150, 169, *176,* 193, 194, 197, *200*
Duit, R., 66, 70, *84, 85*
Dunn, C. S., 194, *199*
Dyche, S., 12, 13, *19,* 91, 93, 105–107, 109–111, *115*

E

Easley, J., 67, *84,* 150, *176*
Eaton, J. F., 110, 112, *114*

Eichinger, D. C., 118, 125, *145*
Engel-Clough, E., 67, *84*
Erickson, F., 66, 69, 81, *84*
Erickson, G. L., 126, *145,* 181, 194, *200*
Eylon, B., 117–123, 125, 126, 132, 139, 142, *145*

F

Feher, E., 81, *84*
Fehr, E., 113, *114*
Feltovich, P. J., 6, *18,* 250, *254*
Fensham, P. J., 67, 69, 73, 74, 78, 82, *83, 84*
Fiel, R. L., 11, *18*
Flavell, J., 212, *216*
Forman, 248
Frederickson, J. R., 16, *19,* 244, 250, 251, *256*
French, L. A., 30, *35*
Freyberg, P., 119, 129, *147,* 251, *255*
Funk, H. J., 11, *18*
Furio Mas, C. J., 119, *145*
Fuson, J., 94, *114*

G

Gabel, D. L., 103, *114,* 125, 139, 140, *145, 146*
Gamalski, J. M., 54, *62*
Gardner, P. L., 82, *84*
Garrard, K., 212, *217*
Gauld, C., 66, 67, *84*
Gellert, E., 181, *200*
Georgiady, N. P., 207, *216*
Gertzog, W. A., 14, *19,* 49, *63,* 91, *114,* 120, 129, *147*
Gick, M. L., 222, *239, 240*
Gilbert, J., 66, 67, 74, *84*
Giuliani, G., 30, *35*
Glaser, R., 6, *18,* 250, *254*
Glasersfeld, E. V., 69, 78, 84
Glynn, S. M., 4, 9, 10, 16, *18, 19,* 221, 222, 230, *239, 240*
Goetz, E. T., 35
Goldberg, F., 81, *84*
Gorodetshy, M., 127, *146*
Gowin, D. B., 48, *63,* 78, *85,* 137, 139, *146,* 183, 194, *201*
Grant, R., 206, *217*
Greminger, J., 54, *62*

Griffin, H. C., 73, *85*
Griffiths, A. K., 125, 126, *146*
Grob, K., 67, *85*
Gunstone, R. F., 28, 30, *35*, 71–73, 77, 78, 79, 82, *83*, *84*
Gussarsky, E., 127, *146*

H

Hashweh, M. Z., 66, 73, 82, *84*
Hall, L. X., 30, *35*
Hallden, O., 77, *84*
Halpern, D., 222, *240*
Hanesian, H., 176, *200*
Harris, H. H., 119, *145*
Hayes, D., 222, *240*
Hendrich, D., 152, 169, *176*
Henson, P., 50
Herron, J., 140, *146*
Hertz-Lazarowitz, R., 31, *36*
Hesse, J. J., 50, 60, *63*, 117, 129, 143, *146*
Hesse, M. B., 220, *240*
Hewitt, P. G., 9, 228, 230–232, *240*
Hewson, M. G. A., 50, *63*, 143, *146*
Hewson, P. W., 14, *19*, 50, *63*, 120, 143, *146*, *147*, 194, *200*, 251, 252, *254*, *256*
Hills, G. L., 66, 67, *84*
Hobbs, E. D., 181, *200*
Hochman, G., 187, *200*
Hoffman, R. R., 12, *19*
Holton, G., 219, 220, *240*
Holubec, E., 30, *35*
Holyoak, K. J., 222, *239*, *240*
Horowitz, P., 245, *256*
Howe, A., 150, *176*
Hunn, D., 125, 139, *146*
Hurd, P. D., 212, *216*

I

Inhelder, B., 121, *216*

J

Jahoda, G., 180, *200*
Jans, H. H., 11, *18*
Johansen, G. T., 139, *146*

Johnson, C. N., 181, *200*
Johnson, D. W., 30, 31, *35*, *36,* 248, *254*
Johnson, R., 30, 31, *35*, *36*, 248, *254*
Johnston, J., 128, *146*
Jones, L. L., 136, 137, *147*
Jung, W., 69, *85*
Jungwirth, E., 182, *200*

K

Kagan, S., 31, *36*
Kargbo, D. B., 181, *200*
Karplus, R., 61, *62*
Kelly, G. A., 67, 69, 77, *85*
Kelly, P. J., 181, 182, *200*
Kendall, D. C., 181, *201*
Kinnear, J., 246, 247, 253, *255*
Kipman, D., 126, 127, 134, 136, *147*
Kleinman, R. W., 73, *85*
Klopfer, L. E., 28, 30, *35*, 81, *85*
Konigsberg Kerner, N., 73, *85*
Kozma, R. B., 128, *146*
Krajcik, J. S., 124, 134, 135, 140, 142, 143, *146*, *147*
Kreitler, H., 181, *200*
Kreitler, S., 181, *200*
Kuehn, C., *115*
Kuhn, T. S., 72, 77, *85*, 150, *176*

L

Ladd, G., 226, *239*
Lane, E., 251, *255*
Larkin, J. H., 242, 250, *255*
Lavender, J., 189, *200*
Lawson, A. E., 110, *114*
Layman, J. W., 134, 143, *146*
Lee, O., 118, 125, *145*
Lehman, J. R., 241, *255*
Lepper, M. R., 254, *255*
Lewis, E. L., 129, 132, 134, 143, *146*
Linn, M. C., 81, *85*, 119, 126, 129–132, 134, 139, 143, *145*, *146*
Longden, B., 246, *255*
Lovell, K., 206, *216*
Lowyck, J., 79, *85*
Lunetta, V. N., 249–251, *255*

M

Mager, R. F., 194, *200*
Mali, G. B., 150, *176*
Malone, T. W., 254, *255*
Mangano, N., 222, *239*
Marek, E. A., 106, *114*
Martin, F. L., 189, *201*
Marton, F., 79, *85*
McCloskey, M., 16, *19*, 150, 169, *177*
McDermott, J., 250, *255*
Meyer, B. J. F., 222, *239*
Miller, F., 227, *240*
Minstrell, J., 44, 49, 51, 52, *63*
Mintzes, J. J., 181, 182, 194, *199*, *201*, 202
Mitchell, I., 78, 83
Mitchell, J., 80, 82, *85*
Mokros, J. R., 134, *146*
Moore, J. E., 181, *201*
Moses, A., 226, *239*
Musonda, D., 142, *146*
Muth, K. D., 4, 9, *19*, 221, 222, 230, *240*

N

Nagy, M. H., 181, *201*
Nakhleh, M. B., 127, *146*
Natadze, R. G., 183, *201*
Neimark, E. D., 11, *19*
Neuberger, H. T., 182, *201*
Newman, S. E., 53, 55, 56, *63*
Niedderer, H., 81, *85*
Northfield, D. J., 77, 79, *84*
Novak, D., 31, *35*, *85*
Novak, J. D., 48, 53, *63*, 78, *85*, 137, 139, 142, *146*, 150, 169, *177*, 179, 183, 194, *200*, *201*
Novick, S., 50, *63*, 112, *114*, 125, 129, 130, *146*, *147*, 251, *255*
Nussbaum, J., 50, 54, *63*, *114*, 125, 129, 130, *146*, *147*, 150, 169, *177*, 194, *201*, 251, *255*

O

Ogborn, J., 81, *83*
Okey, J. R., 11, *18*, 111, *115*, 212, *216*, *217*
Oldham, V., 129, 130, *145*, 194, *200*

Oppenheimer, R., 220, *240*
Osborne, R., 67, 74, *84*, 119, 125, 129, *147*, 150, *177*
Osborne, R. J., 117–119, *147*, 251, *255*

P

Padilla, M., 212, *216*, *217*
Pankratius, W. J., 7, 8, 137, *147*
Papert, S., 242, *255*
Pea, R., 242, 248, *255*
Penland, M. J., 222, *239*
Perez, J. H., 119, *145*
Perret-Clermont, A. N., 30, *36*
Peters, H., 135, *147*, 251, *255*
Peterson, R. F., 127, *147*
Pfundt, H., 66, 70, *85*
Piaget, J., 53, *63*, 94, *114*, 150, *177*, 180, 181, *201*, 206, 212, *216*, *217*, 248, *255*
Pines, A. L., 117, 118, 129, *147*
Polya, G., 219, *240*
Pope, M., 69, *85*
Porter, C. S., 181, *201*
Posner, G. J., 14, 15, *19*, 91, *114*, 120, 129, *147*
Posner, J., 50, *63*
Potter, G., *35*, 40
Poulos, S., 150, 169, *177*
Preece, P., 75, *85*
Preston, K. R., 125, 126, *146*

R

Raph, J., 206, *217*
Renner, J. W., 106, 109, 110, *114*, *217*, 249, *255*
Resnick, L. B., 54, *63*, *201*, 242, *255*
Reynolds R. E., *35*
Rhoneck, C. V., 67, *85*
Rice, K., 113, *114*
Rice, R., 81, *84*
Rogers, E. M., 227, *240*
Romano, L. G., 207, *216*
Roth, K. J., 52, 56, 60, *62*, 117, 129, *145*
Rowell, J. A., 111, *114*
Roy, P., 30, *35*
Russell, R. W., 180, *201*

Rutherford, F. J., 219, 220, *240*
Ryman, D., 183, *201*

S

Saltiel, E., 76, *85*
Samuel, K. V., 125, 139, 140, *145*, *146*
Scanlon, E., 81, *84*
Scardamalia, M., 56, *63*
Schallert, D. L., *35*
Schilder, P., 181, *201*
Schmuck, R., 31, *36*
Schneider, 110
Schrader, C., 139, 140, *145*
Schullum, B., 125, *147*
Schwab, J. J., 47, *63*
Schwebel, M., 206, *217*
Semrud-Clikeman, M., 9, *19*, 230, *240*
Shafer, T. H., 194, *199*
Sharan, S., 31, *36*
Shayer, M., 78, *83*
Shepherd, D. L., 109, 110, *114*
Sherwood, R., 140, *145*
Silberstein, J., 117–123, 125, 126, 132, 142, *145*
Simmons, P. E., 247, 249, 250, 253, *255*
Simon, D. P., 250, *255*
Simon, H. A., 250, *255*
Simpson, R. D., 208, *217*
Singer, H., 222, *239*
Slavin, R. E., 30, 31, *36*
Smith, C., 16, *19*
Smith, E. L., 13, *18*, 49, 52, 61, 62, *63*, 110, 112, *114*
Smith, K., 30, *36*
Smith, M. K., 227, *240*
Smith, S. G., 136, 137, *147*
Sneider, C., 150, 169, *177*
Snider, B., 142, *147*
Solomon, C. A., 28, *35*
Songer, N. B., 126, 130, 134, 143, *146*
Sprague, C. S., 11, *18*
Squires, D., *35*
Staver, J., 206, *217*
Stead, K., 251, *255*
Steinbach, R., 56, *63*
Stensvold, M. S., 139, *147*
Stepans, J. I., 12, 13, *19*, 90, 91, 93, 105–107, 109, 110, 111, *115*

Stewart, J., 246, *255*
Strike, K. A., 14, 15, *19*, 50, *63*, 120, 129, *147*
Strike, R. A., 68, *85*
Sutherland, J., 206, *217*
Sutula, V. D., 140, *147*

T

Tasker, R., 251, *255*
Thompson, P. W., 242, 244, *255*
Tillman, M. H., 222, *240*
Tinker, R. F., 134, *146*
Toulmin, S., 49, 54, 60, *63*
Treagust, D. F., 127, *147*
Trowbridge, J. E., 182, *201*

V

Veath, M. L., 113, *114*
Viennot, L., 16, *19*, 76, *85*, 150, 177
Vosniadou, S., 16, *19*, 129, 134, 136, 140, *147*, 150, 152, 154, 162, 169, 172, 174, *177*, 221, 222, *240*
Vygotsky, L., 30, *36*, 69, *85*

W

Wandersee, J. H., 104, *115*, 182, 192, 197, *201*, *202*
Watson, F. G., 219, 220, *240*
Watts, M., 66, *84*
Watzlawick, P., 65, *85*
Webb, C., 31, *36*
Wechsler, D., 181, *201*
Weiss, I. R., 241, *256*
Wellman, H. M., 181, *200*
West, L. H. T., 117, 118, 129, *147*
White, B. Y., 16, *19*, 150, 169, *177*, 244, 245, 248, 250, 251, *256*
White, C., 222, *239*
White, J., 16, *19*
White, R., 28, *35*
White, R. T., 71–73, 78, 82, *83–85*
Williamson, P. A., 180, *202*
Wilson, J. T., 139, *147*
Winter, 90
Wise, K. C., 111, *115*

Wiser, M., 16, *19*, 126, 127, 134, 136, *147*
Wittrock, M. C., 150, *177*, 223, *240*
Wood-Robinson, C., 181, 182, *200*
Woodrow, J. E. J., 248, *256*

Y

Yager, R. E., 142, *147*

Yap, K. C., 11, *19*
Yarroch, W. L., 117, 119, 122, 123, *147*
Yeany, R. H., 11, *19*

Z

Za'rour, G. I., 112, *115*
Zietsman, A. I., 15, *18*, 222, *239*, 251, 252, *256*

Subject Index

A

Academic task, 22, 23, 30, 31, 32, 37
Action research, 78
Affective, 82
Affective outcomes, 243–248
Alternative conceptions, 179
  intuitive biology, 181
  naive theories, 179, 180
Alternative frameworks, (*see also* Naive
  conception) 49, 67, 68, 80
Analogical reasoning, 222
Analogy, 9, 220, 223
  analog, 223
  dangers of analogies, 227
  multiple analogies, 237
Arguments for an activity approach, 205
  affective goals—success in science, 208
  constructivism, 206
  development of logical thought, 205
  doing and understanding, 207
  physical and emotional nature of learner,
  207
  promotion of creative thinking, 208
Attitudes, 79, 82

C

Chemical concepts, understanding of, 118,
  119

acid and base chemistry, understanding
  of, 127
chemical change, understanding of, 118,
  120
chemical reactions, understanding of, 119,
  120
  chemist's understanding, 120, 121
  student's understanding, 119, 112
combustion, understanding of, 119, 120
covalent bonding, understanding of, 127
equilibrium, understanding of, 128
particulate nature of matter,
  understanding of, 123, 135
Chemistry, 253
Chemistry curriculum, 141
  chemistry textbooks, 141
Children's biology concepts, 179, 180, 182,
  197
  animal classification, 182, 183–185, 194,
    196, 197–198
  evolution, 181, 182
  heredity, 181, 182
  human body, 181–182, 185–189
    cardiovascular system, 182, 185–189,
      195, 198
    reproduction, 181–182
  life, 180–181
  photosynthesis, 182, 189–192, 193, 196,
    198–199
Children's science, 67
Clinical interviews, 53, 183, 196

Coaching, 53, 55–61
Cognitive apprenticeship, 53, 55, 56, 61
Cognition enhancer, 241
Cognitive, 82
Cognitive change
  learning cycle, 21, 33, 37
    assess, 22, 33, 38, 40
    elaborate, 22, 23, 38, 39
    engage, 22, 23, 31, 32, 37
Cognitive conflict, 72
Cognitive model, 10
Cognitive outcomes, 243–248
  conceptual change research, 251
    children's views, 251
    criticisms, 252
    naive theories, 252
    scientists' views, 251
  mega-microworld, 242
    ThinkerTools, 244
  Newtonian physics, 244
  optics microworld, 253
  textured microworld, 243
Cognitive processes, 5
Cognitive science, 69
Cognitive structure, 47
Community, 47, 54–56, 61
Computer, 81
Computer microworld, 242
  artificial reality, 241, 250
    geometry computer microworld, 244,
      254
    Logo turtles, 242
    Motions microworld, 244
    QUEST, 244, 250
Computer simulation, 243
  genetics, 246
    Birdbreed, 246–247
    Catlab, 246–247
  physics, 251
Computing technologies and uses, 241
  computer literacy, 249
  microcomputers, 241
    surveys, 241
  software uses, 241
    barriers to use, 248–249
    surveys, 241
Concept mapping, 6
Concept maps, 48, 49, 183, 194, 195
Concepts, 219
Conceptual change, 14, 49, 50, 52–57, 61, 62,
  66, 70, 72, 77, 81, 82 180–181, 192–
  199, 251–252

examples of, 49
problem of, 49
requirements for, 50
  dissatisfaction, 50
  fruitfulness, 50–52, 60, 62
  intelligible alternative, 50, 51
  plausibility, 46, 50–52, 60
teaching, 129, 142, 192–199
  conceptual objectives, 194–195
  eliciting student ideas, 196–197
  multisensory experiences, 194, 196
  restructuring student ideas, 197–199
teaching strategy, 252
  microcomputer simulations, 252
theory, 180–181
Conceptual development, 179
Conceptual ecology, 120
Conceptual frameworks, 65–71, 71, 74, 77,
  80, 82, 120, 122, 123, 128
Conceptual networks, 6
Conceptual understanding, 3, 118, 127, 128,
  134, 136, 140, 141
Conducting an experiment, 213
Connectedness, 46, 47, 49, 54
Construction, 16
Construction of construction, 79, 80
Constructing meanings, 192–194
Constructivism, 248
  radical, 69
Constructivistic science instruction, 80, 83
Constructivistic view, 66, 68, 69, 70, 73, 77,
  78, 80, 82, 83
Curriculum, 4
  teacher-centered curriculum, 4
  textbook-centered curriculum, 4

D

Development,
  cognitive, 30, 31
  inquiry skill, 31
  learning-to-learn skill, 23, 30, 31
  problem-solving skill, 30, 31
  thinking skill, 31
Discourse, 43, 60, 61
Discrepant event, 50

E

Elaborative processes, 9

Establishing a problem, 56–59
Ethnographic studies, 238
Everyday experiences, 74
Everyday language, 74
Evolutionary epistemology, 75
Examples, 225
Executive control, 10
Expert practice, 55
Explanatory ideal, 60

F

Fading, 57–60
Force, 44–46, 48–52, 55, 57–61
    balanced forces 48, 50, 51, 57, 59, 60
    reaction force, 46, 51, 52, 60
    unbalanced forces, 48, 57, 59, 60
Frames, 47
Friction, 48, 49, 57–61
Function of scientific knowledge 46, 53–56
    control, 54, 56, 58
    description, 54, 56–58
    explanation, 51, 52, 54, 56, 58, 60, 61
    prediction, 54, 56, 58

G

Genetics, 246–247
Geometry, 244
Gravity, 44, 45, 48–50, 59

H

Hermeneutics, 69
Historical conceptions, 76, 77

I

Implementing a process approach, 213
Information processing system, 9, 10
Information processing theories, 69
Innate structures, 74, 75
Instructional techniques, 137
    analogies, 140
    concept maps, 129, 137
        hierarchical diagrams, 137
    discrepant events, 131
    exposing events, 130
    predictions, 129

redescription of chemical problems, 139
Integrated understanding, 117, 119, 120, 122,
    137, 141, 143
Internal consistency, 55, 61

K

Kinds of activities, 208
    open-ended activities, 209
    recipe labs, 208
        content activities, 209
        process activities, 209
Knowledge, 26
    community 24, 33
    expert/novice, 25
    personal, 24, 28, 29
    scientific, 24, 25

L

Learning, 5, 222
Learning environments, 242
Long-term memory, 9, 11

M

Meaningful learning, 47, 56, 223
Meaningfulness, 6
Media, 79
Mental models, 254
Metacognition, 82
Metacognitive, 78, 83
Metaknowledge, 81
Metalearning, 77, 78
Minitheory, 67, 68
Misconceptions, 13, 67, 75, 101, 234
Misunderstanding, 226
Modeling, 53, 55–61
Models, 11
    personal models, 12
    scientific models, 12

N

Naive conception, 49, 52, 57
Negotiation, 81
New technologies, 132
    microcomputer-based laboratories, 133

laboratory tool, 133
simulations, 134
  microworlds, 134
  videodisc technologies, 136
Newton's Second Law, 49
Newton's Third Law, 46

O

Objectives, 57, 58, 59
Observation and conception, 70–73
Organizational processes, 6

P

Parsimony, 55, 61
Perception, 5
Personal knowledge, 117, 129, 143
  spontaneous knowledge, 117
  personal understanding, 117, 127
Phenomenology, 69
Photosynthesis, 49
Physical science, 229
Physical science concepts, understanding of,
  119
  heat energy, understanding of, 126
  physical change, understanding of, 117, 118
  temperature, understanding of, 126
Physics, 229, 244
  circuit behavior, 250
    engineers, 250
    models of electric current: OHM'S
      Law, 251
    qualitative physical models, 250
    QUEST, 244
  Newtonian physics, 244
  optics, 253
    optics microworld, 252
    ThinkerTools, 244
Preconceptions, 6
Prior Knowledge, 46, 48–50, 56, 57
Process-oriented instruction, 3
Process skills, 10

Q

Qualitative research, 69

R

Reconstruction, 16
Relational learning, 6
Relations, 223
Rote learning, 47

S

Scaffolding, 56, 57, 61
Schemata, 47
Science
  biological, 36
  nature of science, 33
  physical, 28, 29
  school science, 23, 24, 33
  scientific argumentation, 23, 24, 33
  scientific evidence, 23, 24, 33
  scientific inquiry, 23, 24
Science process skills, 209
  importance of process, 212
  problem solving, 210
Scientific knowledge, 117, 129
  chemical knowledge, 118, 120
  formal knowledge, 118
Scientific models, 131, 135
Scientific reasoning, 10
Scientists' models, 249
  qualitative models, 249
  quantitative models, 249
  quantitative reasoning, 250
  students' models, 250
Sense making, 49, 52
Sensual impressions, 74
Social constructivist, 43, 53–55, 61
Social context, 46, 47, 53, 54
Social interaction, 25, 30–32
  adult-child, 30
  peer-peer, 31
  teacher initiated, 32
Structure of knowledge, 47, 49, 53–55
Students' beliefs related to structure and
  behavior of matter, 98
Students' role, 248
  qualitative reasoning, 250
Students' thinking related to physics
  phenomena associated to weather,
  93
Students' views on sinking and floating, 91

T

Teachers, 3, 233
Teachers' conceptions, 78, 79, 80
Teacher's instruction, 248
  cooperative learning, 248
  divergent questions, 249
  learning cycle, 249
  teacher's role, 248
Teaching, 14
Teaching model, 112
Teaching methods/strategies, 21, 31, 33
Teaching strategies, 81, 107
  instructional cycle, 22, 37
    evaluation of learning, 22, 38, 40
    monitoring interactions, 22, 23, 38, 39
    setting academic tasks, 22
  theory-based, 21
  traditional/conventional, 28, 29
Teaching with analogies, 219
Text, 221
Textbooks, 4, 222
Theory(ies), 11

learning, 25, 31
  behavioral psychological, 31
  cognitive psychological, 25, 31
  constructivist, 27
  social psychological, 30, 31
  personal, 12
  scientific, 12, 30
  spontaneous/personal, 27–30
Thinking out loud, 4

U

Understanding, 23, 43, 46, 47, 49, 52–56, 61
  conceptual, 25, 30, 31
  personal, 29
  scientific, 30
Usefulness, 46, 53, 61

W

Working memory, 9, 10